### THE GUTENBERG ELEGIES

In *The Gutenburg Elegies*, renowned critic Sven Birkerts argues that we are living in a state of intellectual emergency – an emergency caused by our willingness to embrace new technologies at the expense of the printed word. As we rush to get 'on line', as we make the transition from book to screen, we are turning against some of the core premises of humanism – indeed, we are putting the idea of individualism itself under threat. The printed page and the circuit driven information technologies are *not* kindred – for Birkerts they represent fundamentally opposed forces. In their inevitable confrontation our deepest values will be tested.

Birkerts begins his exploration from the reader's perspective, first in several highly personal accounts of his own passion for the book, then in an examination of what he calls 'the ulterior life of reading'. Against this, Birkerts sets out the contours of the transformed landscape. In his highly provocative essay 'Into the Electronic Millenium' and in meditations on CD-ROM, hypertext, and audio books, he plumbs the impact of emerging technologies on the once stable reader-writer exchange. He follows these with a look at the changing climate of criticism and literary practice, and concludes with a blistering indictment of our willingness to strike a Faustian pact with a seductive devil.

Sven Birkerts is the author of three books of criticism, most recently *American Energies: Essays on Fiction*. He has won the National Book Critics Circle Citation for Excellence in Reviewing, a P.E.N. Spielvogel/Diamondstein Special Citation for *The Electric Life: Essays on Modern Poetry*, and Lila Wallace – Reader's Digest Foundation and Guggenheim fellowships. His essays and reviews have appeared in *The New York Times Book Review*, *The Atlantic*, *Harper's*, and *The New Republic*.

# The Gutenberg Elegies

*The Fate of Reading in an Electronic Age*

Sven Birkerts

*faber and faber*

First published in 1994
by Faber and Faber Inc
First published in Great Britain in 1996
by Faber and Faber Limited
3 Queen Square London WC1N 3AU

Printed in England by Clays Ltd, St Ives plc

© Sven Birkerts

Sven Birkerts is hereby identified as author of this work
in acccordance with Section 77 of the
Copyright, Designs and Patents Act 1988

A CIP catalogue record for this book
is available from the British Library

ISBN 0–571–19045–6

2 4 6 8 10 9 7 5 3 1

*To our newcomer, Liam Thomas, and to the rest of my family, all three generations.*

*I also wish to thank the Lila Wallace–Reader's Digest Foundation for generous support during the writing of this book, and my editor, Fiona McCrae, for spurring me on.*

# Contents

**Part III    Critical Mass: Three Meditations**

# The Gutenberg Elegies

*"What hath God wrought?"*
—Samuel Morse (in his first telegraph message)

# Introduction:

## *The Reading Wars*

THE PREMISE THAT FUELED the writing of these essays—and which also holds them together—is simple, if drastic, and needs to be declared straightaway: Over the past few decades, in the blink of the eye of history, our culture has begun to go through what promises to be a total metamorphosis. The influx of electronic communications and information processing technologies, abetted by the steady improvement of the microprocessor, has rapidly brought on a condition of critical mass. Suddenly it feels like everything is poised for change; the slower world that many of us grew up with dwindles in the rearview mirror. The stable hierarchies of the printed page—one of the defining norms of that world—are being superseded by the rush of impulses through freshly minted circuits. The displacement of the page by the screen is not yet total (as evidenced by the book you are holding)—it may never be total—but the large-scale tendency in that direction has to be obvious to anyone who looks. The shift is, of course, only part of a larger transformation that embraces whole economies and affects people at every level. But, living as we do in the midst of innumerable affiliated webs, we can say that changes in the immediate sphere of print refer outward to the totality; they map on a smaller scale the riot of societal forces.

I cannot confront the big picture—I have neither the temerity nor the technological expertise. Instead, I have chosen to focus on the various ways in which literary practice, mainly reading, registers and transmits the shocks of the new. I do this in two stages. I begin by setting out an informal and highly subjective ecology of reading, an ecology extrapolated from my own experience as a reader, and then I introduce the various elements, or forces, that threaten that frail set of balances. My discussions of reading will be seen to shade quite readily at times into discussions of writing or, later, criticism. This is not inadvertent sloppiness, but a recognition of the natural kinship of the various facets of literary exchange.

I have been developing my ideas on paper and in conversation for several years now and I have come to inhabit my assumptions like a comfortable room. They are so familiar, so self-evident to me that I am always taken aback to find that, to say the least, they are not universally shared. The so-called "Luddite" stance is not especially popular these days, at least among intellectually "progressive" people. These progressives tend to equate technological primitivism, or recidivism, with conservatism of the N.R.A. stripe. The implication would seem to be that the new technology has a strictly liberal pedigree. But a moment's contemplation of the electronic ministries of the televangelists or resources of our Defense Department think tanks ought to disabuse us of that notion. I don't think the technology question breaks down along conventional political lines.

Closer to home, I see many of my culturally savvy friends and colleagues carrying on as if very little is really changing, as if we are living in the midst of a fundamentally static environment. They greet my assertions with shrugs and impatient expressions that say, "Are you *still* carping about computers and television?" And no matter what perspectives or evidence I offer, I am met with the "it's just" response. The word processor, the laptop? "It's just a tool, a more efficient way of . . ." Electronic bulletin boards and networks? "They're just other ways for people to connect." The prospect of books on disk? "What's the difference? The *words* don't change . . ." These are often the same people who insist that writers are flourishing, that publishing is healthy, and that readers are reading like never before. I sometimes wonder if my thoughtful friends and I are living in the same world.

These people, my affable adversaries in argument, including all of the well-meaning empiricists who like to assert that "the more things change, the more they stay the same," make up the first tier of my targeted readers. It is their expressions and their rebuttals, real or imagined, that I have in mind as I write. I have thought long and hard about their refusal—or inability—to grant me my thesis of a millennial transformation of society. Are they, I wonder, suffering from the empiricist's particular nearsightedness, or am I entertaining a delusion? Naturally I prefer to think that the problem lies with them—that they cannot credit what they cannot *see* happening, and that they cannot see the transformation going on around us because they cannot pry themselves free from their synchronic worldview. They are not, most of them, interested in projecting backward and forward in time—they prefer the here and now.

I would ask these same people to conceive of a time-lapse view of American domestic life—a vast motion study that would track a citizen or group of citizens through, say, four decades of American life. Let them watch what happens to the phenomenology of living; how since the 1950s countless technologies have been introduced and accommodated and how the fundamental transactions of existence have thereby been altered. At midcentury the average household had a radio and a rotary phone, and a small group of pioneers owned black and white televisions. In the 1990s, looking to the same sample milieu, we find several color TVs with remotes, with VCRs, with Nintendo capacities; personal computers, modems, fax machines; cellular phones, answering machines, car phones, CD players, camcorders . . . When the time-lapse is sufficiently accelerated, the drama of the transformation stands revealed. In less than a half century we have moved from a condition of essential isolation into one of intense and almost unbroken mediation. A finely filamented electronic scrim has slipped between ourselves and the so-called "outside world." The idea of spending a day, never mind a week, out of the range of all our devices sounds bold, even risky.

Only part of this great change impinges directly upon the literary enterprise. But the overall rescripting of all societal premises is bound to affect reading and writing immensely. The formerly stable system—the axis with writer at one end, editor, publisher, and bookseller in the middle, and reader at the other end—is slowly being bent into a pretzel. What the writer writes, how he writes and gets edited, printed, and sold, and then read—all of the old assumptions are under siege. And these are just the outward manifestations. Still deeper shifts are taking place in the subjective realm. As the printed book, and the ways of the book—of writing and reading—are modified, as electronic communications assert dominance, the "feel" of the literary engagement is altered. Reading and writing come to *mean* differently; they acquire new significations. As the world hurtles on toward its mysterious rendezvous, the old act of slowly reading a serious book becomes an elegiac exercise. As we ponder that act, profound questions must arise about our avowedly humanistic values, about spiritual versus material concerns, and about subjectivity itself.

I consider these matters and many others in the essays that follow. I do not pretend to be disinterested, however. Indeed, I have tried hard to resist the tone of a man who tries to find some good in everything. I speak as an unregenerate reader, one who still believes that language and not technology is the true evolutionary miracle. I have not yet given up on the idea that the experience of literature offers a kind of wisdom that cannot be discovered elsewhere; that there is profundity in the verbal encounter itself, never mind what further profundities the author has to offer; and that for a host of reasons the bound book is the ideal vehicle for the written word.

These are, in some ways, pessimistic perspectives. Pessimistic, certainly, if we measure the state of things according to the old humanist assumptions about the sovereignty of the individual. These essays are extrapolations, predictions, warnings. But they are counterbalanced—not refuted, alas—by a number of pieces that were written in a spirit of celebration. When intimations of the brave new future began to drag me down, I had recourse to the place of nourishment. I read and thought about reading, and I indulged my long-standing predilections in a number of reflections on the subject. These represent the faithful heart of this not always cheerful project.

Although this book does have a central premise, it is not what my five-year-old daughter would call a "chapter book." That is to say, the argument is not conducted in linear fashion, but rather by way of what I think of as organic clusters. Each essay was conceived as a freestanding entity; each emerged from its own private compulsion. But as many of the essays depend on the central premise in one way or another, certain thematic recurrences are inevitable. To eliminate these would be to compromise the individual essays. My hope—my faith—is that the recurrences are not simply repetitions but are in fact differently angled approaches to a cultural situation which cannot be sufficiently remarked. I ask similar indulgence, while offering no excuses, for the mixture of discursive and autobiographical—or disinterested and interested—strategies. My investment in the topic of reading is too deep and too partisan to allow me the detachment of the watchful bystander. The more confiding essays at the beginning of the book should be seen as the soil in which the seeds of the later meditations were embedded. Everything here ultimately originates in the private self—that of the dreamy fellow with an open book in his lap.

# PART I

# The Reading Self

# 1

# MahVuhHuhPuh

I T WAS VIRGINIA WOOLF who started me thinking about thinking again, set me to weighing the relative merits of the abstract ana-
lytical mode against the attractions of a more oblique and subjective
approach. The comparison was ventured for interest alone. Abstract
analysis has been closed to me for some time—I find I can no longer
chase the isolated hare. Problems and questions seem to come toward
me in clusters. They appear inextricably imbedded in circumstance and
I cannot pry them loose to think about them. Nor can I help factoring in
my own angle of regard. All is relative, relational, Einsteinian. Thinking
is now something I partake in, not something I do. It is a complex narrative proposition, and I am as interested in the variables of the process
as I am in the outcome. I am an essayist, it seems, and not a philosopher.

I have had these various distinctions in mind for some time now,
but only as a fidgety scatter of inklings. The magnet that pulled them
into a shape was Woolf's classic essay, *A Room of One's Own*. Not the
*what* of it, but the *how*. Reading the prose, I confronted a paradox that
pulled me upright in my chair. Woolf's ideas are, in fact, few and fairly
obvious—at least from our historical vantage. Yet the *thinking*, the presence of animate thought on the page, is striking. How do we sort that?
How can a piece of writing have simple ideas and still infect the reader
with the excitement of its thinking? The answer, I'd say, is that ideas are
not the sum and substance of thought; rather, thought is as much about
the motion across the water as it is about the stepping stones that allow
it. It is an intricate choreography of movement, transition, and repose, a
revelation of the musculature of mind. And this, abundantly and exalt-

11

ingly, is what I find in Woolf's prose. She supplies the context, shows the problem as well as her relation to it. Then, as she narrates her growing engagement, she exposes something more thrilling and valuable than any mere concept could be. She reveals how incidental experience can encounter the receptive sensibility and activate the mainspring of creativity.

I cannot cite enough text here to convince you of my point, but I can suggest the flavor of her musing, her particular way of intertwining the speculative with the reportorial. Woolf has, she informs us at the outset, agreed to present her views on the subject of women and fiction. In the early pages of her essay she rehearses her own perplexity. She is a writer looking for an idea. What she does is not so very different from the classic college freshman maneuver of writing a paper on the problem she is having writing a paper. But Woolf is Woolf, and her stylistic verve is unexcelled:

> Here then I was (call me Mary Beton, Mary Seton, Mary Carmichael or by any name you please—it is not a matter of any importance) sitting on the banks of a river a week or two ago in fine October weather, lost in thought. That collar I have spoken of, women and fiction, the need of coming to some conclusion on a subject that raises all sorts of prejudices and passions, bowed my head to the ground. To the right and left bushes of some sort, golden and crimson, glowed with color, even it seemed burned with the heat, of fire. On the further bank willows wept in perpetual lamentation, their hair about their shoulders. The river reflected whatever it chose of sky and bridge and burning tree, and when the undergraduate had oared his boat through the reflections they closed again, completely, as if he had never been. There one might have sat the clock round lost in thought. Thought—to call it by a prouder name than it deserved—let its line down into the stream. It swayed, minute after minute, hither and thither among the reflections and the weeds, letting the water lift it and sink it, until—you know the little tug—the sudden conglomeration of an idea at the end of one's line: and then the cautious hauling of it in, and the careful laying of it out? Alas, laid on the grass how small, how insignificant this thought of mine looked; the sort of fish that a good fisherman puts back into the

water so that it may grow fatter and be one day worth cooking and eating.

Soon enough, Woolf will rise and attempt to cross a patch of lawn, only to encounter a zealous beadle, who will not only shoo her back toward authorized turf, but will initiate her reverie on male power and privilege. This is her triumph: the trust in serendipity, which proves, when unmasked, to be an absolute faith in the transformative powers of the creative intellect. *A Room of One's Own,* whatever it says about women, men, writing, and society, is also a perfect demonstration of what might be called "magpie aesthetics." Woolf is the bricoleuse, cobbling with whatever is to hand; she is the flâneuse, redeeming the slight and incidental by creating the context of its true significance. She models another path for mind and sensibility, suggests procedures that we might consider implementing for ourselves now that the philosophers, the old lovers of truth, have followed the narrowing track of abstraction to the craggy places up above the timberline.

By now the astute reader will have picked up on my game—that I am interested not only in celebrating Woolf's cunningly sidelong approach, but that I am trying, in my own ungainly way, to imitate it. Woolf had her "collar" (women and fiction) thrust upon her; I have wriggled into mine—let's call it *reading and meaning*—of my own volition. I know that I face an impossible task. Who can hope to say anything conclusive on so vast a subject? But I opted for vastness precisely because it would allow me to explore this unfamiliar essayistic method. A method predicated not upon conclusiveness but upon exploratory digressiveness; a method which proposes that thinking is not simply utilitarian, but can also be a kind of narrative travel that allows for picnics along the way.

I invoke Woolf as the instigating presence. Her example sets the key signature for an inquiry into the place of reading and sensibility in what is becoming an electronic culture. Within the scheme I have in mind, Woolf stands very much at one limit. Indeed, her work is an emblem for some of the very things that are under threat in our age: differentiated subjectivity, reverie, verbal articulation, mental passion . . .

Before I go on, I must make a paradoxical admission: I was spurred to read *A Room of One's Own* by watching a televised adaptation of the book. On the program, Eileen Atkins, playing the part of Woolf, soliloquized for a full hour. Her address, supposedly directed at an audience of women at Girton College, was composed of extracted passages from the text. Armed with minimal props and a rather extraordinary repertoire of gestures, Atkins held forth. And I, wedged into my corner of the couch, was mesmerized. By the acting, sure, but more by the sheer power and beauty of the spoken word. Here, without seeming archaic or excessively theatrical, was a language such as one never hears—certainly not on TV. I was riveted. And as soon as the show was over I went to find the book.

*A Room of One's Own,* I'm happy to say, stood up to its television rendition—indeed, galloped right past it. And it has spent many nights since on my bedside table. But the paradox remains: Just as Woolf's charged prose shows us what is possible with language, so it also forces us to face the utter impoverishment of our own discourse. And as we seek to explain how it is that flatness and dullness carry the day, we have to lay at least part of the blame at the feet of our omnipotent media systems. And yet, and yet . . . here I found myself reintroduced to the power of Woolf by the culprit technology itself.

This is the sort of thing I tend to think about. I ponder the paradox—stare at it as if it were an object on the desk in front of me. I stare and wait for ideas and intuitions to gather, but I do not unpack my instruments of reason. For, as I see it, this little triad—of me, TV, and book—potentially touches every aspect of our contemporary lives and our experience of meaning. To think about the matter analytically would be to break the filaments of the web.

I will therefore set down what amount to a few anecdotal provocations and go wandering about in their midst. All of my points of focus have, as you will see, some connection to my immediate daily experience; they are embedded in the context of my life. But they also have a discernible link. For I *have* been going around for quite some time with a single question—a single imprecisely general question—in my mind. The interrogation mark has been turned upside down and, to follow Woolf, lowered into the waters of my ordinary days. It is always there, and, from time to time, for whatever reason, it captures the attention of some swimming thing. I feel a tug: The paper is produced, the note gets scribbled, and the hook is thrown back out.

The question, again, is, "What is the place of reading, and of the reading sensibility, in our culture as it has become?" And, like most of the questions I ponder seriously, this one has been around long enough to have become a conspicuous topographical feature of my mental landscape. In my lifetime I have witnessed and participated in what amounts to a massive shift, a wholesale transformation of what I think of as the age-old ways of being. The primary human relations—to space, time, nature, and to other people—have been subjected to a warping pressure that is something new under the sun. Those who argue that the very nature of history is change—that change is constant—are missing the point. Our era has seen an escalation of the rate of change so drastic that all possibilities of evolutionary accommodation have been short-circuited. The advent of the computer and the astonishing sophistication achieved by our electronic communications media have together turned a range of isolated changes into something systemic. The way that people experience the world has altered more in the last fifty years than in the many centuries preceding ours. The eruptions in the early part of our century—the time of world wars and emergent modernity—were premonitions of a sort. Since World War II we have stepped, collectively, out of an ancient and familiar solitude and into an enormous web of imponderable linkages. We have created the technology that not only enables us to change our basic nature, but that is making such change all but inevitable. This is why I take reading—reading construed broadly—as my subject. Reading, for me, is one activity that inscribes the limit of the old conception of the individual and his relation to the world. It is precisely where reading leaves off, where it is supplanted by other modes of processing and transmitting experience, that the new dispensation can be said to begin.

None of this, I'm afraid, will seem very obvious to the citizen of the late twentieth century. If it did, there would be more outcry, more debate. The changes are keyed to generational transitions in computational power; they come in ghostly increments, but their effect is to alter our lives on every front. Public awareness of this expresses itself obliquely, often unconsciously, as nostalgia—a phenomenon which the media brokers are all too aware of. They hurry to supply us with the necessary balm: media productions and fashions that harken back reassuringly to eras that we perceive as less threatening, less cataclysmic. But this is another subject. We are, on a conscious level, blinkered to change. We adapt to the local disturbances. We train ourselves to computer literacy, find ways to speed up our performance, accept higher levels of stress as a kind of necessary tax burden, but by and large we ignore the massive transformations taking place in the background. This is entirely understandable. The present hastens us forward, at every moment sponging up what preceded it. Only when we wrench ourselves free and perform the ceremony of memory do we grasp the extent of the change. In our lives, in the world. Then indeed we may ask ourselves where we are headed and what is the meaning of this great metamorphosis of the familiar.

I was recently reading a novel by Graham Swift entitled *Ever After*. At one point, the narrator, an adult looking back upon his youth, recalls how he used to race on his bike to a private lookout post from which he could watch the great steam engines go hurtling past. Calling upon the privileged hindsight of his narrator, Swift writes:

> Between Aldermaston Wharf and Midgham, where the Reading-to-Newbury line clipped the side of the hill and entered a short cutting—a favorite spot for these enthralled vigils, so limply known as "train-spotting"—I could look out on a vista which might have formed the model for one of those contrived scenes in a children's encyclopedia, depicting the theme of "Old and New." River, canal and railway line were all in view. At a single moment it would have been perfectly possible to see, in the background, the old watermill on the Kennet, with a horse working the field before it; in the middle distance, a barge on the canal; and in the foreground, a train racing for the cutting; while no less than three road bridges provided a fair opportunity for some gleaming motor car (complete with an inanely grinning couple in the front seats) to be brought simultaneously into the picture.
>
> I must have seen it once—many times—that living palimpsest. And no doubt I should have been struck by some prescient, elegiac pang at the sight of these great expresses steaming only to their own oblivion, and taking with them a whole lost age.

I found the passage a compelling analogy of our own situation, only instead of modes of transport in the palimpsest I would place book, video monitor, and any of the various interactive hypertext technologies now popping up in the marketplace. Looking up from Swift's page, I wondered what it would be like to look back upon our own cultural moment from a vantage of, say, thirty years. Are we not in a similar transitional phase, except that what is roaring by, destined for imminent historical oblivion, is the whole familiar tradition of the book? All around us, already in place, are the technologies that will render it antiquated.

In the fall of 1992 I taught a course called "The American Short Story" to undergraduates at a local college. I assembled a set of readings that I thought would appeal to the tastes of the average undergraduate and felt relatively confident. We would begin with Washington Irving, then move on quickly to Hawthorne, Poe, James, and Jewett, before connecting with the progressively more accessible works of our century. I had expected that my students would enjoy "The Legend of Sleepy Hollow," be amused by its caricatures and ghost-story element. Nothing of the kind. Without exception they found the story over-long, verbose, a chore. I wrote their reactions off to the fact that it was the first assignment and that most students would not have hit their reading stride yet. When we got to Hawthorne and Poe I had the illusion that things were going a bit better.

But then came Henry James's "Brooksmith" and I was completely derailed. I began the class, as I always do, by soliciting casual responses of the "I liked it" and "I hated it" sort. My students could barely muster the energy for a thumbs-up or -down. It was as though some pneumatic pump had sucked out the last dregs of their spirits. "Bad day, huh?" I ventured. Persistent questioning revealed that it was the reading that had undone them. But why? What was the problem? I had to get to the bottom of their stupefaction before this relatively—*I thought*—available tale.

I asked: Was it a difficulty with the language, the style of writing? Nods all around. Well, let's be more specific. Was it vocabulary, sentence length, syntax? "Yeah, sort of," said one student, "but it was more just the whole thing." Hmmmmm. Well then, I said, we should consider this. I questioned whether they understood the basic plot. Sure, they said. A butler's master dies and the butler can't find another place as good. He loses one job after another—usually because he quits—then falls into despair and disappears, probably to end it all. "You don't find this moving?" One or two students conceded the pathos of the situation, but then the complaints resurfaced, with the original complainer chiming in again that it was not so much the story as "the whole thing."

The whole thing. *What* whole thing? My tone must have reflected my agitation, my impatience with their imprecision. But then, after endless going around, it stood revealed: These students were entirely defeated by James's prose—the medium of it—as well as by the assumptions that underlie it. It was not the vocabulary, for they could make out most of the words; and not altogether the syntax, although here they admitted to discomfort, occasional abandoned sentences. What they really could not abide was what the vocabulary, the syntax, the ironic indirection, and so forth, were communicating. *They didn't get it*, and their not getting it angered them, and they expressed their anger by drawing around themselves a cowl of ill-tempered apathy. Students whom I knew to be quick and resourceful in other situations suddenly retreated into glum illiteracy. "I dunno," said the spokesman, "the whole thing just bugged me—I couldn't get into it."

Disastrous though the class had been, I drove home in an excited mood. What had happened, I started to realize, was that I had encountered a conceptual ledge, one that may mark a break in historical continuity. This was more than just a bad class—it was a corroboration of something I had been on the verge of grasping for years. You could have drawn a lightbulb over my head and turned it on.

What is this ledge, and what does it have to do with the topic I've embarked upon? To answer the second question: Everything. As I wrote before: the world we have known, the world of our myths and references and shared assumptions, is being changed by a powerful, if often intangible, set of forces. We are living in the midst of a momentous paradigm shift. My classroom experience, which in fact represents hundreds of classroom experiences, can be approached diagnostically.

This is not a simple case of students versus Henry James. We are not concerned with an isolated clash of sensibilities, his and theirs. Rather, we are standing in one spot along a ledge—or, better, a fault line—dividing one order from another. In place of James we could as easily put Joyce or Woolf or Shakespeare or Ralph Ellison. It would be the same. The point is that the collective experience of these students, most of whom were born in the early 1970s, has rendered a vast part of our cultural heritage utterly alien. *That* is the breaking point: it describes where their understandings and aptitudes give out. What is at issue is not diction, not syntax, but everything that diction and syntax serve. Which is to say, an entire system of beliefs, values, and cultural aspirations.

In Henry James are distilled many of the elements I would discuss. He is inward and subtle, a master of ironies and indirections; his work manifests a care for the range of moral distinctions. And one cannot "get" him without paying heed to the least twist and turn of the language. James's world, and the dramas that take place in that world, are predicated on the idea of individuals in an organic relation to their society. In his universe, each one of those individuals are still surrounded by an aura of importance; their actions and decisions are felt to count for something.

I know that the society of James's day was also repressive to many, and was, further, invested in certain now-discredited assumptions of empire. I am not arguing for its return, certainly not in that form. But this was not the point, at least not in the discussions I then pursued with my students. For we did, after our disastrous James session, begin to question not only our various readings, but also the reading act itself and their relation to it. And what emerged was this: that they were not, with a few exceptions, readers—never had been; that they had always occupied themselves with music, TV, and videos; that they had difficulty slowing down enough to concentrate on prose of any density; that they had problems with what they thought of as archaic diction, with allusions, with vocabulary that seemed "pretentious"; that they were especially uncomfortable with indirect or interior passages, indeed with any deviations from straight plot; and that they were put off by ironic tone because it flaunted superiority and made them feel that they were missing something. The list is partial.

All of this confirmed my longstanding suspicion that, having grown up in an electronic culture, my students would naturally exhibit certain aptitudes and lack others. But the implications, as I began to realize, were rather staggering, especially if one thinks of this not as a temporary generational disability, but rather as a permanent turn. If this were true of my twenty-five undergraduates, I reasoned, many of them from relatively advantaged backgrounds, then it was probably true for most of their generation. And not only theirs, but for the generations on either side of them as well. What this meant was not, narrowly, that a large sector of our population would not be able to enjoy certain works of literature, but that a much more serious situation was developing. For, in fact, our entire collective subjective history—the soul of our societal body—is encoded in print. Is encoded, and has for countless generations been passed along by way of the word, mainly through books. I'm not talking about facts and information here, but about the somewhat more elusive soft data, the expressions that tell us who we are and who we have been, that are the record of individuals living in different epochs—that are, in effect, the cumulative speculations of the species. If a person turns from print—finding it too slow, too hard, irrelevant to the excitements of the present—then what happens to that person's sense of culture and continuity?

These are issues too large for mere analysis; they are over-determined. There is no way to fish out one strand and think it through. Yet think we must, even if we have to be clumsy and obvious at times. We are living in a society and culture that is in dissolution. Pack this paragraph with your own headlines about crime, eroded values, educational decline, what have you. There are many causes, many explanations. But behind them all, vague and menacing, is this recognition: that the understandings and assumptions that were formerly operative in society no longer feel valid. Things have shifted; they keep shifting. We all feel a desire for connection, for meaning, but we don't seem to know what to connect with what, and we are utterly at sea about our place as individuals in the world at large. The maps no longer describe the terrain we inhabit. There is no clear path to the future. We trust that the species will blunder on, but we don't know where *to*. We feel imprisoned in a momentum that is not of our own making.

I am not about to suggest that all of this comes of not reading Henry

James. But I will say that *of* all this comes not being *able* to read James or any other emissary from that recent but rapidly vanishing world. Our historically sudden transition into an electronic culture has thrust us into a place of unknowing. We have been stripped not only of familiar habits and ways, but of familiar points of moral and psychological reference. Looking out at our society, we see no real leaders, no larger figures of wisdom. Not a brave new world at all, but a fearful one.

The notion of historical change compels and vexes me. I am not so much interested in this war or that treaty or invention, although obviously these are critical factors. What I brood about has more to do with the phenomenology of everyday life. How it is that the world greets the senses differently—is experienced differently—from epoch to epoch. We know about certain ways in which the world has changed since, say, 1890, but do we know how the *feeling* of life has changed? We can isolate the more objective sorts of phenomena, cite improvements in transportation, industrial innovations, and so on, but we have no reliable access to the subjective realm. When older people sigh and say that "life was different back then," we may instinctively agree, but how can we grasp exactly what that difference means?

On the other hand, we all inhabit multiple time zones. We have the world of our daily present, which usually claims most of our attention, but we are also wrapped in shadowy bands of the past. First, we have the layers of our own history. The older we get, the more substantial grows the shadow—and the greater the gap between the world as we know it now and the world as it used to be. At the outer perimeter, that indistinct mass of memories shades together with another mass. These are the memories we grew up among. They belong to our parents and grandparents. Our picture of the world, how it is and how it used to be, is necessarily tinged with what we absorbed from innumerable references and anecdotes, from the *then* that preceded us.

Thus, as a man in my early forties, I already carry a substantial temporal baggage. I am a citizen of the *now*, reading the daily paper, sliding my embossed card into the money machine at the bank, and renting a video for the evening's relaxation. But I am also other selves: a late starter, a casualty of the culture wars of the 1960s, an alienated adolescent sopping up pop culture and dreaming of escape, an American kid

21

growing up in the 1950s, playing touch football and watching "I Love Lucy." An American kid? I should say a kid trying very hard to be an American kid. For although I was born here, both my parents were from the old country, Latvia, and my childhood was both subtly and overtly permeated by their experience—their stories of growing up in Riga, of war and dispersal. And how it was for them naturally became a part of how it was for me.

Nor did it end there. I also grew up with grandparents. And from them I imbibed still another sense of time. Visiting their home, I circulated among their artifacts, heard their reminiscences. Through them I made contact, however indirectly, with a world utterly unlike anything I know now: a world at once more solid and grim, a world that held gaps and spaces and distances. Although my grandparents both grew up in towns, they had roots in rural places. Their stories were filled with farm and country lore. Indeed, until quite late in their lives they had no car, no TV. Even the telephone had something newfangled about it. Their anecdotes unfolded in a different order, at a different pace. They had one foot in the modern era and one foot back in the real past. By that I mean the past that had seen generation upon generation living more or less in the same way—absorbing incremental change, yes, but otherwise bound to a set of fundamental rhythms.

There is a difference between this sort of reflection and that more-piercing awareness we call nostalgia. Nostalgia is immediate, and tends to be more localized. As often as not, it is triggered by an experiential short-circuit; our awareness of the present is suddenly interrupted by an image, a feeling, or a sensation from the past. A song on the radio, an old photograph discovered in the pages of a book. The past catches us by surprise and we are filled with longing: for that thing, that person, that place, but more for the selves that we were then.

Like everyone else, I am subject to these intrusions. I distinguish them from the more sustained sorts of excavations that I have been undertaking recently. I am not in search of private sensation, but of a kind of understanding. I want to know what life may have been like during a certain epoch, what daily living may have felt like, so that I can make a comparison with the present. Why? I suppose because I believe that there is a secret to be found, a clue that will help me to solve the mystery of the present.

It happened that while I was in this season of thinking about time and the life of the past I rented a video of a film called *Fools of Fortune,* based on a novel by William Trevor. It was a desperate grab, really, a bid to cancel the residue of an enervating day. But as soon as I popped the cassette into the player I felt my obsessions again coalesce. The opening moments of the film reproduced what were meant to be bits of old 8-mm footage. Jerky, erratic, bleached and pocked by time. A child toddling forward across a grand lawn, a manor house in the background. A woman in a garden chair with period clothing and hairstyle. All cinematic artifice, of course, but I was entirely susceptible to it.

The film depicted Ireland in the early years of our century, during the time of the civil war. I was most struck by what seemed its real sensitivity to the conditions of the provincial life it recorded. Lingering shots of silent rooms, of people working in uninterrupted solitude, of people walking and walking, carts slowly rolling. I may be tailoring my memory of the film to fit my need, but never mind. And never mind the fact that I was sitting in my 1990s electronic cottage, watching actors in a commercial production on my videocassette player. For a few moments I succumbed to the intended illusion: I was looking through a window at the actual past, at things as they had once been. I was overwhelmed, really, by the realization of change. In a matter of decades—from the time of my grandparents to the time of the present—we have, all of us, passed through the looking glass.

At one point in the film the main character walks along the side of a brick building, toward the town square. An unremarkable scene, transitional filler. Yet this was, for some reason, the moment that awakened me. I thought: If I could just imagine myself completely into this scene, see my surroundings as if through the eyes of this person, then I would know something. I tried to perform the exercise in different ways. First, by taking a blind leap backward, restricting myself to just those things he might have encountered, imagining for myself the dung and coal-smoke scent of the spring air, the feel of rounded cobblestones under my shoes, a surrounding silence broken by the sounds of hammers, cartwheels, and hooves. A nearly impossible maneuver, but attempting it I realized how much has to be forcibly expunged from awareness.

I have also tried working myself back gradually from present to past, peeling off the layers one by one: taking away televisions and telephones (all things "tele-"), airplanes, cars, plastics, synthetic fibers, efficient sanitation, asphalt, wristwatches, and ballpoint pens, and on and on. The effect is quite extraordinary. I feel a progressive widening of space and increase of silence, as well as a growing specific gravity in objects. As I move more deeply into the past, I feel the encroachment of place; the specifics of locale get more and more prominent as the distance to the horizon increases. So many things need to be reconstituted: the presence of neighbors; the kinds of knowledge that come from living a whole life within a narrow compass; the aura of unattainable distance that attaches to the names of faraway places—India, Ceylon, Africa . . . And what was it like to live so close to death? And what about everything else: the feel of woven cloth, the different taste of food, drink, pipe tobacco? From the center of the life I imagine, a life not even a century old, I find it impossible to conceive of the life I am living now. The looking glass works both ways.

The chain of association is the lifeline, or fate, of thought. One thing leads to another; ideas gather out of impressions and begin to guide the steps in mysterious ways. After my experience of watching *Fools of Fortune,* I decided that I should find a novel from the period. To read it with an eye for those very "background" features—to derive some further sense of the feel of life in a pre-electronic age. I picked up Thomas Hardy's *Jude the Obscure.*

Read this way, with as much attention paid to the conditions of life as to the lives themselves, *Jude* becomes another window opening upon *how it was.* From the very first sentences, the spell of the past is woven:

> The schoolmaster was leaving the village, and everybody seemed sorry. The miller at Cresscombe lent him the small white tilted cart and horse to carry his goods to the city of his destination, about twenty miles off, such a vehicle proving of quite sufficient size for the departing teacher's effects.

To enter the work at all we need to put our present-day sense of things in suspension; we have to, in effect, reposition the horizon and reconceive all of our assumptions about the relations between things. Hardy's twenty miles are not ours. The pedagogue does not pile his belongings into the back of a Jeep Cherokee. His "effects" fit easily into a small horse-drawn cart he has borrowed. The city, called Christminster in the novel, is within walking distance of the village of Marygreen, but the distance means something. Soon enough, Hardy's Jude will stand on a nearby hill straining to catch a glimpse of that city's spires. He will dream of one day going there: to Jude it is the far edge of the world. Not because he could not with some pluck walk there to see it himself, but because he knows, as does everyone, that places are self-contained. Christminster is not just a point on a grid, it is a small world with its own laws, its own vortex of energies; it is *other*. And reading *Jude* we begin to grasp distinctions of this sort.

It would take too long to address as they deserve the myriad ways in which Jude's world is different from ours. But as we read we are gradually engulfed by a half-familiar set of sensations. Because the characters walk, we walk; because they linger by roadsides or in market squares, we do too. And by subtle stages we are overwhelmed. Overwhelmed by the size of the world. If Christminster is a trip, then London, hardly even mentioned, is a journey. And America, or any other country, is a voyage. The globe expands, and at the same time our sense of silence deepens. No background hum, no ambient noise. When people communicate, it is face to face. Or else by letter. There are no telephones or cars to hurriedly bridge the spatial gaps. We hear voices, and we hear footsteps die away in the distance. Days pass at a pace we can hardly imagine. A letter arrives and it is an event. The sound of paper unfolding, of wind in the trees outside the door. And then the things, their *thingness*. Jude's little hoard of Greek and Latin grammars, the smudgy books he had scrimped to buy—books he carried with him until his dying day. His stoneworking tools: well cared for, much prized. I suddenly think of lines from Elizabeth Bishop's poem "Crusoe in England." The castaway has returned "home" after his long years on the island:

Now I live here, another island,
that doesn't seem like one, but who decides?
My blood was full of them; my brain
bred islands. But that archipelago
has petered out. I'm old.
I'm bored, too, drinking my real tea,
surrounded by uninteresting lumber.
The knife there on the shelf—
it reeked of meaning, like a crucifix.
It lived. How many years did I
beg it, implore it, not to break?
I knew each nick and scratch by heart,
the bluish blade, the broken tip,
the lines of wood-grain on the handle . . .
Now it won't look at me at all.
The living soul has dribbled away.
My eyes rest on it and pass on.

This is it, no? The densities of meaning once conferred, since leached out. Our passage into bright contemporaneity has carried a price: The more complex and sophisticated our systems of lateral access, the more we sacrifice in the way of depth. Read *Jude the Obscure* and you will be struck, I think, by the material particularity of Hardy's world. You will feel the heft of things, the solidity. You will also feel the stasis, the near-intolerable boredom of boundedness.

Advantages and disadvantages—how could it be otherwise? I speak as if longingly of those times, but would I trade the speed and access and comfort of my life for the rudeness and singularity of that? I doubt it. But then, I have the benefit of hindsight. I am in the position of the adult who is asked if he would return once and for all to his childhood. The answer is yes and no.

And the purpose of this rambling excursion? Am I simply lamenting the loss of something I could not bear to recover—a gone world? No. What I intended, in the obscure way one intends these things when writing, was to wander away from the specter of my American short story class, wander until the reader's memory traces should have all but faded, and then to bring the image of those students forward again. To try one more time to make something of my intuition: that their unease before Henry James's "Brooksmith" has a larger significance, that it is not just another instance of young minds being put off by James's assumptions of civilization, but rather that that unease illuminates something central about our cultural condition and its prospects.

Obviously it is too simplistic to blame the students' discomfiture, not just with James but with demanding texts in general, upon any one thing, such as television, video games, inadequate secondary schools, or what have you. To do so would be to miss the larger point: that the situation is total and arises from systemic changes affecting the culture at every level. And while the situation thus defies ready analysis, it nevertheless has the greatest consequences for all of us and must somehow be addressed. We are at a watershed point. One way of processing information is yielding to another. Bound up with each is a huge array of aptitudes, assumptions, and understandings about the world.

We can think of the matter in terms of gains and losses. The gains of electronic postmodernity could be said to include, for individuals, (a) an increased awareness of the "big picture," a global perspective that admits the extraordinary complexity of interrelations; (b) an expanded neural capacity, an ability to accommodate a broad range of stimuli simultaneously; (c) a relativistic comprehension of situations that promotes the erosion of old biases and often expresses itself as tolerance; and (d) a matter-of-fact and unencumbered sort of readiness, a willingness to try new situations and arrangements.

In the loss column, meanwhile, are (a) a fragmented sense of time and a loss of the so-called duration experience, that depth phenomenon we associate with reverie; (b) a reduced attention span and a general impatience with sustained inquiry; (c) a shattered faith in institutions and in the explanatory narratives that formerly gave shape to subjective experience; (d) a divorce from the past, from a vital sense of history as a cumulative or organic process; (e) an estrangement from geographic place and community; and (f) an absence of any strong vision of a personal or collective future.

These are, granted, enormous generalizations. But they record what a great many of my students have said of themselves and their own experiences. For, apart from talking about their responses to texts, we talked a good deal about their lives. They were as interested as I was in discussing how their sense of the world had bearing on their reading. What surprised me was the degree to which their own view of themselves was critical.

But these are all abstract considerations while the pressure that compels me to write this is very much rooted in daily experience and in my own fears. I worry not only that the world will become increasingly alien and inhospitable to me, but also that I will be gradually coerced into living against my natural grain, forced to adapt to a pace and a level of technological complexity that does not suit me, and driven to interact with others in certain prescribed ways. I tried to live without a telephone answering machine for a time and was made to feel like a pariah. I type these words on an IBM Selectric and feel positively antediluvian: My editors let me know that my quaint Luddite habits are gumming up the works, slowing things down for them.

These are trivial examples, but they are indicative. On one level or another we make our adjustments; we shrug and bow to progress. But the fact is that with each capitulation we are drawn more deeply into the web. True, none of the isolated changes make that much difference— but the increasing enmeshment does. The more deeply we are implicated, the more we forfeit in the way of personal initiative and agency; the more we become part of a species-organism. Every acquiescence to the circuitry is marked by a shrinkage of the sphere of autonomous selfhood.

As a writer I naturally feel uneasy. These large-scale changes bode ill for authorship, at least of the kind I would pursue. There are, we know this, fewer and fewer readers for serious works. Publishers are increasingly reluctant to underwrite the publication of a book that will sell only a few thousand copies. But very few works of any artistic importance sell more than that. And those few thousand readers—a great many of them, it turns out, are middle-aged or older. The younger generations have not caught the habit.

I rue all of this, but I can take it. Reading and writing will last long enough to cover my stay here below. Indeed, I have resolved to make the crisis—I see it as such—my subject. But I also look toward the future as a father. I have a five-year-old daughter and cannot but think of the ways in which her life will be different than mine. And when, in my darker moods, I contemplate the forces that will determine so much of her experience, her subjective outlook, I feel a sharp sense of regret. Then it seems to me that unless her mother and I are able to equip her with an extraordinary doggedness and with a strong appetite for what is unique and vital, she will be swept up in the tide of the homogeneous. If she goes to a school where reading is not prized, if she follows the non-reading horde of her peers, where will she find the incentive, the desire to read on her own? And if she does not read on her own, where will she find the nutrients she needs in order to evolve an independent identity?

We do what we can, and we try to do it in a noncoercive way. We promote the pleasures of the book by example, by forever reading. And we try to make the encounter enjoyable. We buy books, borrow them from the library, and read to her regularly. But we also try to avoid any association of the medicinal—that books are good for her and that reading is a duty. So far it seems to be working. She is eager; she recognizes that books are a place away from routine, a place associated with dreams and fantasies.

On the one side, then, is the reading encounter, the private resource. On the other is the culture at large, and the highly seductive glitter of mass-produced entertainment. We are not so foolish as to prohibit it, but I sometimes wonder if we are being as wise as we might be in not curtailing it more. We have entered the world of Disney, and I am seized by the fear that there might be no way out. This past season it was *Beauty and the Beast*. I don't just mean that we saw the movie in the theater once or twice, which would have been the beginning and end of it when I was a child; we saw the movie three, four, five times. We bought the book, illustrated with stills from the movie, and we read that, and looked through it, half a hundred times. The cassette of the songs was purchased and played until the emulsion on the tape wore thin. Then, for Christmas, the video. Another thirty viewings, maybe more. And then the ice show with the *Beauty and the Beast* theme, and the accessories (flashlight, cup) that can perch on the shelf alongside the plastic *Beauty and the Beast* toys given out at Burger King.

Today as never before in human history the child lives in an entertainment environment, among myriad spinoffs and products and commercial references, all of which reinforce the power, or should I say tyranny, of the movie. I relent in the face of it. I was raised quite strictly so I am, in my turn, lenient. I don't have the heart to deny my daughter what she covets and what all her friends have. I see the pleasure she takes in occupying this vivid universe and I want her to have it. I tell myself that it will feed her imagination and that she will soon enough grow into more intricate and demanding fantasies.

And then I despair. I conjure up a whole generation of children enslaved by a single carefully scripted, lushly animated narrative. Not even a narrative created by a single artist, but a team product. A studio job. And I wonder what tale or rhyme or private fantasy will be able to compete with the high-powered rendition from Hollywood's top talents. Is her imagination being awakened, or stultified, locked forever on a kind of assembly-line track? What is the effect of these dozens and dozens of repetitions? What are the overt and subliminal messages she is taking in? What is she learning about men, women, love, honor, and all the rest? Is she incorporating into her deepest subjective structure a set of glib clichés? Will she and her millions of peers, that huge constituency that comprises our future and that is underwriting the global growth of the Disney empire—will all of these kids march forward into adulthood as Disney automatons, with cookie-cut responses to the world they encounter?

I have these fears, and yet I remain permissive. I suppose that is in part because I believe that mass culture is so pervasive these days that it is folly to try to hide from it; that if I do curtail it I will invest it with all that much more appeal. But my permissiveness also depends upon a kind of wager, or a profession of faith. I let the rivers of popular culture (the less-polluted ones) flow freely around my daughter. But at the same time I do everything I can to introduce her to books and stories. I trust that in the free market of the child's imagination these more traditional goods are interesting and unique enough to hold their own. No less important, I stake myself on the basic vitality and independence of that child's soul. I cannot allow that we are so limited, so acquiescent in our basic makeup that we can be stamped to shape like identical cogwheels by the commercial machinery, however powerful that machinery may be.

The good and the true, I believe, will win out. But for that to happen there must be exposure. The child needs to know the range of pleasures. There is room for *Beauty and the Beast* à la Disney, but only when the field includes the best that has been imagined and written through the ages. I believe, I believe—help mine unbelief.

The form of my meditation has been—as I warned—loose. Liberated by the example of Woolf, I have at times let the line of thought go trailing away. But there is also a point to these musings. To put it simply: We have, perhaps without noticing, slipped over a crucial threshold. We have rather abruptly replaced our time-honored and slow-to-evolve modes of communication and interaction with new modes. We have in significant ways surmounted the constraints imposed by nature, in the process altering our relation to time, space, and to each other. We have scarcely begun to assess the impact of these transformations—that will be the work of generations. What I have tried to suggest is that some of our fundamental assumptions about identity and subjective meaning need to be examined carefully. For, by moving from the order of print to the electronic, we risk the loss of the sense of obstacle as well as the feel of the particular that have characterized our experience over millennia. We are poised at the brink of what may prove to be a kind of species mutation. We had better consider carefully what this means.

I have been accused of being alarmist and conservative and prey to excessive nostalgia. And I accuse myself of cowardly pessimism. Why can't I embrace the necessity of historical progress? I have my reasons.

1. I believe that what distinguishes us as a species is not our technological prowess, but rather our extraordinary ability to confer meaning on our experience and to search for clues about our purpose from the world around us.

2. I believe, too, that meaning of this kind—call it "existential" meaning—has from the beginning been the product of our other great distinguishing aptitude: the ability to communicate symbolically through language. Indeed, language is the soil, the seedbed, of meaning. And the works of language, our literatures, have been the repository of our collective speculation.

3. Literature holds meaning not as a content that can be abstracted

and summarized, but as experience. It is a participatory arena. Through the process of reading we slip out of our customary time orientation, marked by distractedness and surficiality, into the realm of duration. Only in the duration state is experience present as meaning. Only in this state are we prepared to consider our lives under what the philosophers used to call "the aspect of eternity," to question our origins and destinations, and to conceive of ourselves as souls.

I am not going to argue against the power and usefulness of electronic technologies. Nor am I going to suggest that we try to turn back or dismantle what we have wrought in the interests of an intensified relation to meaning. But I would urge that we not fall all over ourselves in our haste to filter all of our experience through circuitries. We are in some danger of believing that the speed and wizardry of our gadgets have freed us from the sometimes arduous work of turning pages in silence.

I keep a file at home entitled "The Reading Wars"—there I save newspaper clippings and relevant notes I've jotted down. The title captures my sense of urgency, my sense that there is a battle going on. On bad days I think it's hopeless, that the forces pulling us away from print—and from ourselves—are too strong; that it is inevitable that generation by generation all independence and idiosyncrasy and depth will be worn away; that we will move ever more surely in lockstep, turning ourselves into creatures of the hive, living some sort of diluted universal dream in a perpetual present. When that fear threatens to lay me low, I try to remember to turn my head. There, pinned to my bulletin board, is a sheet of white paper covered with crayon marks. Crude letters, runes on a cave wall. M's and V's and H's and P's—repeated over and over. My daughter's work. She came to it by herself. One afternoon she marched into my study with the page extended proudly. She wanted to know what she had written. How to answer? You wrote "MahmahmahVuhvuhvuhHuhhuhhuhPuhpuhpuh"? Or act the indecipherable adult and say: "You just helped your dad finish something he's been working on for weeks"? I said neither. I complimented her work and let her help me pin it to the bulletin board.

# 2

# The Paper Chase:

## *An Autobiographical Fragment*

M ANY YEARS AGO, when I was still in college and affecting paperbacks in my back pockets and dreaming of the great novels I
would one day produce, I went to hear Anthony Burgess speak on "The
Writer's Life." The man was, as one might expect, a charming racon-
teur, and he carried on with great authority about the perils and
perquisites of literary careers. I have forgotten most of what was said,
but I do remember that at one point Burgess joked about his experiences as a book reviewer. Every day, he said, the postman would bring
him parcels of bright new review copies. These he would pile neatly in
the hallway by his front door until he had a tall stack, at which point he
would cart them down to the local bookseller and "flog" them for
pocket money. I didn't know the slang idiom "flog" then, but it had a
raffish ring to it and I thought, "Yes, that's quite a racket." And for a
long time I thought nothing more about it.

I thought no more about it because I had bigger fish to fry. I was in-
cubating important creative works and all other writing endeavors
seemed insignificant in comparison. Besides, I knew that book reviewing was not a vocation that one aspired to; rather, one did it with the left
hand while doing worthier things with the right.

I can almost see myself as I was then. Stubbled, slouching, eager
above all else to be perceived as different—in the crowd but not of it, a
young writer not about to waste his time on the lower part of the mountain. And if I pick that afternoon lecture as a place to start from it is because I am now that thing I so confidently scorned, a book reviewer. It
has taken me almost twenty years to free myself of the idea that writing

about novels represents the defeat of the would-be novelist. And even now I'm not completely liberated. When people ask me what I do, I usually say I'm an essayist or a critic. More honorable terms, both, and they mostly fit. They almost conceal the fact that the greater part of what I do is read and write about books.

There is a path, then, from A to B, from disaffected renegade to reviewer, though of course it neither begins right at A nor ends obligingly at B. As paths go it is a meandering thing, with many twists and divagations, each describing some choice made at a crucial moment. Back then, when the whole idea of a path was hazy, I did not think of myself as following or making any sort of track. I wandered to and fro in the realm of the immediate, moving toward what I liked and striking out against whatever displeased me. Retrospect alters everything. Looking through the aperture of time is like watching a movement from a great altitude. What felt like blundering starts to look like a fate.

That stubbled poseur, that angry and no-doubt-irritating nineteen-year-old—where did he get the idea that he wanted to write? Why that and not filmmaking or professing law or practicing psychotherapy? To ask this is naturally to initiate a regress, to scramble all the way back to the psyche in formation. Why words on a page, why a desire to write fiction?

There is one obvious answer: that the urge was a direct outgrowth of a love of reading, a determination to master the source of that pleasure—but this answer hardly exhausts the matter. Why did I become such a reader in the first place? What made me so susceptible to the figments I coaxed from the printed page? Was it something innate in my disposition (both grandparents on my father's side had been literary people back in Latvia), or some fortuitous early exposure (the fact that my mother delighted in reading me stories)? Or were the influences of greater psychological complexity, having to do with the fact that our family spoke another language (Latvian) at home, a fact that marked my childhood deeply and filled me with a sense of being different? Or was reading just my way of blocking out family tensions—my father's strictness, the unpredictable flaring of his temper? I would have to circle all of the above.

But to list determinants in this way, even to think of them as factors in isolation, must misrepresent the experience. True, these were all things that pushed me toward books—toward an "other" place away from my immediate surroundings—but what made me a reader were the experiences I got from the books themselves. An obvious assertion, but a true one. It is easy enough in retrospect to see a book as a screen, a shield, an escape, but at the time there was just the magic—the startling and renewable discovery that a page covered with black markings could, with a slight mental exertion, be converted into an environment, an inward depth populated with characters and animated by diverse excitements. A world inside the world, secret and concealable. A world that I could carry about as a private resonance, a daydream, even when I was not reading. A moveable feast.

From the time of earliest childhood, I was enthralled by books. First just by their material mysteries. I studied pages of print and illustrations, stared myself into the wells of fantasy that are the hallmark of the awakening inner life. Mostly there was pleasure, but not always. I remember a true paralytic terror brought on by the cartoon dalmations pictured on the endpapers of my Golden Books. For a time I refused to be alone in the room with the books, even when the covers were safely closed. Ascribing power to likeness, I thought the dogs would slip free of their confinement and come baying after me.

But that was the exception. Dreamy sensuousness generally prevailed. A page was a field studded with tantalizing signs and a book was a vast play structure riddled with openings and crevices I could get inside. This notion of hiding, secreting myself in a text was important to me—it underlies to this day my sense of a book as a refuge. That I could not yet translate the letters into words and meanings only added to the grave mysteriousness of the artifact. On the far side of that plane of scrambled markings was a complete other world. And then one day the path came clear. I was in the first grade. I went over and around and suddenly *through* the enormous letter shapes of Kipling's *Jungle Book*. The first sentence, that is. I read! And from that moment on, the look of a word became a window onto its meaningful depths.

Once I got underway, I was an interested, eager, but not terribly precocious reader—I was no Susan Sontag knocking back nutritive classics while still in grade school. I was a dreamer and books were my tools for dreaming. I read the ones that were more or less suited to my age and did so devotedly. Books about Indian chiefs, explorers, and dogs; biographies of inventors and athletes; the pasteurized versions of London and Poe that came via the Scholastic Book Club. I had the first real thrill of ownership in second or third grade, when the teacher broke open the first shipment and handed each of us in the class the books we had ordered. Later it was the Hardy Boys, with their illustrated covers and crisp blue spines; then James Bond, the slim little pocketbooks reeking of sexual innuendo and high-class gadgetry. Not until I was in junior high did I begin to make contact with some of the so-called "better" books—by Salinger, Wolfe, Steinbeck and others. But even then I had no idea of bettering myself. I was simply looking for novels with characters whose lives could absorb mine for a few hours.

That demand has not changed much over the years. What have changed are my empathic capacities. I have gradually grown interested in lives that are utterly different from my own. I find that I have little difficulty now slipping into the skin of Emperor Hadrian or Clarissa Dalloway or anyone else, provided the narrative is psychologically compelling and credible. But when I was ten or twelve or fourteen I needed to hear what other young men, my age or a few years older, had to say about things. I looked to Tom Sawyer, later to Holden Caulfield and Eugene Gant and the heroes of William Goldman's novels. I prowled the aisles of Readmore Books, the local temple to the mass market paperback, searching for books with a certain kind of cover—usually a rendering of a moody-looking young man with some suggestion of meditated rebellion in his stance. Interestingly enough, there were quite a few books that fit the bill, from William Goldman's *Temple of Gold* to Romain Gary's *Ski Bum* to Harold Robbins's *Stone for Danny Fisher*. The approach of the late-1960s counterculture could have been discerned here by anyone with a grasp of how images translated into collective attitudes, and vice versa. Although I did not know it then, I was on the cusp of my own rebellion, slowly readying myself for a major bout of acting out. When the time came, two or three years later, my guides would be Jack Kerouac, Ken Kesey, Richard Fariña, Kurt Vonnegut, Norman Mailer, Henry Miller, and others.

The reading I did in late boyhood and early adolescence was passionate and private, carried on at high heat. When I went to my room and opened a book, it was to seal myself off as fully as possible in another place. I was not reading, as now, with only one part of the self. I was there body and soul, living vicariously. When Finney died at the end of John Knowles's *Separate Peace* I cried scalding tears, unable to believe that the whole world did not grind to a sorrowful halt. That was then. Books no longer tap my emotions quite so directly; I am rarely brought to tears or fury. But what I have not lost is a churning anxiety, an almost intolerable sensation that sometimes has me drawing breaths to steady myself. There is something about the reading act that cuts through the sheath of distractedness that usually envelops me. It is as if I can suddenly feel the pure flow of time behind the stationary letters. Vertigo is not a comfortable sensation, but I keep seeking it out, taking it as an inoculation against what a Latin poet called *lacrimae rerum,* "the tears of things."

I remember so clearly the shock I would feel whenever I looked up from the vortex of the page and faced the strangely immobile world around me. My room, the trees outside the window—everything seemed so dense, so saturated with itself. Never since have I known it so intensely, this colliding of realities, the current of mystery leaping the gap between them. In affording this dissociation, reading was like a drug. I knew even then, in my early teen years, that what I did in my privacy was in some way a betrayal of the dominant order of things, an excitement slightly suspect at its core.

This last is a complex business, intensified for me by my father's attitudes. In my childhood, my father was a stern man with a quick temper and an impatient disdain for anything that smacked of reverie or private absorption, almost as if these states in some way challenged his authority. I find his attitude strange, the more so since he idolized his mother, who was one of the most bookish people I have ever known. Indeed, when we first traveled to Riga to visit her, when I first stepped through the door into her apartment, I was stunned. I suddenly understood a great deal about my own genetic inheritance. As I took in the walls of books, the piles of journals and papers on every available surface, I saw the signs of a mania I knew all too well.

But my father was nothing like his mother in this respect. He was a man out in the world, a problem-solver. He had the idea that a boy should be outside in the fresh air, playing, doing chores, whatever. For him there was something against nature in the sight of a healthy individual sitting by himself with a book in his lap. This shouldn't surprise anyone—it is the prevalent bias in our culture. Doing is prized over being or thinking. Reading is something you do because it has been assigned in school, or because all other options have been exhausted—no more chores to do, all other games and activities put away.

It says a great deal about the dynamics of our family that my mother was—and remains—a devoted reader. She read for pleasure, for company, and for escape. Novels, biographies, popular histories—there was never a time when she did not have at least one book going. My father had long since given up any idea he might have had of reforming her (into what?), but to this day he continues to mock what he considers to be her absorption in secondhand experience.

Naturally books became something of a battleground—although no one ever admitted this directly. When I read I was, in my father's understanding of things, siding not only with my mother but with the feminine principle itself, never mind that I might have been reading Hemingway or Thomas Wolfe or Ian Fleming. And whenever the jibes began ("What are you doing on the couch in the middle of the day? You need something to do? *I'll* give you something to do"), my mother, no doubt recognizing a sidelong swipe at herself, would rush to my defense. At which point I had to recognize that I was being caught up in what looked like a traditional "mama's boy" scenario. And I did *not* want to be seen by anyone, especially my father, as a mama's boy.

I therefore began to be more careful about my reading. Although I could still be spotted with a book in my hand, my real reading life, the main current of it, flowed on behind closed doors. If that life was not secret, it was private. I read when my parents were away; I read late into the night. Befitting my usual pattern, I was outwardly yielding to my father while inwardly rebelling. By cultivating a hidden reading life I was, in one sense, acceding to his view that there was something not altogether savory about the way I was using the best energies of my youth. But I was also thereby giving the act a more privileged place in my life; I was investing it with some of the cachet of the prohibited. If reading was worth guarding and being secretive about, there had to be genuine power in it.

So I read. I moved into the space of reading as into a dazzling counterworld. I loved just thinking about books, their wonderful ciphering of thought and sensation. I was pleased by the fact that from a distance, even from a nearby but disinterested vantage, every page looked more or less the same. A piano roll waiting for its sprockets. But for the devoted user of the code that same page was experience itself. I understood that this was something almost completely beyond legislation. No one, not even another reader reading the same words, could know what those signs created once they traveled up the eyebeam.

And the connection of all this to the writing urge? Again, the precise origins are hard to trace. The roots extend back into earliest childhood where only the faintest hints of inclination are ever discernible. Certainly both the desire and the ability to write are closely bound up with the love of the word. Love? Wouldn't it be more accurate to speak in terms of pleasure, of sensuousness, of finding joy in the making and hearing of meaningful sounds? My situation was complicated and no doubt intensified by my relation to the words, by the fact that my first language was Latvian, the language of home, and that immersion in English only came once I was old enough to play with the neighborhood kids and start school.

I don't have any clear memories of learning English or of making some difficult transition from native to adopted tongue. I don't recall stammering or looking for words I didn't have, or suffering ridicule from my preschool peers. But I do know that for a long time, for much of my childhood, I felt that English was not mine, that it belonged to *them*. The fact that I traded in one language for another as soon as I set foot in our house underscored what I knew from the start: We were different. I envied the slangy ease of others, envied it in the basic way that all kids envy the looks or toys of their more fortunate playmates. I heard, or I imagined, how they were at home in their speech, and I wanted it.

By the time I was in second grade I could mimic them perfectly, saying "betcha" and "wanna" without a betraying flicker. But deep down I knew that my possession of the idioms of the kid world was second-hand. Unlike them, I could step back from myself and experience what W. E. B. Du Bois in another context called "double consciousness." I watched myself playing the role of the normal American kid.

Did this sharpen my sense of English? How could it not? I was bent upon blending in, upon never giving away what I knew to be my outsider status. Looking back now it seems a small issue, but then it was my life. Everything depended upon acceptance by others. I became, in my way, a student of inflection, a scholar of offhand delivery. And I managed it well. Still, I had my private agonies. Whenever either of my parents came in contact with my friends, even with other adults, I winced at their accents. Both spoke English in a way that called attention to the fact that they were foreigners. Every fumble they made, every syntactical misstep, threatened the edifice I was building for myself. And yet, the odd thing is, I don't remember any of my friends making cracks or comments about the way my parents spoke—I inflicted all the lashes myself.

The drive to write declared itself only gradually. Just as I was not a devourer of classics at a young age, so too I was not one of those gifted children who are forever making up stories or creating little books. I did take a real interest in writing school reports and papers, but of course I concealed it. Like everyone else, I groaned when a new writing assignment was announced. But behind the mask I was glad. I liked my handwriting and quite enjoyed the physical transcription of materials for reports. I was also compulsive. I prized neatness and if a handwritten page did not look right I would tear it up and start again. I remember toiling over vast projects on the human body, the Olympics, and my state of choice, Oregon. I copied out far more information than I had to. I had discovered something gratifying in the act of inscribing signs on a page in an orderly way. The basic warps of character are there from the start and we do not outgrow them easily; drafting these words into a spiral notebook, I find that both the compulsiveness and pleasure remain.

The more purposeful, creative kind of writing became important to me once I started junior high school. In response to a class assignment for English—write a description of someone you know—I produced an utterly fictitious portrait of my grandfather, my mother's father, endowing him with a white beard, a pipe, and a fund of stories about far-away places he had explored. In fact, he was clean-shaven, nonsmoking, and quite private about his past experiences. My teacher entered the sketch in a citywide writing contest and stunned me one day by announcing before the whole class that I had won a gold key. How little encouragement it sometimes takes. From that day on, I have thought of myself as a writer.

"A writer". . . I hasten to say that my view of what a writer is and does has changed a good deal since those days. I have not, I'm glad to say, purged myself entirely of the idealized images I once had, but those images have been overtaken (swamped, really) by the more prosaic parts of the daily demand. Nowadays being a writer is mainly about the realities of producing new work and finding outlets for it. But when I was in my teens, work was the least of it. Indeed, I saw the writing itself as the necessary by-product of the image. To *be* a writer—that is, to live that particular relation of self to the world—that was what mattered. If one lived the right way, then the prose would just somehow be there. And I viewed writers less in terms of what they had written than in terms of the facts of their biographies. Did they honor the vocation with their way of living? I read the author notes on dust jackets, and I meditated over the photographs, zeroing in not just on the faces, but the backgrounds as well. Was the Aegean visible through the window? Was that a whiskey bottle, a lion's hide? Long before I had read a word by Hemingway I knew the lore—the wars, the wives, the marlins, the wild nights of drinking in exotic locales.

Not only was my image-worship terminally adolescent, but it also marked a complete inversion of what I later learned were the accepted values—I was exalting the artist over the art. But I don't want to scoff too much at my fixation, for underneath the hero-worship (or maybe at the core of it) was a recognition that I still endorse. Namely, that to be a writer was not just to produce words—books—as other professionals produce car designs or legal agreements. Rather, it was to position oneself independently, at an angle to society; it was to live in a different and possibly dangerous way in the service of a vision. It sounds grandiose, but I think there is also a truth there, one we too readily pride ourselves on having outgrown. Don't we still search for it as we read? Isn't this independence, this outsider's perspective, part of what we trust the writer to supply as an intrinsic component of any book? Don't we still, at some level, need our dreams of writers and their mysterious art?

Back then, of course, I thought of danger in mainly physical terms —Hemingway carrying stretchers or hunting tigers, Knut Hamsun riding across the American plains on top of a freight train—and vision was something utter and absolute, a near-hallucinatory way of seeing the world (I harkened to Rimbaud's idea of "the complete derangement of the senses"). But with some modification of terms, allowing that a sense of danger can accompany a psychological or moral struggle, and that vision need not require insane magnifications of the ordinary, I find that I can still embrace the conception.

All of this is a roundabout way of saying that through my teens I thought and fantasized a great deal about being a writer, but I did not actually write very much. Like most members of the self-styled "bohemian" fringe, or "artsy" crowd, I kept a sheaf of loosely metered, Ferlinghetti-inspired poetry, adding lines and images to it whenever the heavens dictated. And there was a similarly loose "idea journal" to which I contributed long free-associative paragraphs about my growing sense of alienation from all accepted authorities (I almost wrote "from Amerika," but this activity was underway before the counterculture announced itself). But I had no higher discipline, no will yet to produce finished work.

Nor, if the truth be told, did I read omnivorously. I dabbled in books constantly, started a great many, but I was much keener on fingering the pages, studying the covers and prefaces. I was far too daunted by all that I had not read to confine myself to the hard work of reading any one book—except those that I saw as pertaining directly to my life: books by Hesse, Salinger, Kerouac, and a very few others.

I find it hard to look back on those years without embarrassment. The identifications and gestures were all so romantic, and enacted at such a pitch. But I also have to believe that this is where some of the most revealing clues about the character are to be found. Don't we reveal our essential selves most explicitly in the unguarded enthusiasms of our teenage years? Isn't that why the memories later fill us with such a prickly sense of shame?

I remember perfectly the intoxication I felt at the mere contemplation of certain writers. They were my rock stars (though rock stars were my "rock stars," too); their lives and their writings fused into emblematic images. Hesse the ascetic wanderer; Hamsun the wounded but stoical romantic (think of *Pan*'s hero, Glahn, shooting his beloved dog and having it delivered to the woman who spurned him); Wolfe the appetitive giant . . . I accumulated lore. I made these individuals, all of them, into patron saints; I stocked myself with images for every contingency: writer as brawler, as lover, as contemplative. Where does it all originate, this innocent adolescent ardor that can contort our lives permanently?

When I was in high school it was Kerouac more than the others who possessed me. I'm sure that my experience was hardly unique. I was sixteen years old, seething with notions and desperate to break from the constraints of schoolwork and curfews. I was already picking up advance vibrations of what would soon emerge full-blown as the counterculture. I listened to Bob Dylan and the Kinks, kept my ear glued to Detroit's new FM stations; I studied the hair, clothes, and attitude signals on the albums I was buying. I was chafing at parental restrictions—my father's response to these same atmospheric rumblings was to clamp down, to turn stricter and more sarcastic. When I spotted a copy of *On the Road* in my mother's bookcase (a friend had given it to her), I was touched off like tinder. The title alone got me excited. I can't begin to recreate the feeling now, but once those three words were a telegraphic condensation of all my craving for motion and open spaces. I browsed the first sentences right there by the upstairs bookcase and was swept up by an almost intolerable excitement:

> I first met Dean not long after my wife and I split up. I had just gotten over a serious illness that I won't bother to talk about, except that it had to do with the miserably weary split-up and my feeling that everything was dead. With the coming of Dean Moriarty began the part of my life you could call my life on the road.

43

Who can ever account for how certain books come along to ignite a reader's soul? Where are the studies of incendiary books and susceptible readers? My contact with *On the Road* shook me awake. It sent me out the door and into an extended fantasia of hitching and bumming and collecting adventures. In our imitations, my friends and I were the sincerest flatterers. We drove around through the long summer nights, drinking beer and sputtering to each other about the lives we would live as soon as we hit the road ourselves. We smoked and drank, postured and lied. We only half-jokingly called each other "Dean" and "Sal," and we kept stoking up the promise of times to come. Soon. When we finished school, when we got away from home.

Does Kerouac count as a literary influence? I would have to say yes, even though we were hardly subjecting the text to dispassionate aesthetic inquiry. Although most of my response was primitively imitative—I wanted to be those characters, to have their lives—some deeper writerly connection was also made. Part of the glamour of that book, at least for me, lay in the fact that Sal Paradise was a writer, or a would-be writer. He had adventures, thrillingly sordid adventures with truck drivers, waitresses, and drunks, but they were more than a string of vanishing episodes. They were his *material*. I knew that after his travels he returned to the desk and smelted his experiences into prose—probably like the very prose that had me so excited. So, the imitative impulse was not discharged for me by hitchhiking, drinking, and having strange encounters—it extended into my desire to write about everything that happened to me.

I still have my notebooks from those days. If I were able to bear it, I could read the long and overly lyrical entries that reflect my desire to be a certain kind of writer—entries that, so clearly now, show my influences. In high school it was mainly Kerouac, with some strong meditative accents derived from my readings of Hesse. Later, in the early years of college, it was Henry Miller; for a long time his angry rakishness was irresistible to me. I see now that the Miller intoxication was a carrying on of the Kerouac fantasy in a slightly different key. Kerouac was America, the West; Miller was the slums of Paris. Never had indigence sounded so good. Miller made living on the edge of starvation in a foreign city seem like the finest thing one could aspire to. During my freshman year at the University of Michigan, I made elaborate plans to quit school and expatriate myself to Europe. And the following summer I tried to set the plan into motion. I saved up money from a janitor job and got myself across the ocean. I followed the itinerary of the times— hitching from Amsterdam to Paris to Barcelona—and paid my romantic dues, scrounging food, sleeping in barns, even spending a few hours in jail on the island of Ibiza. But when the time came to declare myself, to write the letter saying that I was never coming home, my nerve failed me. The following September I was back in class.

Here—I can see it—the reading and writing memoir threatens to shade into general autobiography. How could it not? Everything about those years of urgent self-making was tied up with fantasy (and a narcissism I can hardly stand to think about). And for me, more than music or drugs or politics or the ferment of pop culture, books were the engine of that fantasy. How readily I slipped into the lives of certain literary characters—Rupert Birkin, Paul Morel, Hans Castorp, Holden Caulfield . . . Then I believed that it was the genius of the author that allowed me such identification. Now I am less sure. I deem it more likely that at that stage of life I possessed a rather extraordinary will to identify—an ability, now much diminished, to project my clamorous ego into available fictional personae. Whatever the fuel, it sponsored a range of intense involvements—very nearly impersonations—before it was used up. Now when I read I appreciate allusions, savor subtleties of expression and thematic ambiguities; I grasp the fine points of technique and heed the structural signals. But I sometimes feel I would trade these more refined siftings for my old uncritical engagement in an instant.

Looking back in this way, trying to explain myself to myself, I discover that it is very easy—and tempting—to produce a self-caricature. To simplify and to highlight. One doesn't need a biographer to come along to smudge the true picture of how it was—one does it oneself. Year after year I have been telling stories on myself, working up a fond portrait of the artist as a young man. I have, I can see now, patronized myself at every turn. I have conflated my memories with a generic image drawn from my various readings and I have come to believe in my own creation. The restless dreamer, the would-be adventurer. To be sure, there was some of that. From childhood on I had struck private poses and inhabited outlandish fantasies. And certainly the fantasy I inhabited in college had these elements in abundance. But there were other, less image-driven sides to my nature. I did, in bursts, pursue my studies. And I did, somehow, manage to pick up a more sober and conventional sort of bookishness. I remember that I had a great desire not just to be thought of as intelligent and well-read, but to really *be* those things. I compiled extensive lists of books I knew I ought to have read if I were to consider myself educated, and I did, from time to time, gather my will to assault them.

At some point in my sophomore year I began to spend my free time in libraries and in the campus bookstores. Not yet reading, but just walking around, snooping, browsing cover copy and snatches from introductions. When it was all too much, I would carry my mania out into the streets, walking wherever my steps took me, my brain reeling as I tried to factor the growing realization of my own ignorance into the scheme of writing and adventuring I had set for myself. Rhetorically I want to make a show of asking "Who *was* that person?" But I know him very well.

Thinking about my experiences in this way, from present into past, I look for tendencies, lines of force; I try to think of events that may have had some strong determining effect. What I find, however, is not so much a set of explicit causes—meetings with remarkable people, sudden reversals of fortune—as the steady working of inscrutable pressures. As important as anything else, and very hard to account for, was this growing compulsion to be around books. Although I had always liked libraries and bookstores—as a kid I had stood in the local bookshop and tried to read my way through the Hardy Boys books I didn't own—this level of obsession was something new. And it would eventually determine more about the direction of my life than my four misguided years of college.

What was happening? Quite suddenly, or so it seems now, I was putting in hours in bookstores. Moving my way slowly through fiction, criticism, poetry, philosophy . . . I was also spending many of my evenings on the fifth floor of the graduate library, sidestepping to and fro in the deserted aisles, gathering piles of European literature (poets, obscure surrealists, second-tier geniuses like Reverdy and Lautréamont), hauling my stack to the nearest available study carrel to inspect it.

And my social life? It was narrow but intense, and books were involved there as well. My girlfriend, S., was a fellow English major and a great reader, and if we didn't talk a great deal about literature, we had learned to read our own books in tandem. Or so I remember it: the two of us sprawled at opposite ends of the couch in her apartment. My best friend in those days, Whitney, was likewise bookish. We would sit in his deep armchairs drinking from a big jug of wine, smoking with the beautiful abandon of youth, and talking book talk. Whatever *that* was. Mainly it was naming favorites and playing "have you read?" and mapping out reading paths for the future, writing down all of the books we needed to get and read. And then, as a kind of punctuation, one of us might grab something from a shelf and say "Wait, listen to this!" I was living at a certain pitch and was ready for the next event—my discovery of secondhand books.

In the early 1970s, Ann Arbor had not yet blossomed into the great book town it is today. The one used bookstore was the Wooden Spoon, a dark little place many blocks from campus in an area of bars and resale shops. This probably accounts for my late encounter with the place—it was not an area I frequented. But my own readiness enters the picture. If I had wandered into the Wooden Spoon before the book fever captured me, I might have been impervious to its attractions. I might have gathered in a strong impression of dust and cat piss and left. But my visit turned out to be a conversion experience of sorts.

The proprietress of the shop was a woman named Dee Marshall. Dee must have been in her fifties, and she had some problem with her eyes—an off-kilter gaze, magnified pupils aswim behind thick lenses. She was something of an Ann Arbor character. She applied her red lipstick generously and sloppily, smoked long cigarettes that were forever ashing into her lap, and she drank. This I knew not only from her breathily gushing manner, but also because Dave, her assistant, would announce her condition in a theatrical stage whisper whenever I came through the door—which soon became daily. "She's blotto!" he would mouth behind Dee's back. If she noticed she did not let on. Drunk or sober, she sat in the chair by the window with a burning cigarette between her fingers and an open book in her lap.

The atmosphere was pure Tennessee Williams—scroungy cats, smoke, gin bottles in drawers—and to me it was like an elixir. Even the books, which I now recognize as the usual sort of secondhand stock, partook of the aura. I was ecstatic. I pawed my way through everything, even the boxes in the back room, and I started buying. Here were books I could afford. Big hardcovers for a dollar or two, paperbacks for pocket change. I became a daily customer, then a fixture. Before long, Dee was taking me with her on her rounds through the neighborhood thrift shops. I carried her bags and boxes and she repaid me with store credit.

Not that she would have needed to pay me anything, for, day by day, I was picking up the rudiments of the trade. And, though Dee was often in her cups, she was intelligent, funny, and, like most true book lovers, delighted to share anything she knew. From her I learned how to read a title page, identify a first-edition colophon, and check the *Bookman's Price Index* to establish value. She steered me away from countless "trophies" I brought her—first editions of unimportant books—and rewarded me with a startlingly girlish squeal when I did find something of real interest.

I was then living in a small room above a delicatessen. Night after night, when I should have been getting ready to go study at the library (after all, I *was* in college), I would come trudging up the dark stairs, through a miasma of corned beef and onion smells, carrying my shopping bags of books. I had outfitted a wall with brick-and-board shelves and was now trying to build a library. The project consumed me more than any course of study ever had. I remember the sense of ritual that attended the daily unpacking of the bags. I would lower myself into my armchair, light up a cigarette, and then, with a sensualist's tense languor, I would unpack the day's purchases and examine them. I was acquiring in all directions—these were the early stages of bibliomania. I picked up novels and books of poetry, biographies, histories, philosophy . . . Each book was a plan, a project, a gesture made toward a future in which I would know everything.

After I had studied each acquisition, fingering the paper, reading the dust jacket minutiae, I would move to the shelves. I arranged and rearranged late into the night, fully enclosed in the glow of my private absorption. I might pull up a chair and just sit, tilting my head to one side and running my gaze along the lettering on the spines. What was going on in my thoughts? Was I even thinking? I would like to believe that I was somehow meditating the shape of my life. But I don't know; I picture only the glare of my architect's lamp and the lazy, concentrated swirl of blue smoke.

I can now recognize a certain long-term consistency in my actions and attitudes. Just as I dreamed of being a writer, a figure out on the societal margins, unaffiliated with offices and institutions, so as a reader I was drawn away from the center. The classroom setting did not kindle my imagination; if a book was on a syllabus, I lost interest. But to be rooting around in dingy basements with a bibulous older woman—that had a romance about it. That was real.

The real was the star I steered by; it was the intangible object of all my searching. And when I began to write fiction during this period, I sought above all to create a texture of tough authenticity. My guide was Hemingway. I wanted the sound and feel of the Nick Adams stories— hard, rueful, bitter, with just a trace of something fine and unspoiled. I spent many months working on a series of understated sketches that featured a character I called simply "Peck" (a discreet allusion to Pechorin, the wounded romantic in Lermontov's *Hero of Our Time*). Peck did nothing. He was a mood, a filter for my observations about the world. "Peck sat at the counter and watched the people through the window . . ." Peck was a young man living on the fringes, waiting for real life to send him something worthy. He drank a great deal of coffee, smoked more than Humphrey Bogart, and carried on clipped conversations only when they were unavoidable.

Some people use mirrors to enhance their lovemaking, others fictionalize images to help them through the day. I developed the tic of translating my most prosaic actions into flat declarative sentences and attributing them to my hero. I would actually walk the streets of Ann Arbor writing his script in my head. "Peck stopped at the corner and waited for the light to change." Nothing ever happened to the fellow— nothing of note. He was trapped by his creator, who was himself trapped in the long loop of college, impatient for his life to really begin.

It was as a frustrated but also cocksure (and Hemingway-besotted) young writer that I went to hear Anthony Burgess tell of his experiences. And when I smirked at his descriptions of the book reviewer's life, it was because I was sure that things far greater than mere literary journalism lay in store for me.

I hold the camera on that disaffected young man, that bundle of spiky attitudes. I can read the pose, the telltale mannerisms. Indeed, I see it reproduced year after year in certain of the students I teach. I look out from the front of the room, note the hunched shoulders, the drifting gaze, the ever so slightly mocking inflection at the corners of the mouth. And though I should know better, I feel judged by it. That arrogance of youth, that narcissistic conviction that one's life will be better, more interesting than the lives of the defeated adults who populate the world—I remember it all so clearly. But while I can say, "That was me just twenty years ago," I still feel triggered. I want them to see me as an exception; I want them to approve of the choices I made. I want them to know, too, that those choices never present themselves as we, flush with omnipotence, imagine they will.

When I finished college in the spring of 1973 I was a book-obsessed young man with big ideas about writing fiction. I read whatever I could find about the writers I most admired, and I still thought in terms of that thing called the Great American Novel. I was also seriously involved with S. We were more or less cohabitating and talking about more complex affiliations. Not marriage—no one thought in terms of marriage back then—but of moving far away and starting up some kind of life together. We were both convinced that we had to get away from the Midwest. Unlike me, S. knew exactly what she wanted. She wanted to be in New England, near the ocean. She spun out her fantasies and I took them on for myself. Anything near the ocean would do. If I squinted into the future I could read my dust jacket copy: "The author lives in isolation on the coast of Maine."

But before that or any other dream could unfurl itself, we needed money. That meant work. We calculated various possibilities on a paper placemat and then made some hard decisions. S. would leave town and move in with her parents while she took a waitress job. I would stay in my room in Ann Arbor and see what I could find.

I handed in applications at several bookstores, and I was asked in for an interview at one the very next day. Borders Book Shop was a new business in town, run by two young brothers from Kentucky. They had burst through one storefront and were opening in a larger place on State Street. They recognized me as a browser—perhaps they saw the fixated look of the addict—and I was hired. What ecstasy! I walked home in the hot afternoon sun grinning at the sidewalk and wishing I had someone to celebrate with.

I knew the world of used books slightly, but among new releases I was a tyro. Where the Wooden Spoon was like something out of an old daguerreotype—slow, dark, and quiet—Borders was all hustle and crackling fluorescents. The brothers kept the staff in motion all day long, unpacking boxes, stocking shelves, sorting backstock, and working the cash registers. We were expected to know titles and references. And, although my years of obsessive browsing helped some, I was once again face to face with my ignorance.

My whole relation to books was changed again. All contemplative distance was shattered. I was not there to thumb through offbeat volumes—I was stacking and sorting the brand-new stuff. Everything was glossy and crisp. And, I thought, cutting-edge. I felt as if everyone were just waking up to books as I was. Suddenly there were thousands of serious readers in town. They thronged the aisles of the store, asked questions, placed orders. The books had an aura, an excitement about them. And just moving the titles back and forth, getting them onto the shelves and into the hands of customers, was an education. For the first time I caught a sense of what a genuine intellectual life might be like. This was a sense I had never had in college, no matter how challenging a given course may have been. *That* was packaged thought, with everything already subjected to institutional dry-cleaning. This was different; this was hands-on. I saw my role as quasi-priestly: I was channeling the nourishing word to the people who wanted it most. I *had* to feel that because, otherwise, I was just putting in time at a low-paying retail job, not at all ministering to the life of the culture or moving along a worthy career path. However, this was 1973 and not many people my age were thinking about careers and long-term initiatives. The haze of marijuana smoke had not yet cleared from Washtenaw County; people still talked about starting communes or trekking overland from Amsterdam to Afghanistan. There was a sense of the future lying open in all directions. And, added to that, a faith that one could dawdle toward it slowly. Everything would be revealed.

My savings accumulated, but slowly. Although the pay at Borders was paltry, my needs were simpler still. I lived the honorable poverty of the counterculture: a cheap room with a bed and dresser, some jeans and shirts. Hamburgers and tuna did for meals, and there was always some change for coffee, cigarettes, and beer. That was my life and I liked it. What made it habitable were three things: the books, the people, and the fantasies. The books, picked up cheaply with my employee discount, kept piling up, and I read erratically in all directions (you cannot be in the book business and escape the mania). The people, apart from S. and a few old friends, were mainly my co-workers at the store. Tom Frick, Larry Shields, Jim Kingsbury . . . We were all to one degree or another print-obsessed; we fired each other with our enthusiasms. Tom Frick liked European novels, science fiction, and hermeticists and mystics of all descriptions. Larry Shields, back from a year in France, was a few beats ahead of everyone on this side of the Atlantic. He talked of structuralism, Lévi-Strauss, Derrida, Althusser, and Lacan—and yet, as hard as I tried to appear alert, I didn't understand a thing he said. I was still reading my way along the outlaw fringe of twentieth-century fiction. We made a strange gabble in the stockroom.

And the fantasies? Although mine were on hold, they enveloped me and filled my conversation. I talked about travel and the eventualities of a writing career. Tom Frick confided a similar bent. Whenever possible, we took our dinner breaks together. We sat at a place called Dominick's and guzzled beer and then floated back to work the evening shift. Things were looser once the bosses were gone. We turned up the radio, joked with customers, and took turns roaming the aisles to find books to inspect. Sometimes we hunched over the world atlas and looked for places to travel to. I made a special study of the indentations of the coast of Maine. I pictured myself living in a simple shingle hut—writing, full of purpose and concentration.

The fantasy, parts of it, very nearly came true. After endless planning, and then endless hesitating (for S. could not tell her parents that we were moving out together), we got ourselves out of the Midwest. I don't remember giving notice or leaving, but I do remember a late-night going-away party in a place called the Pretzel Bell. Departure was swallowed up in toasts and insults. There was the jumpcut of a short flight and I was in Boston, killing time while I waited for S.'s plane.

I traveled light. Long before I left my room above the deli, I saw that I was going to have to divest myself. I suffered as I combed through my shelves, trying to reduce a full wall down to a stack that I could jam into my knapsack. I sifted and sorted, and, with each new sortie, invoked a different set of criteria. Books I loved, books that inspired me, books that I would finally get myself to read . . . And then I gave it all up. The only solution was to take nothing, to trust to serendipity—I would find what I needed when I needed it. I boxed up my library to store at my parents' house, pausing as I packed away my prizes, my Hamsun, my Miller, my Strindberg, my Agee, my nice hardcover editions of Thoreau, Whitman, and Emerson—books I'd read and books I still meant to get to. I observed then and I have confirmed many times since: A book never looks more alluring, more essential, than when it is about to get packed away in a box.

I can now bracket this moment of leaving Ann Arbor and pointing myself East as revelatory. I see the two opposite sides of my nature converging and grinding like millstones. One side stationary, orderly, bound to (or enslaved by) print; the other bent upon movement and action, on putting the claims of experience before the claims of reflection. While surrounded by my books and papers I lived with a certain vision of myself—as a reader, a thinker, an introvert. To get myself out of Ann Arbor and into a new situation, however, I had to abandon that self-image and reactivate the fantasies of earlier years. I thought about Kerouac again, and Miller and Hemingway and Hamsun—all the writers who had to break from their verbal solitudes in order to renew themselves. I would do the same.

And indeed, several months after landing at Logan Airport, more or less as planned, S. and I found ourselves renting an off-season shingled cottage on the southern coast of Maine, and driving an ancient but functional red Saab that we had bought for a few hundred dollars. We both had enough savings to last through spring and summer if we were frugal. In other words, there was no excuse now for not writing. The soothing futurity at the core of the fantasy was gone.

At first there was no problem. I revelled boyishly in our idyll and avoided unease for at least a month. The dream script was coming to pass and I told myself to trust it. It was early spring. Here we were in a small cozy house right across the street from the ocean. A few minutes' walk brought us from the beach to a vast headland of barnacled rocks and tide pools. I rolled up my jeans and chanted half-remembered lines from Dylan Thomas. Having grown up inland, I was awed by the sheer fact of the ocean. I spent every available minute monitoring it, walking up and down the beach, coining images that I trusted myself to remember later. As I lay in bed at night, I listened to the surf—I was overwhelmed by a sense of bounty. And so it was—for that while. I keep the fond memories. S. and I were in our early twenties, living under a momentary enchantment and supposing that it would just continue.

My unease announced itself gradually. The *now what?* could not be kept at bay forever. I had shorn myself of my books and my papers; I had opened up great vaults of time for myself and had proclaimed far and wide my plans to write. I could no longer ignore my green Olivetti parked in the corner with the airline tag still dangling from its handle.

That spring and summer, more intensely than ever before, I went up against the white page—the glare of it, the depth, the mocking stillness. I'd had no problem filling pages with my Peck ruminations before, but now I had no interest in reanimating the fellow. Peck belonged back there—to college, to Ann Arbor mindstates. I had broken those moorings. I had moved to a beautiful and quiet place to see if I could make myself into a writer, and the pressure of the move—the sense that the whole of my future hung in the balance—was crippling. I rolled clean pages into the machine, stared at them until the eye-motes started swimming, then rolled them out again. I wrote longhand. I tried out terse openings for what I hoped might, with some coaxing, become stories. No luck. The best I could do was to compose, with great gritting effort, feeling like Flaubert in one of his famous *marinades,* short descriptive paragraphs about the ocean. Images of waves leaving their white scrawl on rocks, enthralled hymns to repetition.

I lived in Maine for two years, and when I finally returned to Ann Arbor—broke and heartsick—I carried all of my writings from that time in a notebook-sized bundle. My quiet, highly polished ocean meditations. To give myself the illusion that I had accomplished something, I made up two little booklets. One went to S.—a kind of *in memoriam* to our time of happiness—and the other is in a suitcase in my attic.

The writing dream appeared to fizzle, it's true, but the reading was a revelation. It was during that time in Maine that I first broke through to what I think of as the deeper place of reading, that subjective clearing on the far side of all distraction. For once I was not confronted daily with the daunting wall of unread classics. I had nothing, a small wedge of a shelf where paperbacks gradually accumulated. I bought all of my books at a small roadside thrift shop near Ogunquit. For some reason the owner always had boxes of quality paperbacks at good prices. Every Saturday I made the drive, fingers crossed against engine trouble, and returned with whatever odd and appealing things I turned up. This was an era of unstructured wandering, one of the happiest reading periods in my life so far. I read Claude Lévi-Strauss's *Tristes Tropiques* (Larry Shields's influence), Gauguin's *Noa Noa*, and Norman O. Brown's *Life Against Death*. I soaked myself in the most miscellaneous oddities: Oswald Spengler, Robert Coover, biographies of Picasso and Cézanne, novels by D. H. Lawrence and the writers of the Latin American "boom" . . . And, if my method was erratic and my coverage hit-or-miss, I was nonetheless reading deeply. Those were wonderfully solitary years— they felt, in some ways, like a recovery of childhood. We had no friends to socialize with. Once a week, usually on Saturdays, S.'s sister and her husband would drive up from New Hampshire. The four of us cooked lobster, drank wine, and played Scrabble into the night. But that was it. Otherwise, silence. I could open the covers on a book and read uninterruptedly for hours. When I wanted a break I would go up the street to the tiny post office and peer through the porthole of our box to see if any of my Ann Arbor friends had written.

After some months, when the end of the funds was in sight, long after we had begun shopping at a discount store that sold dented cans and slightly compromised produce, S. took a waitressing job at a local restaurant. I found part-time work at a local college, writing press releases about school activities. But whatever happened outwardly, inwardly I was plummeting further into my private world. I read, made futile notes toward ambitious writing projects, waited for the spark that would carry me from planning into actual production. When I tired of drafting notes, I pushed the notebook aside and went back to my reading. As the light darkened outside the window, I made myself a sandwich, another cup of instant coffee. A walk to clear the head and then back to the book. And when I could no longer abide the sight of print, I would move my chair up to the bedroom window and watch for the distinctive headlights of the Saab to appear far down the ocean stretch.

That time now seems like an extended reverie, a dreamy bath in the self that will never—and maybe ought never—be repeated. I took myself away from the clamorous world and went inward. I lived out a complete cycle, one that began as a sort of enchantment, deepened into an internally productive period of meditation, and then swung me around full circle and forced me to leave. The last phrase arrived quite suddenly. I woke up one day and found that my way of living had become intolerable. I couldn't think, couldn't write; everything felt sluggish. Night after night I sat at my improvised desk. Instead of trying to work, I nursed my anguish. I scribbled desperate pages and tore them up. I wrote letters. My head was suddenly full of fantasies about an opposite kind of life—with people, lights, music, a turbulence I could thrust myself into. The lighthouse I could see blinking in the distance, out at the tip of the headland—at first such a thrillingly authentic touch—now just marked out the extent of the surrounding emptiness. I had to leave.

S. and I had agonized discussions with long silences and hurt looks. She did not want to go back to Michigan, not even for a season. She was just beginning to find the life she had always wanted. I could not imagine staying through another winter. We argued, cried, agreed at last to a "temporary" separation, both of us knowing (she rather more than I) that it was not going to be temporary. I packed my knapsack, coaxed a friend to come out for a visit. When he left to go back to Michigan, I rode with him. I turned around in the front seat and watched the small cluster of buildings recede. One turn and we were headed inland.

Once in Michigan, I returned to Ann Arbor. I had no ideas, no direction, but I would have to find a way to make money. I sold an old leatherbound edition of Tobias Smollett I had hoarded away, and paid the first month's rent on a tiny room in a boarding house. I went to Borders—in my absence the brothers had expanded into a hangar-sized space—and talked my way back into a job. I was directed to the mezzanine, where I sat for some months at a small counter and sold remainders. I willed myself out of bed in the morning and I willed myself through every waking moment. Every night I drank my quarts of beer and fought off the impulse to catch the first bus back East.

I was twenty-four years old and I had run aground. This was now my life, selling remainders by day and lying propped up in bed through the long nights. When I had saved a few dollars I bought myself a ten-speed bike. And then, whenever I felt restless or pained—in the early mornings or at night—I rode around the streets of the town and out into the surrounding countryside. It seems to me now that I was always either hunched over the mezzanine register or over the handlebars of my bike. Cruising at night, I stopped more than once at a phone booth and dialed my old number. I knew there would be no answer, but the ringing connected me. I pictured the phone, heard the reverberations through the rooms of the apartment.

Then, once, I called in the afternoon and S. picked up. Her voice sounded pained and before she even drew a breath and spelled things out for me, I knew. She was seeing someone else. Had been, yes, but nothing had happened while I was still living there. And the weave of that part of the past came loose—I understood nothing. Two months later she was married. I was at point zero.

I say all this in order to account for the mania that ensued. Basically, I was rescued by books. I don't know whether it was because I had impressed them as an employee, or because they couldn't bear to watch me sulking by the remainder stacks, but one day Tom and Louis Borders asked me into their office and offered me a new job. The old storefront across the street was a used and rare book shop. The brothers owned the operation but they were not happy with the managers. They had one person in mind as a replacement; would I be interested in being the other?

The invitation was a godsend. All at once, unexpectedly, my life had direction and momentum. I woke up in the morning and instead of turning to S., my thoughts went right to the tasks at hand. The shop, Charing Cross, was in total disarray. Tom and Louis had explained the finances; we had gone over the stock. They believed the place could be salvaged. As it happened, I needed a mess to clean up; so did George, my new partner. Charing Cross became a sluice for all of our dammed-up energies and frustrations.

Wry, prickly, compulsive, disputatious, George was a Renaissance scholar, a recent ex–grad student with an enormous love for the printed word. Though he was only a few years older than I, he was already something of a polymath. This was obvious immediately, and not only from his conversation. As soon as it was settled that we were going to be partners, he invited me over to his place for dinner. He cooked, from scratch, a five-course Chinese dinner (he had studied with a chef), played me selections from his record library (Haydn quartets, Eric Dolphy, soundtracks from Italian films), regaled me with gossip from his former department (none of which I understood or cared about), and proudly walked me around his library. Every inch of his four-room apartment was given over to books. He had constructed special shelves in the most unlikely places—in the space above the kitchen entry, in the narrows between windows. And everything was filed impeccably. His Renaissance texts, classics (in the original Greek and Latin as well as in translation), books on the history of science, on music, English detective novels, cookbooks . . . *And* he knew what was between the covers. Thumbing through random volumes I saw passages annotated in his fastidious, slightly feminine hand. He fed me dumplings, poured wines, and I walked home in a daze. I climbed my stairs and then stood in my closet of a room gaping at the row of paperbacks I had assembled across the top of my dresser.

My two years at Charing Cross were a deep detour into obsession. I gave myself over completely to business and to books. First, there was the job of turning the shop back into a going concern. George had as many notions as I did; our energies converged. And for a few months in the beginning we all but lived on-site: redesigning the floor space, building new bookcases, answering calls about libraries and collections for

sale. The Borders gave us some money to work with and we threw ourselves at the challenge. It was some time before we both realized that the
business would take as much energy as we were willing to give for as
long as we were willing to give it.

Waking early had become a reflex for me. My breakup with S. had
destroyed my former sleep patterns. Now at the first flicker of consciousness I hurried out of bed and dressed. If I lay still for even a moment the old depression would overtake me. The secret, I told myself,
was to keep moving, to stay busy until I could no longer keep my eyes
open. Thus, I was usually in the shop with my coffee as the sun was
breaking over the rooftops on State Street, hours before we unlocked
the door for our customers. I worked alone, arranging the window display, pricing new acquisitions, setting up the register, and studying
price guides and catalogues. From time to time I would look up and see
some early-morning walker peering in at the books in the window. I felt
reconnected to the world's economy—sad but purposeful.

George, a late riser, would usually find his way in after I had unlocked the front door. He would sit in his chair by the register and carefully pour out a cup of cappuccino from the thermos he always carried
in his bag. This was his hour for gossip and banter, and somehow all of
his friends in town had been alerted. One by one they drifted in, forming a semicircle around George. I fussed and cleaned and helped customers while he gathered steam for the day. And then, suddenly, it
would be time for business. The friends went off to their jobs and
classes, the top was screwed back onto the thermos bottle. The co-
managers were now ready to plan out their buying rounds. We had lists
of people to call and places to visit. We both loved the chase: walking
into a widow's attic, taking a call from a retiring professor, arriving with
our pickup truck at some out-of-the-way library sale. As soon as we
could we hired a full-time assistant to mind the store while we made our
buys.

I was learning more than I ever thought possible—on every level. As
George and I drove around, we naturally talked. More accurately, *he*
talked. He liked having an eager listener who plied him with questions—about books, music, travel, graduate school . . . He told me how
he had quit mid-dissertation because of bad blood with his committee.

He had trouble writing, trouble staying within the limits of his chosen topic. I listened, and began to see that under the mainly genial persona was an angry and often resentful man. This might have explained his trouble with women. Although George was not especially good-looking—he was stocky and balding—he always had intelligent and attractive women coming around to see him. I watched how it happened. He lured them in with his talk—he was marvelously witty—and then he fell in love. Or what he called love. It never failed: The relationships started fast, riding on the tide of talk and good food, until it was time for something more serious to happen. Then, who knows why, George balked. There were hurt feelings, recriminations, blazing arguments in the aisles of the store. Ann Arbor was full of people who crossed the street when they saw George coming.

I, too, was intoxicated, intellectually seduced by his talk. He could be a bit of a pedant, but I admired and encouraged the pedantry. I was hot to learn things and here was the teacher I had been looking for. If George taught me anything—any big thing, that is, apart from the thousand little things—it was that knowledge was less a means to an end than a matter of self-cultivation, a way of transforming the experience of the daily. To be curious, to study, to find out—this was the path to the world. Knowledge exposed connections, imparted significance to the incidental. It was one thing to drive through Detroit lamenting the urban blight outside the car windows, quite another to understand what you were looking at in terms of labor migrations from the Deep South, the history of American race relations, the evolution of the western city since the Industrial Revolution, the politics of trade unions . . . George commanded these perspectives, or appeared to. He talked about Marx and Engels, Louis Sullivan, Louis Mumford, Renaissance aesthetics, and George Gissing. As I drove and he talked, he worked the radio dial, pulling in jazz and classical stations, interrupting his own disquisition to give me a mini-lecture on bebop syncopation, or classical phrasing as Charles Rosen had defined it. I lumbered in his wake—eager, envious, determined that one day I would know just as much.

The other part of my education came, naturally, from books. Aside from reading them, I was learning by buying, handling, pricing and selling them. Working in a bookstore affords a matchless sense of the big picture. Through stocking and sorting titles I started to see recurrences, interrelations, and, in time, arcs of connection. I read flap copy, and dipped in to sample. I heard the comments of customers and noted who was buying what. Out of this, somehow, came a grasp of the divisions and subdivisions of knowledge and a more refined sense of the important writers and thinkers in each field.

Inevitably, George and I started picking up books for ourselves. I soon realized that one of George's main incentives for taking the job was that it would allow him to build up his library. I was far behind him but anxious to get started.

We had an understanding that after a successful buy we would reward ourselves with a few books we wanted for ourselves. The store was now booming along, and we felt no compunctions on this score. I took my lead from George. Instead of just picking up literary works, I branched out. I wanted to know everything—I thought I could see how all fields were connected. And here was the chance of a lifetime to build up a library. I carted home histories, books of philosophy, editions of the classics, not to mention all of the novels and books of poetry that struck my fancy. I felt the old book sickness beginning to grip me.

I told myself I was happy. I had a new life, and I could feel the heartache ebbing away. I was doing something I liked, making good money, and meeting interesting people. Being around George had awakened me. I shook my head in disbelief when I counted out the months and realized that just one year ago I had been living in Maine, dragging my way through my melancholy isolation, trying to figure out what to do with myself.

But it was also true that, since leaving Maine those long months ago, I had not stopped moving. I was sleeping little, had lost close to thirty pounds, and hardly ever paused to take stock of my inner life. It had been a year since I had been calm enough to read a book cover to cover, much less sit down to do any writing. I felt some deep twinges about this. I worried that I might be turning into a bookstore junkie. This was a definite type—George and I met dozens in our travels. Characters with bad posture and anxious demeanors, men and women who seemed to do nothing but prowl around books, buying and selling, always looking for the rarities, the edition of *Tamerlane* that was going to turn up in the very next bargain basement crate. I could not let this happen to me.

I made a genuine effort to wind myself down. Now that the shop was running smoothly, with good book sources and a steady clientele, I could relax my vigilance. I began to take occasional days off. I stopped letting myself through the door at sunup. I got myself reading and started thinking about writing again. It was the great cycle of my life (though I couldn't yet see it as such): After throwing myself outward— I told myself I had done it to save myself—I drew inward. I began working through some of the books I had requisitioned for my own library. I turned to the philosophers and psychologists of love, read Kierkegaard, Pavese, Stendhal, Tolstoy, Ford Madox Ford—and I read poetry. I made my way to Donne and Shakespeare and Hardy, then to Auden, Muir, Roethke, Lowell, and Bishop. For the first time ever I immersed myself in the poetic element. I read poetry when I got up, and during my lunch break, and before I turned out the light at night. And then, from sheer imitative pressure, I began to write poems. Disconsolate lines about loss and betrayal. Everything I had repressed after my breakup with S. came flooding forth. I wrote and wrote, and I stuffed the poems away where no one would see them.

At this point in my life I had a providential encounter. Like many others in the Ann Arbor community, I had followed closely the case of the poet Joseph Brodsky—his trial, his exile, his arrival in the U.S., then in our town. I had read what little had been translated and felt the grip of it (it helped that so many of Brodsky's early poems were likewise about loss and betrayal). I had even seen the poet walk past the window of the shop once or twice. One Sunday morning I was in Borders buying a newspaper when I noticed Brodsky standing by the counter. He was asking the clerk for a copy of *The Education of Henry Adams* and the clerk was patiently explaining that the book was out of stock. There was some confusion, as Brodsky's English was not quite up to the exchange. In what was for me an uncharacteristically forward gesture, I stepped over and said, "I can get you the book."

We crossed State Street together. Brodsky waited in front of the store while I turned off the alarm and let myself in. I returned a moment later with the book. "For you," I said, awkwardly. He was no less awkward about receiving it. We stood by the window for a few minutes. He asked me if I wrote poetry. I demurred, said I was mainly a reader. Who did I read? Brodsky started firing off names. Did I know Vasko Popa, Miroslav Holub, Tomas Tranströmer, Zbigniew Herbert . . . ? I nodded, shook my head no, nodded. I had no idea how to respond. I could not believe that Brodsky cared what I thought. And then, as I was standing there, it came to me with great clarity: The poet was lonely. He was drilling me with questions because he wanted to talk to someone. I invited him to join me at my sister's apartment for lunch. He agreed readily and ended up sitting on her couch for much of the afternoon, drinking coffee and smoking.

On the strength of that meeting and the friendliness that grew up around it, I asked Brodsky if I could audit his seminar in twentieth-century poetry. He welcomed me, and so two afternoons a week I left the store and found my way to a windowless conference room where a handful of graduate students fidgeted around an enormous table. Although Brodsky had not yet forged a teaching style, and though classes often consisted of long silences following in the wake of some vexing query—"Who is the darker poet, Mandelstam or Montale?"—I felt a familiar dizziness. Something new was in the air; my life was headed toward change. Immobilized like the others in the deepening silence, embarrassed and fearful, I nonetheless caught the virus. Brodsky's passion for poets, poetry, and the written word in general had a transfiguring power for me. What else but literature could possibly matter? "Choice?" he might ask. "For the writer there is no choice." I walked home from the classes both excited and irritated with myself. I had let my ambition languish; I had settled for less. I saw Brodsky's devotion, felt the radiation of his intensity, and said, "I want that."

Another shift thus began, gradually. I did not stop hunting for books with George or working late nights in the store basement pricing stock. I was still bringing piles of books to my room and trying to discipline myself to several hours of daily study. I made lists of what I needed to read and then checked off titles as I finished them. But I had begun again to entertain the possibility that bookselling was not going to be my life, that I was not yet ready to abandon my dream of being a writer.

At that point—I was twenty-six—I was seeing a young woman

named P. She and I had met during those first disconsolate months when I sold remainders at Borders, and while we both knew that ours would not be a relationship for the ages, we started to spend more time together. After some months—I was well into my Charing Cross obsession by then—we agreed that I would move in with her. I lugged my boxes of books up her stairs and set up my shelves along the walls of the bedroom. I specify this because it was in that bedroom one afternoon, staring at the spines of my books, that I experienced a most vivid and distressing awakening. The message was blunt, and as clear as if a voice had spoken into my ear: *If you don't get away from Charing Cross you will never be a writer.* I paced back and forth in that room, arguing the pros and cons with myself, knowing even as I did so that I would be leaving. Oddly—or maybe not—I retain a perfect impression of the room, the day: I see the afternoon light on the wallpaper and feel the agitated silence around me. By evening I had decided: I would leave the shop and go somewhere; I would write a novel.

In my experience, decisions like this have a subversive effect. One determined action and everything changes. I must have been ready, for a tap of the hammer brought the whole edifice of my life down around me. Suddenly everything pointed to my leaving. I gave my notice to Tom and Louis, and then, with some real trepidation, I told George. He was surprised and hurt, but he put a bright sarcastic face on things. He humored me about my plans for writing a novel, and assured me that I would be back in a few months. We quipped our way around the awkwardness of saying goodbye, and then I was gone.

I ended up going to Boston, in part because I had liked the city when S. and I visited it from Maine, but also because P. had decided to go to graduate school there. We did not make our plans together, as a couple, but they evolved in parallel formation. She would have her place, I would have mine. Also, I would be arriving somewhat later. I was going to use some of the money I had saved to travel in Europe. I would use the rest to set myself up, to buy six months for writing.

It was late October when I arrived at Logan Airport en route from Rome. Travel had jarred me loose from my Ann Arbor ways. I was back in an ascetic mode: I had a backpack full of clothes and my green

Olivetti. There were a few books secreted among the shirts, but the rest of my library was in Michigan, boxed, to be shipped east as needed. I was absolutely set on making a new life for myself—again. I had a bottle of Four Roses that I had bought in the duty-free shop and I sat on a deserted curb swigging from it, waiting for P. to come pick me up.

The next day, dizzy from jet lag and my fantasies of complete self-renovation, I read the listings in the *Boston Globe* and searched for a room to rent. I found one quickly—four walls, a bed, a deal dresser, a tiny bedside table, and a huge walk-in closet lit by a bare hanging bulb. I moved in immediately. That is, I hiked over from P.'s place, unpacked my knapsack, and carried the bedside table into the closet. Now I had a room and a study, and I was quite pleased with myself. I opened my typewriter case, set out a stack of paper, and went back to stay with P. The next morning I would begin.

I was a model of self-discipline. Much as I wanted to explore Boston and its bookstores, I made a punitive writing schedule and kept to it. I sat in that bulb-lit closet for most of every day, six days a week, most of that winter, breaking off only to cross the street for a sandwich and coffee, or to air my thoughts. I had an idea for a novel, an idea I had incubated while traveling in Italy. I would tell the story of a relationship and its aftermath, of a young man who returned to his family home in Maine after finding out that his girl (with whom he had lived in Michigan) was seeing someone else. I worked obsessively, pouring myself into the words, and while I cannot remember much about the feeling of writing, I do recall the room down to its scuffed floorboards. It was the archetypal transient's bolt-hole, the kind of place one lands after some major reversal of fortune. There were coughing noises from the adjacent rooms, clanging radiators, and deep ruts worn into the hallway carpet. Whenever I got stuck in my work I would follow the ruts down the stairs and out. I logged a good many hours walking up and down alongside the Beacon Street trolley tracks. In the evening, when the day's pages were done, I hiked across Brookline to P.'s apartment. I didn't have the fortitude to pass a whole night in the rooming house.

I finished the novel—writing and rewriting—in about six months. A short period, but I had been working at a white heat. Moreover, it was not exactly *The Magic Mountain* I was writing. *The Glass,* so called because the key scene took place in a mirror-walled restaurant, weighed in at less than a hundred and fifty pages. When I finished, ceremoniously writing THE END on the last page, I went to buy a lottery ticket. I had the idea that my final page count was going to be a winner. A friend from Ann Arbor who had just moved to town gave me five dollars to play the same number for him.

We didn't hit.

The very next night my Michigan friend and P. sat together on her couch while I read *The Glass* from start to finish. Apparently I didn't worry about how P. might receive these images of heartbreak, this dark valentine to another. The whole recitation took hours, and I am still mortified whenever I think of my two loyal friends listening all the way through and then trying to act properly enthusiastic afterward. I think I knew the truth even as I gave voice to the early pages. It was a clinker. A private, embittered expression—a tomb for my hurt feelings. I read on, sick with the feeling that a half year's work had come to nothing.

Up until then, until I finished my novel, or novella, I had, without thinking much about it, felt myself in possession of large amounts of time. I had the idea that life, real life, still lay in wait; that all things were possible. When I finished my project and felt the failure of it—felt it like a silent ax-blow—all that changed. A new desperation came into my life, a sense that in terms of figuring things out and getting them under-way it was growing late. Twilight in the evening lands. I was twenty-seven. I had exiled myself from what had been in many respects an ideal situation. I had made big noises about writing a novel—and I had not come through. That is, I found that I did not have it in me to write fic-tion. I was too much trapped in the circuit of myself; I was utterly lack-ing the novelist's necessary negative capability. This was a bruising realization, and the pain of it deepened as time passed.

The next few years were the worst yet. I shelved my writing and put my typewriter away. As soon as I ran out of money, I went back to work-ing in bookstores. I did a stint at George Gloss's Brattle Book Shop (a Boston legend), another in the basement of a new Barnes & Noble superstore. After buying whole libraries, sometimes for thousands of dollars, I now found myself donning a beige clerk's jacket and stacking remainders on tables. But I had ruled out going back. (It would not have been possible, really. George, too, had left the shop and was moving around from place to place.) It was a dreary time. P. and I split up. I answered an ad in the newspaper and wound up sharing an apartment in Cambridge with a reclusive young poet. The situation was fine by me, for I was feeling more than a touch reclusive myself. I ate my meals—canned soups, tuna sandwiches—and retreated to my room.

I have only very general memories from that time. One is that nearly every night I would lie awake fighting down the feeling that something terrible was going to happen—in my life, in the world. When the Three Mile Island disaster struck I saw both a confirmation of my fears and a harbinger for the future. I worried that I might have some kind of a breakdown. I would stretch out in the dark and listen to classical music on the all-night station, waiting for the window square to lighten and my anxiety to abate.

More benignly, I remember that I once again undertook to reconstitute my library. I bought books at work and asked my parents to ship some of my boxes to me. I was back to shelf-grazing: sitting, smoking, staring at the spines of my books. But I also read. Though I was quite depressed (I never admitted this at the time), I did find my way back to the page. Indeed, I read more seriously and ambitiously than I had for a long time. Walter Benjamin, Robert Musil, Malcolm Lowry, Max Frisch, Marguerite Yourcenar—many Europeans, many of the writers Brodsky had mentioned. They were also, almost without exception, dark writers attuned to the atrocities of history and charged with nameless existential forebodings. Their brooding nourished me and gave me a somewhat different sense of the writer's mission.

They also returned me to writing. They detonated the cloudy and volatile mixture I had been carrying inside me for years. It was all very unexpected. I had a realization, and then, right on its heels, an impulse. For some months I had been reading through the translated work of Robert Musil—his stories, his *Young Törless,* and the three volumes of his unfinished masterpiece, *The Man Without Qualities.* The book jackets carried endorsements from esteemed critics citing him as one of the towering figures of twentieth-century literature. I was caught up in the work and wanted to know more. But as I searched the libraries and bibliographies I discovered that there was next to nothing available in English. A few scholarly monographs, some dissertations. And then flashed the proverbial lightbulb: I had read the work, I had ideas—maybe *I* could write something.

We all know the cinema clichés of inspiration: the exhilarating montage shots of the wire-haired inventor working through the night, the clock hands on the wall revolving like propellers. I sat at the desk I had built into the corner of my room and I worked. I went through the books and copied out lengthy passages I wanted to quote. I filled sheets of paper with ideas, drew connecting arrows. And then, relying on my memory of writing college papers, as well as on the example of essays I admired by writers like George Steiner, Susan Sontag, and Brodsky himself, I launched forth. I rolled a clean page into the Olivetti and typed a first sentence.

What I enjoy about this story, which I always tell when someone asks me how I came to writing essays, is its fairy-tale quality. For, no sooner did I begin putting words on the page than I tapped a rightness and ease I had never known before. Writing fiction—or *trying* to write fiction—had never been anything but a chore. A painful process, like carving something hard and rubbery with a dull knife, or trying to extract some impossibly rooted thing from the ground. With fiction, if the words came easily it was a sure sign that I was straying into the purple, resuming the free-association tics from the days when I dumped my angst heedlessly into my journals.

But writing about Musil, free for once of the hovering shades of my various masters, I felt only liberation. It was almost as if I simply tipped the pitcher and poured. I wrote and rewrote, struggled over certain transitions and worried about how I might impart a momentum to the whole—but through the entire process I was never out of earshot of a voice. Not a Muse chanting in my ear, but more like a set of tonal possibilities. I had found, or claimed, a key signature for myself. It constrained me, but it also guided me. From the rhythmic logic of the first few sentences, which came easily, the rest unfolded.

The writing of that essay was deeply gratifying. There were, of course, the immediate pleasures of getting my thoughts into place, quoting my favorite passages, feeling myself free for once to use the language without the clenching sense of fraudulence. But the real joy came with the realization of arrival. I did not know what I would do with the essay—whether I would publish it anywhere—but that hardly mattered. The important thing was that I had answered the question that had been tormenting me for so long. Although I understood nothing about the practical side of the essay-writing racket—how one might go about doing it as a vocation—I knew that I had found the clue, the sign about my future.

Here is the stopping point. One story ends, another begins. If this were a *bildungsroman,* the author would mark the end of the hero's wanderings, find some emblem of passage to sear into the page. But that would make everything too tidy. I did not immediately give up my lifelong fantasy of writing fiction—that would sputter on for years, flaring up into occasional (shelved) short stories. Nor did I straightaway start grinding out essays by the basketful. The movement forward was jerky, rough. But in the deeper sense there was a change, a recognition, and it reshaped my life to the very core.

# 3

# The Owl Has Flown

*Reading has a history. It was not always and everywhere the same. We may think of it as a straightforward process of lifting information from a page; but if we considered it further, we would agree that information must be sifted, sorted, and interpreted. Interpretive schemes belong to cultural configurations, which have varied enormously over time. As our ancestors lived in different mental worlds, they must have read differently, and the history of reading could be as complex as the history of thinking.*

—Robert Darnton, *The Kiss of Lamourette*

Reading and thinking are kindred operations, if only because both are actually and historically invisible. Of the two, reading has the stronger claim to invisibility, for thought at least finds a home from time to time in the written sign, whereas the *reception* of the written sign leaves no trace unless in written accounts after the fact. How do people experience the written word, and how have those experiencings, each necessarily unique, changed in larger collective ways down the centuries? The few indications we have only whet the speculative impulse.

We know from historians, for example, that before the seventh century there were few who read silently (writing some centuries before, Saint Augustine professed astonishment that Saint Ambrose read without moving his lips); that in Europe in the late Middle Ages and after, designated readers often entertained or edified groups at social or work-related gatherings. Then there is the fascinating study of Menocchio, the sixteenth-century miller. Historian Carlo Ginzburg anatomizes his intellectual universe by triangulating between Menocchio's few books and the depositions taken at his trial for heresy. In *The Cheese and the Worms*, Ginzburg combines scholarly excavation with shrewd surmise to suggest how this lettered worker assembled a cosmology—one compounded in part from the rich reserves of the dominantly oral culture, and in part from his intense and methodical, if also fanciful, readings of the few texts he owned.

After Menocchio's day, with the proliferation of mechanically produced books and the general democratization of education, reading not only spread rapidly, but changed its basic nature. As Robert Darnton writes in his essay, "The First Steps Toward a History of Reading," summarizing the conclusions of his fellow historian Rolf Engelsing:

> From the Middle Ages until sometime after 1750, according to
> Engelsing, men read "intensively." They had only a few books—the
> Bible, an almanac, a devotional work or two—and they read them
> over and over again, usually aloud and in groups, so that a narrow
> range of traditional literature became deeply impressed on their con-
> sciousness. By 1800 men were reading "extensively." They read all
> kinds of material, especially periodicals and newspapers, and read it
> only once, and then raced on to the next item.

That centrifugal tendency has of course escalated right into our present, prompted as much by the expansion of higher education and the demands of social and professional commerce as by the astronomical increase in the quantity of available print. Newspapers, magazines, brochures, advertisements, and labels surround us everywhere—surround us, indeed, to the point of having turned our waking environment into a palimpsest of texts to be read, glanced at, or ignored. It is startling to recall the anecdote about the philosopher Erasmus pausing on a muddy thoroughfare to study a rare scrap of printed paper flickering at his feet.

As we now find ourselves at a cultural watershed—as the fundamental process of transmitting information is shifting from mechanical to circuit-driven, from page to screen—it may be time to ask how modifications in our way of reading may impinge upon our mental life. For how we receive information bears vitally on the ways we experience and interpret reality.

What is most conspicuous as we survey the general trajectory of reading across the centuries is what I think of as the gradual displacement of the vertical by the horizontal—the sacrifice of depth to lateral range, or, in Darnton's terms above, a shift from intensive to extensive reading. When books are rare, hard to obtain, and expensive, the reader must compensate through intensified focus, must like Menocchio read the same passages over and over, memorizing, inscribing the words deeply on the slate of the attention, subjecting them to an interpretive pressure not unlike what students of scripture practice upon their texts. This is ferocious reading—prison or "desert island" reading—and where it does not assume depth, it creates it.

In our culture, access is not a problem, but proliferation is. And the reading act is necessarily different than it was in its earliest days. Awed and intimidated by the availability of texts, faced with the all but impossible task of discriminating among them, the reader tends to move across surfaces, skimming, hastening from one site to the next without allowing the words to resonate inwardly. The inscription is light but it covers vast territories: quantity is elevated over quality. The possibility of maximum focus is undercut by the awareness of the unread texts that await. The result is that we know countless more "bits" of information, both important and trivial, than our ancestors. We know them without a stable sense of context, for where the field is that vast all schemes must be seen as provisional. We depend far less on memory; that faculty has all but atrophied from lack of use.

Interestingly, this shift from vertical to horizontal parallels the overall societal shift from bounded lifetimes spent in single locales to lives lived in geographical dispersal amid streams of data. What one loses by forsaking the village and the magnification resulting from the repetition of the familiar, one may recoup by gaining a more inclusive perspective, a sense of the world picture.

This larger access was once regarded as worldliness—one travelled, knew the life of cities, the ways of diverse people . . . It has now become the birthright of anyone who owns a television set. The modern viewer is a cosmopolitan at one remove, at least potentially. He has a window on the whole world, is positioned, no matter how poor or well-to-do, to receive virtually the same infinite stream of data as every other viewer. There is almost nothing in common between the villager conning his book of scriptures by lantern-light and the contemporary apartment dweller riffling the pages of a newspaper while attending to live televised reports from Bosnia.

How is one to assess the relative benefits and liabilities of these intrinsically different situations? How do we square the pluses and minuses of horizontal and vertical awareness? The villager, who knows every scrap of lore about his environs, is blessedly unaware of cataclysms in distant lands. News of the Lisbon earthquake of 1755 took months to travel across Europe. The media-besotted urbanite, by contrast, never loses his awareness of the tremors in different parts of the world.

We may ask, clumsily, which person is happier, or has a more vital grip on experience? The villager may have possessed his world more pungently, more sensuously; he may have found more sense in things owing both to the limited scope of his concern and the depth of his information—not to mention his basic spiritual assumptions. But I also take seriously Marx's quip about the "idiocy of rural life." Circumscribed conditions and habit suggest greater immersion in circumstance, but also dullness and limitation. The lack of a larger perspective hobbles the mind, leads to suspiciousness and wary conservativism; the clichés about peasants are probably not without foundation. But by the same token, the constant availability of data and macroperspectives has its own diminishing returns. After a while the sense of scale is attenuated and a relativism resembling cognitive and moral paralysis may result. When everything is permitted, Nietzsche said, we have nihilism; likewise, when everything is happening everywhere, it gets harder to care about anything. How do we assign value? Where do we find the fixed context that allows us to create a narrative of sense about our lives? Ideally, I suppose, one would have the best of both worlds—the purposeful fixity of the local, fertilized by the availability of enhancing vistas. A natural ecology of information and context.

We are experiencing in our times a loss of depth—a loss, that is, of the very paradigm of depth. A sense of the deep and natural connectedness of things is a function of vertical consciousness. Its apotheosis is what was once called wisdom. Wisdom: the knowing not of facts but of truths about human nature and the processes of life. But swamped by data, and in thrall to the technologies that manipulate it, we no longer think in these larger and necessarily more imprecise terms. In our lateral age, living in the bureaucracies of information, we don't venture a claim to that kind of understanding. Indeed, we tend to act embarrassed around those once-freighted terms—*truth, meaning, soul, destiny* . . . We suspect the people who use such words of being soft and nostalgic. We prefer the deflating one-liner that reassures us that nothing need be taken that seriously; we inhale the atmospheres of irony.

Except, of course, when our systems break down and we hurry to the therapist's office. Then, trying to construct significant narratives that include and explain us, we reach back into that older lexicon. "My life doesn't seem to make sense—things don't seem to mean very much." But the therapist's office is a contained place, a parenthetic enclosure away from the general bustle. Very little of what transpires there is put into social circulation. Few people would risk exposing their vulnerable recognitions to the public glare.

The depth awareness, where it exists, is guarded as a secret. If we have truly wise people among us, they avoid the spotlights—it is part of their wisdom to do so. For the fact is that there is no public space available to individuals who profess the vertical awareness. At best there are pop pulpits, public television slots that can accommodate a Joseph Campbell, Betty Friedan, or Rabbi Kushner.

Wisdom, an ideal that originated in the oral epochs—Solomon and Socrates represent wisdom incarnate, and Athena or Minerva were wisdom deified—is predicated on the assumption that one person can somehow grasp a total picture of life and its laws, comprehending the whole and the relation of parts. To *comprehend*: to "hold together." We once presumed that those parts added up, that there was some purpose or explanation to our being here below. If that purpose could not be fully fathomed, if it rested with God or Providence, it could at least be addressed and questioned.

The explosion of data—along with general societal secularization and the collapse of what the theorists call the "master narratives" (Christian, Marxist, Freudian, humanist . . . )—has all but destroyed the premise of understandability. Inundated by perspectives, by lateral vistas of information that stretch endlessly in every direction, we no longer accept the possibility of assembling a complete picture. Instead of carrying on the ancient project of philosophy—attempting to discover the "truth" of things—we direct our energies to managing information. The computer, our high-speed, accessing, storing, and sorting tool, appears as a godsend. It increasingly determines what kind of information we are willing to traffic in; if something cannot be written in code and transmitted, it cannot be important.

The old growth forests of philosophy have been logged and the owl of Minerva has fled. Wisdom can only survive as a cultural ideal where there is a possibility of vertical consciousness. Wisdom has nothing to do with the gathering or organizing of facts—this is basic. Wisdom is a seeing *through* facts, a penetration to the underlying laws and patterns. It relates the immediate to something larger—to a context, yes, but also to a big picture that refers to human endeavor *sub specie aeternitatis*, under the aspect of eternity. To see through data, one must have something to see through *to*. One must believe in the possibility of a comprehensible whole. In philosophy this is called the "hermeneutic circle" —one needs the ends to know which means to use, and the means to know which ends are possible. And this assumption of ends is what we have lost. It is one thing to absorb a fact, to situate it alongside other facts in a configuration, and quite another to contemplate that fact at leisure, allowing it to declare its connection with other facts, its thematic destiny, its resonance.

Resonance—there is no wisdom without it. Resonance is a natural phenomenon, the shadow of import alongside the body of fact, and it cannot flourish except in deep time. Where time has been commodified, flattened, turned into yet another thing measured, there is no chance that any piece of information can unfold its potential significance. We are destroying this deep time. Not by design, perhaps, but inadvertently. Where the electronic impulse rules, and where the psyche is conditioned to work with data, the experience of deep time is impossible. No deep time, no resonance; no resonance, no wisdom. The only remaining oases are churches (for those who still worship) and the offices of therapists. There, paying dearly for fifty minutes, the client gropes for a sense of coherence and mattering. The therapist listens, not so much explaining as simply fostering the possibility of resonance. She allows the long pauses and silences—a bold subversion of societal expectations—because only where silence is possible can the vertical engagement take place.

There is one other place of sanctuary. Not a physical place—not church or office—but a metaphysical one. Depth survives, condensed and enfolded, in authentic works of art. In anything that can grant us true aesthetic experience. For this experience is vertical; it transpires in deep time and, in a sense, secures that time for us. Immersed in a ballet performance, planted in front of a painting, we shatter the horizontal plane. Not without some expense of energy, however. The more we live according to the lateral orientation, the greater a blow is required, and the more disorienting is the effect. A rather unfortunate vicious cycle can result, for the harder it is to do the work, the less inclined we are to do it. Paradoxically, the harder the work, the more we need to do it. We cannot be put off by the prospect of fatigue or any incentive-withering sense of obligation.

What is true of art is true of serious reading as well. Fewer and fewer people, it seems, have the leisure or the inclination to undertake it. And true reading is hard. Unless we are practiced, we do not just crack the covers and slip into an alternate world. We do not get swept up as readily as we might be by the big-screen excitements of film. But if we do read perseveringly we make available to ourselves, in a most portable form, an ulterior existence. We hold in our hands a way to cut against the momentum of the times. We can resist the skimming tendency and delve; we can restore, if only for a time, the vanishing assumption of coherence. The beauty of the vertical engagement is that it does not have to argue for itself. It is self-contained, a fulfillment.

# 4

# The Woman in the Garden

I HAVE IN MY MIND an image—a painting. Either it really exists, or else I have conjured it up so often that it might as well.

The painting belongs to a familiar genre—that of the pensive figure in the garden. I see a bench, a secluded bower. A woman in Victorian dress is gazing away from a book that she holds in one hand. The image is one of reverie and privilege. But these attributions hardly begin to exhaust its significance. If reverie or privileged leisure were the point, then the book would not figure so profoundly in my mental reconstruction. Indeed, it is the book that finally grips my attention. I have it placed, if not literally then figuratively, in the center of my visual field. At the vanishing point. The painting is, for me, about the book, or about the woman's reading of the book, and though the contents of the pages are as invisible as her thoughts, they (the imagined fact of them) give the image its appeal.

Writing this, I feel as though I'm venturing into a labyrinth I may never exit. Already I find that my thoughts are cross-hatched with corrections and qualifications. For one thing, I suggested just now that the woman was thinking, had thoughts, as she looked away from the page. Not true. The whole point of my summoning her up is to fasten upon a state that is other than thinking. If she were thinking, she would be herself, contained fully within her circuits. But for me the power of the image lies precisely in the fact that she is planted in one reality, the garden setting, while adrift in the spell of another. That of the author's created reality. The business of interpretation gets more complicated when I think that the image was presumably held in mind and executed by a painter working at an easel, and that I have it in my mind not through direct perception, but in memory—or in my imagination.

What compels me is that the painter has tried to find a visible expression for that which lies in the realm of the intangible. Isn't this the most elusive and private of all conditions, that of the self suspended in the medium of language, the particles of the identity wavering in the magnetic current of another's expression? How are we to talk about it?

I zero in on the book itself. It is unmarked, unidentified—a generic signifier. But it does not belong to the ordinary run of signifiers: It is an icon representing an imagined and immaterial order. The book, whatever it is, holds dissolved in its grid of words a set of figments. These the reader will transform into a set of wholly internal sensations and emotions. These will, in turn, prove potent enough to all but eclipse her awareness of the surrounding world. The woman looks up from her book. She looks not *at* the garden but *through* it. What she sees, at most, is a light-shot shimmering of green, nothing more. Of the bench she is entirely oblivious.

I see the book. Inside the book are the words. They are themselves the threshold between the material and immaterial, the outward and the inward. The book is a thing, the page is a thing, as are the letters of the words, pressed to the pages by the printing press. They are tiny weights of ink. But if the physical book can be seen as a signifier, then the words are signifiers raised to the hundredth power. Signification is their essence, their entire reason for being. The word is the serpent eating its tail; it is the sign that disappears in its act of signing—the signing is not complete until the word has disappeared into its puff of meaning. At the instant of apotheosis it ceases to be itself; when it has brokered the transaction, it vanishes, reappearing only when the eye has moved on. This is the paradox of paradoxes: The word is most signifier when it least signifies.

But enough. What about the woman in the garden? About the meaning of reading? What is it we do when we brush our eyes over sheaves of print, and why do so many of us elect to do it for our own pleasure? What is the connection between the reading process and the self? Is this a question that can even be answered? I'm not sure. But if it can't, maybe there are others that can be, such as: What is the difference between the self when reading and when not reading? Or: Where am I when I am involved in a book?

But you can see the problems that arise. This is Einstein's universe. To isolate where I am when reading, I would have to be able to say where I am when I'm not, and this is the psychic equivalent of whirling around in front of the mirror to see what you look like from the back. And there are other difficulties. Like which self to consider—the self as adult mired in the distractions of living? Self as possessed adolescent? Self as child? And what kind of book, what kind of reading? History? Romance? Serious novels?

The last is the easiest to answer. I will confine myself to the literary novel because that, for me, represents reading in its purest form. And what interests me here are not the pedestrian incarnations of the act— reluctant struggles with novels we have no heart for—but its most idealized attainments. The question of which self, meanwhile, brings on more muddles. For I have no doubt but that my self-as-reader has changed as much over time as the other, merely existing self. What's more, not only has my changing self affected the reader-self, but the reverse has surely been true as well. Which leaves us back at the problematic boundary line that separates the one self from the other.

I am well aware of the traditional wisdom about reading and its importance. I've heard all the bromides that get passed along as we imbibe our formal education: That books are good for you; that reading broadens, quickens verbal skills, fosters attentiveness and imagination, and develops the sense of contextual relativism that makes us more empathetic, more inquisitive beings; and that rewards increase with the worthiness of the texts themselves. Indeed, the basic assumption behind most schooling, still, is that a steady application to the so-called "great works" yields an accumulation of facts and perspectives that eventually constitutes an education.

Important as these generalizations are, they do not begin to get at the real heart of reading, or to answer the question of why it matters. The truth lies elsewhere—in a context of self-making that far transcends the imperatives of self-improvement. There is a metaphysics of reading that has to do with a good deal more than any simple broadening of the mind. Rather, it involves a change of state and inner orientation, and if we contemplate the reading process in this light we can hardly get away from introducing the world *soul* (or something very like it) into the conversation. And this, I would say, it what compels me so much about the painting of the woman in the garden: It uses purely pictorial indicators to push the mind past the picture plane and toward a "beyond" that is right here inside.

We tend to think of reading as a means to an end. Like driving, it gets us from here to there. We do it, often, in order to have done it; the act is considered a sponge for contents. When we ask someone "Have you read *Bleak House?*" we are not so much inquiring whether the person has had the *experience* of reading Dickens's novel as asking whether they know the plot and the basic reference points of character and theme. Ours is a checklist sort of culture and our approach to artistic expression cannot be expected to diverge much from our general approach to the business of living.

But such an attitude greatly diminishes the scope and importance of reading. For beyond the obvious instrumentality of the act, the immersing of the self in a text has certain fundamental metaphysical implications. To read, when one does so of one's own free will, is to make a volitional statement, to cast a vote; it is to posit an elsewhere and to set off toward it. And like any traveling, reading is at once a movement and a comment of sorts about the place one has left. To open a book voluntarily is at some level to remark the insufficiency either of one's life or of one's orientation toward it. The distinction must be recognized, for when we read we not only transplant ourselves to the place of the text, but we modify our natural angle of regard upon all things; we reposition the self in order to *see* differently.

Reading is not on a continuum with the other bodily or cognitive acts. It instigates a shift, a change of state—a change analogous to, but not as totally affecting as, the change from wakefulness to sleep. Maybe the meditation state would be a better correlative. In any case, the relative outer tranquility of reading belies the magnitude of the internal transition. When we take up a book we are engaged in, we quite rapidly switch from responding to our immediate surroundings to processing a set of codes and responding to those instead. And as any devoted reader of thrillers can tell you, the coded stimuli can set the heart to racing as reliably as a crisis in the real world.

Reading a novel, then, is not simply a matter of making a connection to another person's expression. Over and above the linguistic connection, the process makes a change in the whole complex of the self. We are, for the duration of our reading, different, and the difference has more to do with the process than with its temporary object—the book being read. As with meditation, both the pulse rate and the breathing seem to alter; the interior rhythms are modified in untold ways.

Then there are the metaphysics. When we enter a novel, no matter what novel, we step into the whole world anew. The complete order of earthly things is implicitly there, even if the protagonist never leaves his bed; it is figured, assumed, in the perceptual scheme. There is only one difference: this is a world held fully in the suspension of a single sensibility—the author's. However much the life in the book may resemble life as it is known to the reader, it is nevertheless irradiated through every part with the intended coherence of its conception. The fictional world is a world with a sponsoring god—or creator—and this is true even where the work argues for the nihilistic chaos of all experience. The author's reality is meaningful—an intended entity—and we soak it up right along with the story line. And for the space of our reading, and perhaps beyond, it changes our relation to all things.

The transition from the world we live in to the world of the book is complex and gradual. We do not open to the first page and find ourselves instantly transported from our surroundings and concerns. What happens is a gradual immersion, an exchange in which we hand over our groundedness in the here and now in order to take up our new groundedness in the elsewhere of the book. The more fully we can accomplish this, the more truly we can be said to be reading. The tree in front of us must dim so that the tree on the page can take on outline and presence. The operation is by no means passive; we collude at every point. We *will* that it be so. We project ourselves at the word and pass through it as through a turnstile. And we do this, often, with an astonishing facility—we must in some way need it. A reader in the full flush of absorption will not be aware of turning words into mental entities. The conversion is automatic, as unconscious as highway driving. We often don't register what we are doing for pages at a time. In this peculiar condition, a misprinted word can be as suddenly jarring as the sight of a hubcap rolling toward us down the center line.

What makes this miracle possible is the shared medium, language. Language is the landmass that is continuous under our feet and the feet of others and allows us to get to each other's places. We bring the words, set in the intensely suggestive sequences and cadences of the writer, into ourselves. We engulf them in our consciousness and then allow ourselves to be affected by them. But reading should not therefore be construed as the simple inscribing of another person's signs upon the blank screen of our receptivity. We don't shut ourselves off and turn the book on; we are never that silent or submissive. Our own subthreshold murmuring continues, but it is pushed into the background by the more articulated, more present language of the book. Notice, however, that when our attention flags, for whatever reason, the self-murmuring rushes in to fill the void. At times we find the two voices—ours and the author's—in dissonant parley. John is confessing his love for Maria and we are simultaneously wondering if the back tire on our car is leaking. If John and Maria fade any further, we may get up to go to the garage.

But is it really so simple? Do we really find two adjacent voices coexisting, the one making room for the other? Isn't there some way in which the two might actually connect, with the author's taking in our own as a kind of tributary? It might be that just as the word-sign dissolves into the concept or picture, so our free-floating consciousness—what I have loosely called the subthreshold murmuring—coalesces around the signals to give them clarity and animation. I do sometimes have the sense that in yielding to a book I am like an orchestra at that moment when it stops its infernal seething and assents to the conductor's baton. Where am I when I'm reading? Isn't this another way of asking what happens to the buzz of consciousness when the writer's language takes possession of us?

The phrasing here is tricky, with concealed assumptions and preconceptions. I wrote "language takes possession" because it seemed to convey the sense I wanted, but on second glance the construction implies passivity before conquest, or outright seduction, when the far more likely scenario is one of collaboration. We don't just allow the writer's words the run of the house—we bring our substance to them and make them live. We are actively present at every moment, scripting and constructing. The writer may tell us, "The mother wore a shabby, discolored dressing gown," but the word canisters are empty until we load them from our private reservoirs. We activate our sense memories and determine the degrees of shabbiness and discoloration, not to mention the styling of the gown. We are bustling in all directions. If the murmur of the self is repressed, it is probably less because our language has been overpowered and more because we are too busy to heed its flickerings. Fully engaged, we work with the writer to build our own book. We preside over the movements in a world that comes into view and vanishes, present into past, just like the one we inhabit when the book is shut. That passing is condensed, foreshortened; compared to the slow sprawl of our own days, we feel as though we are experiencing the essence of time itself.

Reading may be, as I have suggested, the positing of an elsewhere, but the activity is not spatially static—it is a dynamic condition. How shall we characterize that condition? What is it that separate reading acts share that lies beyond the local construction of setting, characters, and narrative circumstances? Is there a fundamental and identifiably constant condition that we return to over and over, one different from all other conditions, from being asleep, from being high, from daydreaming?

I think there is—certainly for me. But years of working in bookstores have convinced me that this fundamental condition is there for others as well—not just a specific inner state, but a need for getting back to it. Readers know it and they seek it out. I study people in the aisles of bookstores all the time. I see them standing in place with their necks tilted at a forty-five degree angle, looking often not for a specific book, but for a book they can trust to do the job. They want plot and character, sure, but what they really want is a vehicle that will bear them off to the reading state.

In this state, when all is clear and right, I feel a connectedness that cannot be duplicated (unless, maybe, when the act of writing is going well). I feel an inside limberness, a sense of being for once in accord with time—real time, deep time. Duration time, within which events resonate and *mean*. When I am at the finest pitch of reading, I feel as if the whole of my life—past as well as unknown future—were somehow available to me. Not in terms of any high-definition particulars (reading is not clairvoyance) but as an object of contemplation. At the same time, I register a definite awareness that I am, in the present, part of a more extensive circuit, a circuit channeling what Wallace Stevens called "the substance in us that prevails."

The state of being elsewhere while reading was once, in childhood, a momentous discovery. The first arrival was so stunning, so pleasant, that I wanted nothing more than a guarantee of return. Escape? Of course. But that does not end the discussion. Here was also the finding of a lens that would give me a different orientation to what was already, though only nascently, the project of my life. Through reading I could reposition the contents of that life along the coordinate axes of urgency and purpose. These two qualities not only determined, or informed, the actions of whatever characters I was reading about, but they exerted pressure on my own life so long as I was bathed in the energies of the book.

If anything has changed about my reading over the years, it is that I value the state a book puts me in more than I value the specific contents. Indeed, I often find that a novel, even a well-written and compelling novel, can become a blur to me soon after I've finished it. I recollect perfectly the feeling of reading it, the mood I occupied, but I am less sure about the narrative details. It is almost as if the book were, as Wittgenstein said of his propositions, a ladder to be climbed and then discarded after it has served its purpose.

No matter what the shape or construction of the ladder, the ideal state of arrival is always the same. Deeply familiar—like the background setting of certain dreams, like travel, like the body sensations of crying.

I would guess that most adults who are now devoted readers began at a young age, and that they formed a good part of their essential selves through interaction with books. That is, they somehow founded their own inwardness, the more reflective component of their self, in the space that reading opened up. The space is implicit in the act of reading: It is created by the act, and the act constantly reinforces it. Again, I use the spatial analogy loosely to represent a way of perceiving the world and of situating the self vis-à-vis experience.

This self-situation of the reader is not a common one in our society. Many perceive it as deviant, even threatening. My intuition is that non-readers (by which I mean those who are able but prefer not to read) tend to see reading as a kind of value judgment upon themselves, as an elitist and exclusionary act. And there is a certain truth in that perception. Reading *is* a judgment. It brands as insufficient the understandings and priorities that govern ordinary life. Reading, pledged to duration, refuses the idea of time as simple succession. Reading argues for a larger conception of the meaningful, and its implicit injunction (seldom heeded even by readers) is that we change our lives, that we strive to live them in the light of meaning. This is not a message that many people want to hear, for the responsibility it imposes is crushingly great.

What reading does, ultimately, is keep alive the dangerous and exhilarating idea that a life is not a sequence of lived moments, but a destiny. That, God or no God, life has a unitary pattern inscribed within it, a pattern that we could discern for ourselves if we could somehow lay the whole of our experience out like a map. And while it may be true that a reader cannot see the full map better than anyone else, he is more likely to live under the supposition that such an informing pattern does exist. He is, by inclination and formation, an explorer of causes and effects and connections through time. He does not live in the present as others do—not quite—because the present is known to be a moving point in the larger scheme he is attentive to.

The time of reading, the time defined by the author's language resonating in the self, is not the world's time, but the soul's. I don't know how else to define the soul in secular terms except as a kind of self-consistent condensation of self. Reading makes this self more present. The energies that otherwise tend to stream outward through a thousand channels of distraction are marshaled by the cadences of the prose; they are brought into focus by the fact that it is an ulterior, and entirely new, world that the reader has entered. The free-floating self—the self we diffusely commune with while driving or walking or puttering in the kitchen—is enlisted in the work of bringing the narrative to life. In the process, we are able to shake off the habitual burden of insufficient meaning and flex our deeper natures. Everything in the book exists under the aspect of meaning; every sentence takes its place in the overall design. To participate in this meaning is to make the radical assumption—for oneself no less than for the characters—that the least moment will take its appointed place in the whole, and that at last all parts of the whole will flash forth their pattern of significance.

This is why the image of the woman in the painting haunts me. I see it as an emblem of paradoxical doubleness, where the physical self is rooted in one world, and the inner self is almost entirely dissolved away from its reliance on the immediate. The figure in the garden thus echoes the paradox of the book itself, which is to be a physical object whose value is found in the invisible play of energies entrapped by its covers.

# 5

# Paging the Self:

## *Privacies of Reading*

I'M GOING TO TAKE IT as an axiom that the act of reading plays a vital role in the forming and conditioning of sensibility in the life of the committed reader. What interests me is to try to puzzle out the nature of that role. But before I do, I feel that I should pause over the word *sensibility*. It is, I realize, a "humanist" term that is slipping from usage; in our age of hard-edged critical terminology it suggests a fin-de-siècle preciosity. What is sensibility, besides being the counterpart to *sense*? It is neither self nor ego; neither identity nor personality. While these are designations for something one either *has* or *is*, sensibility is more of a construct. The old sense of the word is of a refinement or cultivation of presence; it refers to the part of the inner life that is not given but fashioned: a defining, if cloudy, complex of attitudes, predilections and honed responses. And for this very reason I want to have the term available. For while it can be many things, serious reading is above all an agency of self-making. When undertaken freely, the effort of engaging a book shows a desire to actualize and augment certain inner powers. The reader assumes the possibility of deepened self-understanding, and therefore recognizes the self as malleable. Reading is the intimate, perhaps secret, part of a larger project, one that finally has little to do with the more societally oriented conceptions of the individual.

To talk about reading and the part it plays in developing the sensibility I will need to distinguish not only among different kinds of reading, but also to point out some of the ways in which reading changes across the trajectory of the reader's career. The process that begins, in most cases, with being read to, and which activates the most intense sorts of identifications in the independent reading of childhood, is something else again in adolescence, and again in full-fledged maturity, and yet again, I would guess, in later years. But because from adulthood on we are talking about sensibilities that have more or less crystallized, we may gain more by looking at the reading years of childhood and adolescence.

Being read to, while not strictly reading, is nonetheless not an entirely passive absorption either, as any parent can tell you. The child fleshes out the narrative through imaginative projection, and questions the text constantly. "Why is he crying?" "Is she going to get hurt?" She also engages the book itself, looking at the illustrations, monitoring the momentum of the turning pages, and, with the increase of aptitude, noting the correlation between what is being read out and the placement of words on the page. I see my daughter, now five, hovering on the brink of literary independence. She still loves being read to, but she breaks the flow of the story constantly by fastening on some word and working to sound it out. I can almost see the cognitive machinery at work. My hope is that as my daughter acquires mastery over words and meanings she will also discover that specialized and self-directed inwardness that makes private reading so rewarding.

Independent childhood reading seems to continue and elaborate upon the process of imaginative projection initiated through listening. It is, beautifully and openly, a voluntary participation in an ulterior scheme of reality. We might almost call it pure escape, except that getting *away* is probably less important than getting *to*. Early childhood reading is the free indulgence of fantasy and desire, done because it feels good. I remember the sensation of reading (Freudians can note this) as one of returning to a warm and safe environment, one that I had complete control over. When I picked up a book it was as much to get back to something as it was to set off to the new. The last thing the child thinks about is self-improvement; nor is he, in any obvious sense, trying to figure out the terms of existence (though such figuring probably goes on unconsciously).

The main difference between childhood reading and reading undertaken later is that in the former, futurity—the idea of one's life as a project, or adventure, or set of possibilities—has not yet entered the calculation. The child reads within a bubble. He is like Narcissus staring at his lovely image in the water's mirror. He is still sealed off from any notion of the long-term unfolding of the life, except in the perfected terms of fantasy: *I, too, will be a pirate . . .*

The change comes with adolescence, that biological and psychological free-fire zone during which the profoundest existential questions are not only posed, but lived. Who am I? Why am I doing what I'm doing? What *should* I do? What will happen to me? It is in adolescence that most of us grasp that life—our own life—is a problem to be solved, that a set of personal unknowns must now be factored together with the frightening variables of experience. The future suddenly appears—it is the space upon which the answers will be inscribed. The very idea of futurity now becomes charged with electricity.

This self-intensity, which pushes toward the future as toward some kind of release, is highly conducive to reading. The book—the novel, that is—becomes the site for testing transformations. Indeed, whatever else it may be, diversion or escape, the novel at this stage of life is primarily a screen that will accept various versions and projections of the self.

These projections are different from those of the child reader. The child manipulates fantasy stuff that is still undiluted by the reality principle. The boy dreaming of river rafts or space travel is not yet constrained by the impediments that will eventually curb and instruct his desires. Not so for the adolescent. A different reality has announced itself. Socially, sexually, and even within the bosom of the family, that thing grownups call "life" has begun to bare its face.

Adolescence is the ideal laboratory for the study of reading and self-formation. Or maybe I should say, a laboratory for studying the *ideal* impact of reading on that formation. For of course it is no secret that fewer and fewer adolescents now turn to reading on their own. Private reading still exists, but more exclusively—organized sports and "lessons" as well as seductive electronic games have made deep inroads upon the expanses of dreamy solitude that were once the given of preadult years. And it is precisely this reading, not that done for school assignments, that concerns me here.

How does reading work on the psyche during what is surely its most volatile period of change? There is no pinning it down, naturally, but we might begin with the most obvious sort of answer: the role of specific books and characters. We get reports of this influence all the time in interviews and memoirs. The subject (usually someone who has achieved something noteworthy) tells of *living* with Tom Sawyer or David Copperfield or Elizabeth Bennett. There follows the desire to do what Tom did, to be like young Elizabeth. These recognitions are eventually externalized as ideals and in that form guide the behavior along after the spell of the reading passes. I vividly remember situations in which I acted in a certain way—more bravely, more recklessly—because I believed that that was what Jack London would have done (I had all but memorized Irving Stone's romantic biography *Jack London: Sailor on Horseback*). To be sure, books are not the only places where adolescents can look for role models. Ever vigilant, they pick up moves and attitude display from rock stars, athletes, and sulky actors.

But the identifications we take from books go deeper. They form the very basis of childhood play, and run like a stream alongside the less-rooted transactions of adolescence. They often function as a kind of (pardon the jargon) "meta-narrative." If one is *not* Tom Sawyer or Elizabeth Bennett or whoever (and identifications usually are not absolute) one nevertheless performs in a magnetic field that somehow contains them. The admiring reader acts in a world that is half that of the book and half that of the real life circumstance. Every action is ennobled and exaggerated in significance because the reader imagines it brightly transposed onto the field of the book—the field of a higher and more lasting reality.

Later, as adult claims displace childish needs and as the adolescent matures, reading takes on a slightly different function. Now the reader begins to borrow from the book a sense of consequential destiny that is so absent from the daily routine. For what the novel transmits, over and above its plot and character, is the bewitching assumption of connectedness. Purpose. Meaning. The characters and situations, products of the author's creative intention, are knit together into a larger wholeness. The least movement or action *tends toward;* every action is held within the larger context which is implicitly, artistically purposeful. Our own lives may drift every which way toward the future, but the lives of the characters are aimed toward determined ends. As readers we take this in, unconsciously, and we may begin to conceive of our own actions under this same aspect of fatedness. Certainly we do so while we are reading or otherwise still in thrall to the book. And we thereby become important—just when we need to most. Our lives feel pointed toward significance and resolution; we feel ourselves living toward meaning, or at least living in the light of its possibility. I don't know that this more sustained self-charge is available anywhere else but in books. Movies are too compacted and visually determinate to encourage such operations. They don't last long enough, nor do cinematic images impinge on the memory in the same way that do the images we coproduce. And certainly little in the day-to-day world conveys to the adolescent some larger momentum toward meaning. He needs something with which to fend off the most obvious version of futurity, that incarnated in his parents, whose lives must appear tyrannized by empty ritual and pettiness.

My own shields, I remember, were other alienated solitaries. I searched high and low for novels with troubled protagonists. I soothed myself and fortified myself with novels by Thomas Wolfe, William Goldman, J. D. Salinger, and others. Their situations became the stuff of my own cocoon; they were with me as I sharpened my grievances against the world. When I went against my parents and teachers I was drawing strength from their example. I took onto myself some of what I saw as their specialness. They *had* to be special, for they were the subjects of their own books. I was special, too—subject at least of my life.

Again, I am talking about the reading of fiction—novels and stories that are, to a greater or lesser degree, simulations of reality. This does not mean that I am privileging the genre above all others, but there is a very special transformation that takes place when we read fiction that is not experienced in nonfiction. This transformation, or catalyzing action, can be seen to play a vital part in what we might call, grandly, existential self-formation.

When we read a sentence from a work of nonfiction—a history or a study of some topic, say—the words intersect with the psychic continuum, but they do not significantly modify it. We do what we need to in order to pay attention, to receive the information, but we do not reposition the self. Consider, for example, this straightforward sentence from

*The Columbia History of the World*: "When we talk about human evolution, we are dealing with two different kinds of processes: the evolution of the human body and the evolution of human behavior." As we read the words, we decode the syntactical logic of the statement and extract the idea content, the sense. If there is an authorial "voice," we don't focus upon it. The prose is a conveyor for the concept, a means to an end. We make a place for it in that interior zone where we process verbal information, but we don't ourselves change. Unless, of course, we encounter an idea that can be translated into relevant personal terms and thus affect our understanding of ourselves. But even then we react less to the words than to the implications we dig out for ourselves.

Now open a novel:

> If you really want to hear about it, the first thing you'll probably want to know is where I was born, and what my lousy childhood was like, and all that David Copperfield kind of crap, but I don't feel like going into it, if you want to know the truth.

This, too, is information, but it is obviously information of a very different kind. Reading the earlier sentence about evolution, we make no significant internal adjustment because it is not ourselves—as selves—that we hear addressed. In the second sentence, the opening of J. D. Salinger's *Catcher in the Rye,* the voice is primary. The voice proposes a self and we must greet it accordingly. We therefore heed the casual, alienated, determinedly forthright tone and filter the sense of the statement through that. But we cannot heed and filter so long as our own self is in dormancy—either we decide to engage Holden Caulfield's voice or we close the covers on the book.

Salinger, via Holden, posits a world. Holden's world. And the reader who would hear more about it is forced to open up a subjective space large enough to contain it. The opening of that space is the crucial move, for it requires the provisional loosening of whatever fixed attitudes and preconceptions we may have. In that space, two versions of reality will be stirred together—the reader's and the author's. A hybrid life will start up. Not the author's life, not fully the character's, and not quite our own though all these must be present for the mysterious catalysis of reading.

To read the book we must, in effect, bracket off our own reality and replace it with Holden's. Better, we must use what we know of our world to create his. His can only exist at the expense of ours, though—this is the law of fiction. We agree to suspend our self-grounded posture, our place in the "real" world, in order to make room for Holden's alternative sense of things. We create the textures of his reality with what we have learned from our own. But we don't disappear, either. Our awareness, our sense of life, gets filtered into the character, where it becomes strangely detached from us. The novel, in a manner of speaking, smelts its reader, extracting responsive emotions and apprehensions and then showing them forth in an aesthetic frame. Distanced from these parts of ourselves, then, we (especially as adolescents) possess them in a semiobjectified form. We begin to understand how they matter in the larger human ecology.

We don't entirely become Holden, but we abide by the terms of the world he narrates to us, agreeing to its provisions at least for the duration of our reading. We slip free from our most burdensome layer of contingent identity in order to experience the consciousness of another. This consciousness and its world are, in turn, the product of the author's consciousness. And as we read, we find that Holden's (or any character's) world manifests a kind of wholeness. This fictional world has meaning, even if Holden's own life does not appear to. Unconsciously we attune ourselves to the unitary scheme that underlies the disorder he pitches around in. This scheme, like the white page that underlies the printed words, is the surface that holds our projections. And when we close the book, we return to ourselves. Those projections stream back, only now they have been tested and modified into new shapes and they become elements in our understanding of life. We do not learn so much from the novel itself, the lessons of its situations, as we do from having strayed free of our customary boundaries. On return, those boundaries seem more articulated, more our own; we understand their degree of permeability, and this is a vital kind of knowing.

I recall from adolescent reading the powerful sensation of double

THE GUTENBERG ELEGIES

consciousness, how I went about as if in the active possession of a secret. The secret had less to do with whatever specific narrative I was caught up in, and much more with the knowledge that I had a gateway out of the narrow, baffling, and often threatening world of high school.

What does all this have to do with self-formation? How does it differ from simple escape? I have to answer with my own reader's conviction, my sense that sufficient exposure to the coherent and meaningful realities represented in the pages of novels began to lay down the traces of an expectation in me. They awoke a whole set of private determinations about my life in the future—the life I *had* to have. Even when the awareness of meaning or the sense of fatedness were not to be gathered from my surroundings, novels gave me the grounds, the incentive, to live *as if.* Indeed, more than anything else, reading created in me the awareness that life could be lived and known as a unified whole; that the patterns which make meaning are disclosed gradually. That awareness, I admit, gets harder to sustain with the passing of time—life feels much less concentrated as one grows away from the urgencies of adolescence—but I would not dream of surrendering it. Without that faith, that sense of imminent resolution, the events of the day-to-day would be like some vast assortment of colored beads without a string to hold them together.

# 6

# The Shadow Life
# of Reading

READING: THE TERM is as generous and imprecise as "love." So often it means more than just the word-by-word deciphering of the printed page. Although that definition is primary, the word's etymology (from the Anglo-Saxon *raedan,* "to make out, to interpret") points us toward open sea. We use the verb freely to denote diverse and nonspecific involvements with texts. "What are you reading now?" does not usually mean, "What book are you staring at as I address you?" More often it means, "Are you reading your way through any particular book these days?" Implicit is the understanding that most serious reading is an exertion that is interrupted and resumed and which spans an indeterminate amount of time. But there may be a still more general import to the query, allowing me to reply, "I'm reading quite a lot of modern fiction just now."

This elasticity of definition results in a certain linguistic imprecision; since "reading" signifies so many different things, why don't we have a raft of differentiated signifiers, like northern tribes are said to have for snow? But it also suggests a basic truth about the act, which is that in many vital ways it is carried on—continued—when the reader is away from the page. Thus, something more than definitional slackness allows me to tell a friend that I'm reading *The Good Soldier* as we walk down the street together. In some ways I *am* reading the novel as I walk, or nap, or drive to the store for milk. When I am away from the book it lives its shadow life, its afterlife, and *that,* as the believers have always insisted, is the only life that matters.

To say that we are really reading only while our eyes are in motion, only while we are directly under the spell of the language, voicing the words to ourselves, is tantamount to saying that the writer is only writing while he or she is actively putting words onto paper. What writer would not scoff at such a literal, limiting conception? We might reach a more inclusive understanding of reading (and writing) if we think in terms of a continuum. At one end, the writer—the flesh-and-blood individual; at the other, the flesh-and-blood reader. In the center, the words, the turning pages, the decoding intelligence. Writing is the monumentally complex operation whereby experience, insight, and imagination are distilled into language; reading is the equally complex operation that disperses these distilled elements into another person's life. The act only begins with the active deciphering of the symbols. It ends (if reading can be said to end at all) where we cannot easily track it, where the atmospheres of self condense into thought and action.

The ways in which reading fulfills its aims beyond the immediate verbal encounter are necessarily mysterious. In exploring them we explore, though unscientifically, some of the operations of consciousness itself, especially those having to do with perception and memory. We have to ask not only how we translate a symbolic code, but also what is the effect upon us of the translation process and the translated content? How do we make use of our own experience when we engage a novel? To what extent are we present in the content of what we read? How do we store what we've read and how do we draw upon our reading memory over time? For it is one book we close the covers on today, and quite another after some months or years have passed. The words on the page don't change, but we do, and our "reading"—the experience we had over the duration of our encounter with the book—has the plasticity of any memory.

The eyes move, the hand turns the page, but already the shadow life begins. The fact that our beam of focus is necessarily narrow and purposeful, directed at the words right in front of us, raises questions about the working of the reading memory. For we have obviously stored what we have read in the preceding pages—what we are not just now reading is what allows us to understand what we *are* reading. Without this ground, our experience would be like that of Dr. Oliver Sacks's patient for whom every moment was freshly minted because he could not remember anything that had come before.

Our reading memory must be a specialized function of our larger memory system—specialized in that it operates entirely within the sphere of language and language-produced impressions. Contextual and supple, this memory is (has to be) open to continuous modification. Indeed, the process of reading a work of fiction could be described as the creation and constant successive modification of context.

When we are reading a novel we don't, obviously, recall the preceding sentences and paragraphs—not directly. In fact, we don't generally remember the language at all, unless it is dialogue. For reading is a conversion, a turning of codes into contents. What we hold on to are the impressions and images, the overall structures of sense, that we have derived from the words. Depending on the artistic power of the work and our susceptibility to it, we fashion and then sustain a more-or-less vivid reality image.

If we are told in the early pages of a story that it is a rainy night, and if the descriptions have set us inside a drafty old house, then we naturally inhabit that context. Having brought a setting to life in our imaginations, and having invested it with the tones and shadings that are uniquely our own, we sustain it—and trust the author not to frustrate us. This is part of the implicit writer-reader contract. We do not at every moment remember the setting afresh, any more than when we sit in a restaurant we keep recalling that we are in the middle of a city. We work hard to establish the image, and then we move our attention elsewhere; the image becomes part of the context through which we filter what we read. With certain works it may figure as an ever-present backdrop. With others we forget—only when the character stands up to bid his host goodnight do we recollect that the conversation took place in a cluttered kitchen. We may put what we know out of our thoughts (and we will if we are not called upon to use it), but we do not tend to modify what we have been given until we have reason to. This is true not just for setting, but for character and narrative situation as well.

Our reading memory in many ways echoes our experiential memory, but with one crucial difference: Experiential memory is of actual people, places, and things, whereas our reading memory is of those things as we have been induced to create them in our own minds. The latter, in other words, make use of the former, creating a peculiar sort of self-referentiality about our memories of what we've read. The picture is further complicated by the feedback loop: Our real experiences, and hence our memories, are also influenced by what we carry with us from books.

The shadow life of reading begins even while we have the book in hand—begins as soon as we move from the first sentence to the second and start up a memory context. The creation and perpetuation of this context requires that we make a cognitive space, or "open a file," as it were. Here is the power, the seductiveness of the act: When we read, we create and then occupy a hitherto nonexistent interior locale. Regardless of what happens on the page, the simple fact that we have cleared room for these peculiar figments we now preside over gives us a feeling of freedom and control. No less exalting is the sensation of inner and outer worlds coinciding, going on simultaneously, or very nearly so. The awareness is enforced regularly. I am reading, caught up in my book, when the phone rings. I am shocked back into the room, forced to contend with some piece of business. Then, a moment later, I am back. I have jumped from one circuit to another. The book is there, waiting, like one of those rare dreams that I half-awaken from and then reenter. Knowing that I have the option of return, this figurative space within the literal space I occupy, changes my relation to that literal space. I am still contained in the world, but I don't feel trapped in it. Reading creates an imaginary context which then becomes a place of rescue.

We feel the sense of two worlds—the real and the textual—in still other ways when we engage a work over a longer period. From sitting to sitting, dipping in while we ride the bus, installing ourselves more fully before we turn out the lights at night, we are not simply alternating between zones, between life and book. We live in both at once, only at varying levels of simultaneous awareness.

I am just now reading *Dr. Haggard's Disease*, a novel by Patrick McGrath set in England during World War II. It recounts the rather bizarre progress of one man's obsessive passion for a married woman. Halfway through the book, caught up in its tensions, I am sailing along, able to resume progress effortlessly whenever I get a free moment. But the business was not so simple at the outset. As happens whenever I start a new work, I had to put myself through a fairly complicated set of initiatory steps. I cannot just open to page one and begin.

> I was in Elgin, upstairs in my study, gazing at the sea and reflecting, I remember, on a line of Goethe when Mrs. Gregor tapped at the door that Saturday and said there was a young man to see me in the surgery, a pilot. You know how she talks. "A *pilot*, Mrs. Gregor?" I murmured. I hate being disturbed on my Saturday afternoons, especially if Spike is playing up, as he was that day, but of course I limped out onto the landing and made my way downstairs. And you know what that looks like—pathetic bloody display that is, first the good leg, then the bad leg, then the stick, good leg, bad leg, stick, but down I came, down the stairs, old beyond my years and my skin a gray so cachectic it must have suggested even to you that I was in pain, chronic pain, but oh dear boy not pain like yours, just wait now and we'll make it all—go—away—

An easy and engaging opening, really, with a strong sense of mood, a conversational tone, and a beguiling mysteriousness. Moreover, the writing is skilled. I can tell from the "good leg, bad leg" sentence that McGrath is a stylist I can hand myself over to. And yet, as I sit back on a dark winter afternoon, with all comforts provided, and only the torpid stirrings of the cat to interrupt my focus, I find breaking in as arduous as ever.

First, the work of establishing context. I read the opening paragraphs two or three times, not only to get a grip on the setting and to sort out character relations—filling in the "gaps" and "indeterminacies" that the reading theorists discuss—but also to accustom myself to the rhythm and voice of the work. This is a big part of the struggle, just making the transition from not reading to reading. I cannot flip a switch and be *there*. I have to be both relaxed and focused before I can locate myself in the language. The words have to come alive in the ear—I have to hear them and hear them deeply. For this to happen I need to ratchet myself down by degrees. By the third or fourth reading of the passages I feel that I catch it—I am ready.

But the entry problems are not thereby all solved. Indeed, there remains the larger dilemma—whether or not to invest myself in the book. I read the first few pages, try to read them well, to give them every chance. My hesitation does not so much signal the fickleness of my reading temperament as it underscores the importance I grant to the larger process. I know that any novel I decide to give myself over to will be with me not just for the hours or days it takes me to read through, but possibly for a long time after.

I decide to stay with McGrath's novel and I push on, slowly opening the gate into that ulterior realm, that place I will at least partially inhabit as I go about my daily tasks. I now try to let the language extinguish my other awareness as much as possible, to pull the author's world around me entirely. I make myself susceptible to the sounds and rhythms and their endless modulations. I can measure the difficulty of this by noting the extent of my distractedness. I shift around in my seat, keep glancing at my surroundings. The cat has advanced to the foot of the couch and looks at me imploringly. I teeter, one foot in the old place, one in the new. I return to the words, try to hear them—and yes, by degrees they become transparent, a reverberation of sense. When this happens—and with McGrath it happens quite early on—I feel a tug. The chain has settled over the sprockets; there is the feel of meshing, then the forward glide. When I look up again the cat has vanished.

Now I have occupied the book and the book has begun to occupy me. Its atmospheres bleed obscurely into mine. Because I am immersed, I carry the work everywhere, returning to the narrative every time there is an opening in the day. And for the duration of my reading—and maybe less vividly after—I will shift between two centers of awareness, the one required by my more worldly functions, the other felt as a petitioning of my subjective, inward self. I find the back-and-forth movement—an abstract sort of friction—invigorating. Attending to two very different kinds of reality, reconnoitering between inner and outer focus, enriches my overall responsiveness.

In the course of a fifteen-minute subway ride I drop into Haggard's world as into a well. I heed the outside signals only enough to insure that I don't travel on past my stop. Not until I feel the train decelerating do I close the book and look up. For an instant everything swims in a milky sort of haze; then the eyes readjust and the sensations of reading begin to ebb. I look around at the other passengers—the student, the mother fiddling with the strap on her child's knapsack—and I feel irradiated with a benign detachment. The inner and outer are, briefly, in balance. Haggard is as present to me as these people. And that specious equivalence brings me closer to them, though I'm not sure why. Their boundaries seem porous; I have the illusion that I could enter and understand their lives. The feeling passes. The life of the book dims out as I get to my feet and jostle through the doors.

But Haggard does not simply disappear until I next return to the book. When a work compels immersion, it often also has the power to haunt from a distance. I don't just mean that my thoughts now and again turn to the characters and the story—though this, of course, happens all the time—I mean that I feel haunted. Just as in a true "haunt" one feels the presence of spirits from the "other side," so do I sometimes feel the life of the book suddenly invade me. As if, for a moment, that life were my life—the walls come down. This only happens with certain books, but when it does it feels like a gift, a freely given transcendence of self. I'm not sure how to explain it, except maybe as a kind of cognitive "short circuit," where some triggering association suddenly shunts my readerly preoccupations, my subliminal self, into the foreground. Or as a consequence of some linguistic alchemy that brings a portion of the book so vividly to life that it overwhelms the affective centers.

If we postulate that there are two worlds—the "real" and that of the book—then we might say that the printed page, unread, marks the line between them. As a material thing, a paper surface, the page has its place in the former realm; as it is read, and rendered transparent, it becomes an entryway to the latter. The two are not mutually exclusive, of course. I draw on years of observation to make my picture of Haggard toiling down the stairs. I likewise find that my reading constantly impinges on my living: I cannot watch someone hobbling with a cane without thinking of Haggard cussing and heaving.

The page is our platform, the beginning place. When we lift our eyes away we carry the energies of the book inside ourselves as a kind of subsidiary momentum. Some books possess us so thoroughly that for a time we see everything as if through a special lens. How and whether this happens depends on what we are reading and upon our disposition.

There are works I set aside and forget about entirely until I pick them up again. Others hit me like a drug, altering my moods, my perceptions, and ultimately my interactions with others. If I am reading Walker Percy, for instance, everything that happens to me seems like a possible clue in some encompassing existential mystery. Anita Brookner, meanwhile, can have me moping for days over the sorrowful frailty of all human endeavor. Maybe books, like pharmaceuticals, should carry warnings: *May induce sudden fits of hilarity,* or, *Provokes irreverence,* or, *If melancholy persists after reading, consult a qualified therapist.* The books that matter to me—and they are books of all descriptions—are those that galvanize something inside me. I read books to read myself.

There is a great difference, as I have remarked elsewhere, between the influences we take in when we are young and those that come later, after our patterns of response and our defensive structures are more set. Nothing I read now, alas, could affect me the way certain books did when I was in my teens. I fear that I will never be as taken with an author as I once was with D. H. Lawrence or Henry Miller or Thomas Mann. Now when I read a book that matters I feel that I am carrying it around inside me. Then it was the reverse: I was living my life inside the enclosure of the work. *Women in Love* was not just an intense reading experience—it was a powerful initiation. Through the novel, through what I took to be the Lawrentian sensibility in general, I worked out my first substantial thoughts about love, passion, and sexual power. Rupert Birkin throwing stones into a pond was more commandingly present to me than any of the adults who tried to direct my steps. I could not possibly have such a response if I were to read that novel for the first time today. Yes, I know so much more. But to paraphrase T. S. Eliot: Lawrence and the others have everything to do with what I know. Through reading and living I have gradually made myself proof against total ravishment by authors. Yet so vivid are my recollections of that urgency, that sense of consequence, that I foolishly keep looking for it to happen again.

Book to real world, real world to book—I am in perpetual transit. As a veteran of innumerable shuttlings from one place to the other, I make a sharp distinction. To shut the book and step into the day is to make one kind of passage, and to pull away from the day to enter the book is to make quite another. It is much easier, for some reason, to shift from the page to dailiness than it is to accomplish the reverse. There may be a sigh of reluctance, a momentary dissociation, but the lever is readily moved. It is much harder to push it in the other direction. Even if I am entirely engrossed in a novel and eager to get under its spell again, I still find that reentry takes effort. To return to the realm of symbols, however comfortable I am in that realm, always involves a change of circuit and what feels at first like a great deceleration.

But the difficulties in no way dampen my pleasure in making the transition—they may even heighten it, intensifying the involvement once I have resumed. Indeed, the state I occupy while reading often feels more focused, more meaningful, more *real*, than those that comprise most of my nonreading life. I have the same feeling about certain dreams—that they carry me to a truer place.

I don't mean to suggest that the reading encounter is to be preferred to the real encounter, only to say that an hour spent with the right book may offer a more condensed, more affecting inner transaction than what the daily usually allows. Not only is the text a distillation, a dramatic shaping of materials, but to process it we must apply a very exclusive sort of focus. The result is an altered state of awareness, a kindled-up sort of high. But like any high, it must at some point wear off. Reentry—the return to the more dispersed conditions of dailiness—brings on a sense of affective slackening.

The shadow life of reading generally continues on for some time after we have finished the last page. If we have been deeply engaged by the book, we carry its resonance as a kind of echo, thinking again and again of a character, an episode, or, less concretely, about some thematic preoccupation of the author's. After I recently finished V. S. Naipaul's *A Bend in the River*, I found myself brooding for days on the ways in which cultures and value systems come into collision. I brooded abstractly, but I also saw my reading affect my daily perceptions. Riding the subway or walking downtown, I would catch myself monitoring gestures and interchanges between members of different racial and cultural groups. I also read the morning paper differently, looking more closely at reports detailing racial and ethnic frictions. I had absorbed a context which suddenly heightened the "relevance" of this theme.

Long-term effects: the longer the term, the more complex the legacy. Some works, the ones that really reached us, that muscled into our lives, become permanent points of reference. We not only recall them fondly, but we often recall parts of our lives through them. I cannot think of a certain epoch of my adolescence without invoking Jack Kerouac—the man, my *idea* of the man, and of course the books themselves. I read his pages as if they were scripture and then I acted on the excitements that were aroused in me. Later, only slightly more sedately, I took in major infusions of Hemingway, Henry Miller, Hamsun, Lowry . . . For me to think about certain books by these authors is to reconstitute myself at key points of my younger life.

The literature, of course, changes as we change. The words stay fixed, but the meaning moves around us like a shadow. In some cases we outgrow the book; the passages that flamed so brightly seem pallid when we go back to them. When I reread *On the Road* a few years back I was shocked to find how much of the pith had gone out of the novel. It had had a tremendous effect—more than any single thing it guided my attitudes and actions for a time in my late teens—but whatever magic had been there now survived as only a memory of magic.

But there are also books we only begin to catch up to as we mature. I spent long months in college and after trying to take the measure of Joyce's *Ulysses*. Limited as I was in both experience and learning, I naturally fell short. But so intense was my application that I managed to internalize much of the book. And now, unexpectedly, as if governed by some time-release chemical, lines and passages flash their sense at me. I pick up a reference, I grasp the real point of a joke or a pun, I see in some larger way what Joyce was getting at. The once nearly unscaleable wall of language has come down; the book is now more like some vast honeycomb stacked with corridors, mainly accessible. I have done nothing except grow slowly out of some of my ignorance.

V. S. Naipaul, in his essay, "Conrad's Darkness," has assessed his experience over time with that author. Writes Naipaul, "We read at different times for different things. We take to novels our own ideas of what the novel should be; and those ideas are made by our needs, our education, our background or perhaps our ideas of our background. Because we read, really, to find out what we already know, we can take a writer's virtues for granted." As an example, Naipaul cites a passage from the story "Karain," remarking, "It is a passage that, earlier, I would have hurried through: the purple passage, the reflective caption. Now I see a precision in its romanticism, and a great effort of thought and empathy."

But this has more to do with rereading—with thrusting the changed self forward again to encounter the stationary text. What about the influence exerted over time by the original reading of a literary work? I'm thinking not just of the touchstone works, but of the full panoply—all the novels that lay any claim to significance whatsoever. Over the years, for pleasure, to better myself, and also because it is my vocation to review books, I have read hundreds and hundreds of works of fiction. Novels by Saul Bellow, Anne Tyler, Toni Morrison, Robert Musil, Gabriel García Márquez, Jean Stafford, Philip Roth, Thomas Pynchon, Marguerite Duras, Thomas Bernhard, Russell Banks, Christa Wolf . . . I feel happy just starting a list. And I know that my list is my own, unlikely to correspond too closely with anyone else's. With each book completed I feel that I have augmented myself, gained in some understanding or wisdom, however slight. But I have to wonder, as one reading memory folds into another, as the imprint of thousands of impressions harvested from thousands of pages blurs, what has been the purpose? That is, what *has* all of this reading done for me as a person, apart from providing me with untold hours of entertainment and distraction? Where have my reading experiences gone and what have they left me with?

I've already mentioned the "big" books that changed my thinking, that brought me strange and not always welcomed news about human nature—the books that I read before the age of thirty. But what about the towers of printed paper I have scaled since then? What about all the works I ingested in my less-malleable adulthood?

If I ceased to be malleable I did not cease to be susceptible. I did not become so set in my disposition as to be impermeable to influences. It's just that the recognitions prompted in me by these later books were different, less fundamental. Many have enlarged my sense of things without changing me—broadening my sense of history and human relationships, quickening the empathic nerve. *A Bend in the River* made me more attentive to diverse cultural interactions. That same process has been repeated countless times with other works, and in each case my way of looking at the world has been incrementally altered. Novels by Toni Morrison and John Edgar Wideman have not only given me a new sense of racial barriers and how they are experienced by African-Americans, but they have subtly affected my interactions with members of all so-called "minority" groups. The prejudices I acquired in my suburban upbringing had less to do with notions of superiority and inferiority and more to do with difference. The message: These people do not have your history or cultural background and you cannot know their world; by the same token, they cannot know yours. One of the most heartening long-term effects of reading African-American literature has been the erosion of that sense of irreconcilable otherness. True, the lives depicted in many of the works are in certain aspects alien to me. But the fact of the portrayal, the fact that I can enter those lives by way of language, confirms for me the existence of a commonality prior to all cultural divergences. If that commonality were not there, I could not achieve the immersion I do.

This vanquishing of otherness has happened with respect to other cultures, women, previous historical periods, and so on. The process has been gradual. I have not so much had my eyes opened as I have been taught to see more clearly. How would my understanding have changed over the same period if I were not a reader? I can't begin to imagine. How would I think about memory if I knew nothing of Proust? How would I ponder old age and death without the internalized perspectives of Lampedusa, Tolstoy, Lessing, Yourcenar, García Márquez and others? Apart from giving me ideas, books have forced me to create a space for reflection; they have made certain kinds of thinking inevitable.

What we do with our reading experience is, finally, not so much different from what we do with the experience we acquire directly. For one thing, we use it as a basis for interpreting the behavior of people around us. We figure their motivations and construct scenarios of possibility. If I am thrown into a situation in which I have to deal with a person who is terrified of something, I begin by drawing on my own understanding of fear. I try to remember how I felt during various personal crises and use what I know to establish an affective link. But I do not make a deep distinction between what I know from real life and what I know vicariously through reading. Indeed, much of what I know about fear has been distilled from authors as unlike one another as Nadine Gordimer, Charles Dickens, Charlotte Brontë, Joseph Conrad, and Stephen Crane.

How *does* a reading memory differ from the memory of an actual event? This is a murky business and it is made murkier still by the idiosyncratic selectivity of memory. Over time, every reader accrues a kind of sedimentary layer of insights and impressions; he also establishes a vast hoard of very particular recollections. Of scenes, images, and seemingly irrelevant bric-a-brac. As often as not, these are fragments retained for whatever reason from books otherwise forgotten. It is almost as if the ultimate point of certain reading has been the survival of some odd trace. Again, as in life, so in art. Just as most of what happens to us dissolves, becomes part of an inner compost known in generalized terms—"my high school years," "boot camp," and so on—so most of what we have read loses definition and becomes a blurry wash.

Against this unfeatured backdrop emerge the distinct survivals, the details that for one reason or another we recall. They are not always, or even often, the key elements of the work. We preserve them illogically, savoring their perverse irrelevance, in the same way that we recall the cheap plastic lanyard worn by our grade school gym teacher or the face of the man who ran the hamburger stand. Why this and not that? Who can say? But what this eccentric retentiveness underscores is a certain equivalence between life memories and reading memories—they are subject to the same inscrutable laws. Because our reading memories are partly the product of imagined experiences, do we therefore deem them inferior? Or do we grant that the recollection of a detailed imagining is as much a part of our identity as the memory of something that actually took place?

Every reader carries around his or her own store of specific traces which, if they could be inventoried, would be as useful an index of character as any battery of psychological tests. Even a moment's reflection brings them crowding forth: Hans Castorp staring, love-besotted, at Clavdia Chauchat's x-ray image (*The Magic Mountain*); Humbert

Humbert lounging about in his robe on a Sunday morning, alert through every nerve ending to the movements of Lola Haze (*Lolita*); Geoffrey Firmin, the Consul, sitting in the dim recesses of a Mexican cantina, *perfectamente borracho*, trying to make sense of the sudden flesh-and-blood presence of his estranged wife, Yvonne (*Under the Volcano*); Nikki Jumpei gradually becoming aware of the body of a sleeping woman, her nakedness covered with a fine layer of sand (*The Woman in the Dunes*); Avey Johnson, vacationing in the Caribbean, unexpectedly jumping to her feet to join in a ceremonial dance (*Praisesong for the Widow*); Leopold Bloom watching a rat scurry away under a loose monument at Paddy Dignam's funeral (*Ulysses*) . . .

I love this trolling of the memory. With each retrieval I not only re-experience something of the flavor of the book, the dense reality it enfolds, but I also recover, if only fleetingly, the original circumstance of my reading—a train ride, a favorite chair in an old apartment, the atmosphere of a long, disconsolate summer. And in some special cases the reading seems to have sponged up everything around it. I have a more intense memory of hiding in bed with *Humboldt's Gift* and trying to outrun the pain of a breakup than I do of the long depression I moved around in. I read then in order to get away and what I now recall, mainly, is the book that rescued me.

No *quod erat demonstrandum* arrives to round this meditation out. Works of imagination bleed together with the world they extrapolate from. The writing process begins in the writer, the life; it branches off onto paper, into artifice; but the final restless resting place of every written thing is the solitary life of the reader. There it hibernates, a cluster of stray images, forgotten incitements and conversational asides, a mass of shadow wrapping itself around the thoughts and gestures of the self.

# 7

# From the Window
# of a Train

I WAS TRAVELING BY TRAIN from Boston to New York. I make the trip several times a year, and I've found the five-hour run to be ideal for certain kinds of brooding and notetaking. I have never yet stepped out at Penn Station without a few pages of jumpy script packed away in my bag. On this occasion I had the beginnings of something in mind. I was going to try to work up a set of thoughts about a passage in Oscar Wilde's essay, "The Decay of Lying," (the passage where his aesthete, Vivian, insists, "Life imitates Art far more than Art imitates Life"), and as we hurtled along toward Providence I tried to ease myself into the proper state of meditative focus, a receptive, associative casting about. But I was having no luck. Indeed, the harder I tried to get in the right place, the more obstructed I felt. All sorts of thoughts flashed through my mind, but none were the kind I was hoping for. Providence came and went. And as we began the long and exalting sweep along the Connecticut shoreline, I closed my eyes and tried to subdue my frustration.

It was soon after, somewhere in the vicinity of Old Mystic, that a single phrase set up its recursive beat in my head. "The reader and the writer . . ." There was no logic to it; it stuck like one of those songs we obsess on. I mouthed it silently half a hundred times, unsure of its origin or destination; I knew only that it soothed me to say the words. Before long, however, the packaging of sense fell away, leaving me with just the two thudding trochees: reader . . . writer . . . And these I repeated no less compulsively, aware as I did so that their beat fell in synch with the more extended dactyls of the train. And then, without warning, a string of sentences arrived and I hurried to record them in my notebook. But even as I wrote I had the sense that the words were going to be throw-aways. They were too ripe, too purple. But I figured that they were just the locomotive for freight that would arrive later. And so they were. As soon as I got back from New York I sat down and copied out the insti-gating passage and then the thoughts that had massed just behind them:

> Ree-durr-Rye-turr, Ree-durr-Rye-turr . . . A noise and a motion like that of a galloping whirligig, a lone propeller whispering over the meadows of history——something made of two parts conjoined, awkward in repose, but utterly married once set into motion; scarcely audible, certainly alongside the heavy creaking of the world's machinery, but passing along the very spirit breath itself, the long pneumatic hiss on which all meaning rides . . . Ree-durr—Rye-turr . . . The eerie, necessary interchange—a surge of animated air as the one breathes in and the other breathes out . . .

The writer writes and the reader reads—or so it appears. And there the matter rests, for most. But in truth, this simple proposition is a mask for a vast system of ambiguities and entanglements. For it is also true, in a not so very farfetched way, that in writing the writer reads and that in reading the reader writes. The activities are by no means as clear-cut as appearances would lead us to believe.

To put it simply: Writing is not merely the action of moving the pen or hitting the letters on the keyboard, any more than reading is the straightforward ingesting of print through the eyes. Underneath these basic, seemingly definitive physical operations lie other processes.

What the writer does while moving the pen is not invention; the writer does not create the unknown and unforeseen whole cloth out of nothing. Of course we recognize that. *That* is the unrepeatable, para-digm act that we grant to our mythic gods alone. All subsequent acts of creation—if they can be called "creation" at all—are finally an arrang-ing and interpreting of the given. Not so much a bringing-into-being as a recovering of what is in some way already known. The writer, then, places himself in a condition of silent receptivity. He begins by repress-ing or pushing aside all impediments, tries to rid himself of extraneous stimuli. Only then, when the way is clear, do the fine hair-tip extensions of the inner senses begin their tracking process.

The writer looks for the words that will best convey sensations and ideas. These are known to us first as inklings, energy patterns and traces of great distinctness that are inevitably bound up with memories; anything we know is, after all, known through memory. We do not find the units of our expression floating around in the interior space like so many colored balloons, each tethered to its own meaning. More likely they lie embedded in the dense layers of our print memory. But don't imagine this as a dictionary or filing system. Our print memory is probably more like some indeterminate hyperspace filled with linked-up strands of coded matter, except that the matter is invisible—it is all impulse. The whole of our experience is there, disassembled, in saturated bits, ready for any of the myriad new formations that produce yet another version of the past.

Let us say that we are writers and that our aim is to describe a certain setting—an old wooden dock at a lake, for instance. We know, from some composite of our own experiences, the impressions that we are after: a morning silence, the air over the lake like a transparent membrane, the springy give and take of the boards as we walk toward the end of the dock, the sensations of peeling paint and damp, furred wood against our bare feet, the creaking sound, and so on.

To locate these images, these particular nuances, we research our sense memories, applying our attentiveness inward with the same diligence we would apply to the reading of a difficult text. And it's true, we are in some ways treating our experience as a text and setting about to work our way through it. We must, for we cannot have all of the images and sensations we need at our command at once; memory works by association, by accumulation, and by unconscious reconstruction.

First, we try to recall how it was—or, if we are translating experience, might have been—to walk down to the lake in the early morning. We move in sequence, very much as if we were following the logic of another writer's description. We see the dock from the distance, see the mist; we summon, in natural order, what must be the components of the experience. How cool the sand felt, how the boards first took the body's weight. We read ourselves, and then we report on that reading. We call it writing.

And when we do this reporting, we activate the relevant areas of our language memory which include not only all we know of words, but also all we know *through* words. The description we write will inevitably be a composite, a reworking of a hundred-odd descriptions that have dissolved together inside. For I don't think that we ever really forget what we read, any more than we forget what we experience. More likely, we break down the unity of the illusion, preserving the elements along with the mountains of other traces until they become virtually indistinguishable—until what we have read takes on the status of being something that once happened to us.

When we begin to write our description, then, we find that we already have a sense of the kind of shape we want, and some intuition of the pace. This is not because these are necessarily properties of the reality we would render; rather, because we have a very particular expectation built up from everything we have read and internalized. We know just the feeling—the effect—we want. In a sense we proceed toward our expression by trying to read in ourselves the very prose we are about to write. Writing, then, becomes a kind of matching up of the right words to the specific word-impulses that are lined up inside. This is all very Platonic—to see the act of discovery less as an inventing than a recovering, an *anamnesis*. In writing we grope toward what we think of as the inevitable wording, as though the prose were already finished in an inner place we can just barely reach. And when we do succeed, when from time to time we reach it, we know we are beyond revision.

This is where the subterranean influence of reading plays its part. The writers we read furnish us with expectations—they teach us how we like to see and feel and hear and think about things. So while it is true that we wrote the description of the dock, discovered it inside ourselves phrase by phrase, we will, if we are honest, share at least some part of the credit with E. B. White and Eudora Welty and Norman Maclean and Henry David Thoreau and the innumerable others whose words are packed like silt inside us.

We are not done. The other side of the picture—that reading is a kind of writing—is no less persuasive. Once again we locate ourselves in the cloudy zone where language and memory swirl together. The core question is: What do we do with words when we read? I would argue that we make another person's words our own not simply by looking at them but by apprehending, inhabiting, and reinscribing them. "The dock was old and ramshackle. The peeling boards were springy underfoot." We can only take possession of the words by filling them out with our own recollected experience. Once again, those saturated bits are set into motion, combined and recombined. The larger implications of this, bearing on our own sense of the personal past, are quite staggering. It may well be that we do not carry our memories in an existing archive of stored impressions. Isn't it just as likely that we create the past afresh from available components every time we remember? Each memory would then be a story we write for ourselves on the spot. Some of these, through a kind of narrative insistence (shaped, in turn, by obscure needs) become the authorized versions: This is how it *really* was.

In any case, when we read we bring the life—ultimately *our* life—to the words. In tapping our experience thus, reading becomes a steadily unfolding memory event. Which is not to say that we are actively reliving our pasts every time we read a story, but that our associative mechanisms are constantly operative—those "bits" are agitated like the molecules in a pot on the verge of boiling.

This is one of the great incentives and surprises of reading: that we are at all times so close to the subthreshold energies of the self. "The peeling boards were springy underfoot" means nothing much until we have produced the sensations in ourselves—*created* them. To do so we have had to brush against the original traces, whatever it is we carry inside that holds our knowledge of springy boards. In other words, we make the music indicated by the notes. But even more than the musician following a score, we invest ourselves in the act. This investment resembles closely what the writer does in putting words on the page.

Reading and writing—reader and writer. Could it be that at some level the two activities are not all that different, that they are just manifestations of the ebb and flow of our awareness, ways we have of breaking down and recombining the countless interlocking puzzle pieces inside? Every true reader, then, is a writer and every true writer is a reader, and every person engaged in the project of self-awareness is the reader and writer of himself. Writer and reader: They are the recto and verso of language, which is itself the medium of our deeper awareness.

# PART II

# The Electronic Millennium

# 8

# Into the Electronic Millennium

S OME YEARS AGO, a friend and I comanaged a used and rare book shop in Ann Arbor, Michigan. We were often asked to appraise and purchase libraries—by retiring academics, widows, and disgruntled graduate students. One day we took a call from a professor of English at one of the community colleges outside Detroit. When he answered the buzzer I did a double take—he looked to be only a year or two older than we were. "I'm selling everything," he said, leading the way through a large apartment. As he opened the door of his study I felt a nudge from my partner. The room was wall-to-wall books and as neat as a chapel.

The professor had a remarkable collection. It reflected not only the needs of his vocation—he taught nineteenth- and twentieth-century literature—but a book lover's sensibility as well. The shelves were strictly arranged, and the books themselves were in superb condition. When he left the room we set to work inspecting, counting, and estimating. This is always a delicate procedure, for the buyer is at once anxious to avoid insult to the seller and eager to get the goods for the best price. We adopted our usual strategy, working out a lower offer and a more generous fallback price. But there was no need to worry. The professor took our first offer without batting an eye.

As we boxed up the books, we chatted. My partner asked the man if he was moving. "No," he said, "but I am getting out." We both looked up. "Out of the teaching business, I mean. Out of books." He then said that he wanted to show us something. And indeed, as soon as the books were packed and loaded, he led us back through the apartment and down a set of stairs. When we reached the basement, he flicked on the light. There, on a long table, displayed like an exhibit in the Space Museum, was a computer. I didn't know what kind it was then, nor could I tell you now, fifteen years later. But the professor was keen to explain and demonstrate.

While he and my partner hunched over the terminal, I roamed to and fro, inspecting the shelves. It was purely a reflex gesture, for they held nothing but thick binders and paperbound manuals. "I'm changing my life," the ex-professor was saying. "This is definitely where it's all going to happen." He told us that he already had several good job offers. And the books? I asked. Why was he selling them all? He paused for a few beats. "The whole profession represents a lot of pain to me," he said. "I don't want to see any of these books again."

The scene has stuck with me. It is now a kind of marker in my mental life. That afternoon I got my first serious inkling that all was not well in the world of print and letters. All sorts of corroborations followed. Our professor was by no means an isolated case. Over a period of two years we met with several others like him. New men and new women who had glimpsed the future and had decided to get out while the getting was good. The selling off of books was sometimes done for financial reasons, but the need to burn bridges was usually there as well. It was as if heading to the future also required the destruction of tokens from the past.

A change is upon us—nothing could be clearer. The printed word is part of a vestigial order that we are moving away from—by choice and by societal compulsion. I'm not just talking about disaffected academics, either. This shift is happening throughout our culture, away from the patterns and habits of the printed page and toward a new world distinguished by its reliance on electronic communications.

This is not, of course, the first such shift in our long history. In Greece, in the time of Socrates, several centuries after Homer, the dominant oral culture was overtaken by the writing technology. And in Europe another epochal transition was effected in the late fifteenth century after Gutenberg invented movable type. In both cases the long-term societal effects were overwhelming, as they will be for us in the years to come.

The evidence of the change is all around us, though possibly in the manner of the forest that we cannot see for the trees. The electronic media, while conspicuous in gadgetry, are very nearly invisible in their functioning. They have slipped deeply and irrevocably into our midst, creating sluices and circulating through them. I'm not referring to any one product or function in isolation, such as television or fax machines or the networks that make them possible. I mean the interdependent totality that has arisen from the conjoining of parts—the disk drives hooked to modems, transmissions linked to technologies of reception, recording, duplication, and storage. Numbers and codes and frequencies. Buttons and signals. And this is no longer "the future," except for the poor or the self-consciously atavistic—it is now. Next to the new technologies, the scheme of things represented by print and the snail-paced linearity of the reading act looks stodgy and dull. Many educators say that our students are less and less able to read, or analyze, or write with clarity and purpose. Who can blame the students? Everything they meet with in the world around them gives the signal: That was then, and electronic communications are now.

Do I exaggerate? If all this is the case, why haven't we heard more about it? Why hasn't somebody stepped forward with a bow tie and a pointer stick to explain what is going on? Valid questions, but they also beg the question. They assume that we are all plugged into a total system—where else would that "somebody" appear if not on the screen at the communal hearth?

Media theorist Mark Crispin Miller has given one explanation for our situation in his discussions of television in *Boxed In: The Culture of TV.* The medium, he proposes, has long since diffused itself throughout the entire system. Through sheer omnipresence it has vanquished the possibility of comparative perspectives. We cannot see the role that television (or, for our purposes, all electronic communications) has assumed in our lives because there is no independent ledge where we might secure our footing. The medium has absorbed and eradicated the idea of a pretelevision past; in place of what used to be we get an ever-new and ever-renewable present. The only way we can hope to understand what is happening, or what has already happened, is by way of a severe and unnatural dissociation of sensibility.

To get a sense of the enormity of the change, you must force yourself to imagine—deeply and in nontelevisual terms—what the world was like a hundred, even fifty, years ago. If the feat is too difficult, spend some time with a novel from the period. Read between the lines and reconstruct. Move through the sequence of a character's day and then juxtapose the images and sensations you find with those in the life of the average urban or suburban dweller today.

Inevitably, one of the first realizations is that a communications net, a soft and pliable mesh woven from invisible threads, has fallen over everything. The so-called natural world, the place we used to live, which served us so long as the yardstick for all measurements, can now only be perceived through a scrim. Nature was then; this is now. Trees and rocks have receded. And the great geographical Other, the faraway rest of the world, has been transformed by the pure possibility of access. The numbers of distance and time no longer mean what they used to. Every place, once unique, itself, is strangely shot through with radiations from every other place. "There" was then; "here" is now.

Think of it. Fifty to a hundred million people (maybe a conservative estimate) form their ideas about what is going on in America and in the world from the same basic package of edited images—to the extent that the image itself has lost much of its once-fearsome power. Daily newspapers, with their long columns of print, struggle against declining sales. Fewer and fewer people under the age of fifty read them; computers will soon make packaged information a custom product. But if the printed sheet is heading for obsolescence, people are tuning in to the signals. The screen is where the information and entertainment wars will be fought. The communications conglomerates are waging bitter takeover battles in their zeal to establish global empires. As Jonathan Crary has written in "The Eclipse of the Spectacle," "Telecommunications is the new arterial network, analogous in part to what railroads were for capitalism in the nineteenth century. And it is this electronic substitute for geography that corporate and national entities are now carving up." Maybe one reason why the news of the change is not part of the common currency is that such news can only sensibly be communicated through the more analytic sequences of print.

To underscore my point, I have been making it sound as if we were all abruptly walking out of one room and into another, leaving our books to the moths while we settle ourselves in front of our state-of-the-art terminals. The truth is that we are living through a period of overlap; one way of being is pushed athwart another. Antonio Gramsci's often-cited sentence comes inevitably to mind: "The crisis consists precisely in the fact that the old is dying and the new cannot be born; in this interregnum a great variety of morbid symptoms appears." The old surely is dying, but I'm not so sure that the new is having any great difficulty being born. As for the morbid symptoms, these we have in abundance.

The overlap in communications modes, and the ways of living that they are associated with, invites comparison with the transitional epoch in ancient Greek society, certainly in terms of the relative degree of disturbance. Historian Eric Havelock designated that period as one of "proto-literacy," of which his fellow scholar Oswyn Murray has written:

> To him [Havelock] the basic shift from oral to literate culture was a slow process; for centuries, despite the existence of writing, Greece remained essentially an oral culture. This culture was one which depended heavily on the encoding of information in poetic texts, to be learned by rote and to provide a cultural encyclopedia of conduct. It was not until the age of Plato in the fourth century that the dominance of poetry in an oral culture was challenged in the final triumph of literacy.

That challenge came in the form of philosophy, among other things, and poetry has never recovered its cultural primacy. What oral poetry was for the Greeks, printed books in general are for us. But our historical moment, which we might call "proto-electronic," will not require a transition period of two centuries. The very essence of electronic transmissions is to surmount impedances and to hasten transitions. Fifty years, I'm sure, will suffice. As for what the conversion will bring—and *mean*—to us, we might glean a few clues by looking to some of the "morbid symptoms" of the change. But to understand what these portend, we need to remark a few of the more obvious ways in which our various technologies condition our senses and sensibilities.

I won't tire my reader with an extended rehash of the differences between the print orientation and that of electronic systems. Media theorists from Marshall McLuhan to Walter Ong to Neil Postman have discoursed upon these at length. What's more, they are reasonably commonsensical. I therefore will abbreviate.

The order of print is linear, and is bound to logic by the imperatives of syntax. Syntax is the substructure of discourse, a mapping of the ways that the mind makes sense through language. Print communication requires the active engagement of the reader's attention, for reading is fundamentally an act of translation. Symbols are turned into their verbal referents and these are in turn interpreted. The print engagement is essentially private. While it does represent an act of communication, the contents pass from the privacy of the sender to the privacy of the receiver. Print also posits a time axis; the turning of pages, not to mention the vertical descent down the page, is a forward-moving succession, with earlier contents at every point serving as a ground for what follows. Moreover, the printed material is static—it is the reader, not the book, that moves forward. The physical arrangements of print are in accord with our traditional sense of history. Materials are layered; they lend themselves to rereading and to sustained attention. The pace of reading is variable, with progress determined by the reader's focus and comprehension.

The electronic order is in most ways opposite. Information and contents do not simply move from one private space to another, but they travel along a network. Engagement is intrinsically public, taking place within a circuit of larger connectedness. The vast resources of the network are always there, potential, even if they do not impinge on the immediate communication. Electronic communication can be passive, as with television watching, or interactive, as with computers. Contents, unless they are printed out (at which point they become part of the static order of print) are felt to be evanescent. They can be changed or deleted with the stroke of a key. With visual media (television, projected graphs, highlighted "bullets") impression and image take precedence over logic and concept, and detail and linear sequentiality are sacrificed. The pace is rapid, driven by jump-cut increments, and the basic movement is laterally associative rather than vertically cumulative. The presentation structures the reception and, in time, the expectation about how information is organized.

Further, the visual and nonvisual technology in every way encourages in the user a heightened and ever-changing awareness of the present. It works against historical perception, which must depend on the inimical notions of logic and sequential succession. If the print medium exalts the word, fixing it into permanence, the electronic counterpart reduces it to a signal, a means to an end.

Transitions like the one from print to electronic media do not take place without rippling or, more likely, *reweaving* the entire social and cultural web. The tendencies outlined above are already at work. We don't need to look far to find their effects. We can begin with the newspaper headlines and the millennial lamentations sounded in the op-ed pages: that our educational systems are in decline; that our students are less and less able to read and comprehend their required texts, and that their aptitude scores have leveled off well below those of previous generations. Tag-line communication, called "bite-speak" by some, is destroying the last remnants of political discourse; spin doctors and media consultants are our new shamans. As communications empires fight for control of all information outlets, including publishers, the latter have succumbed to the tyranny of the bottom line; they are less and less willing to publish work, however worthy, that will not make a tidy profit. And, on every front, funding for the arts is being cut while the arts themselves appear to be suffering a deep crisis of relevance. And so on.

Every one of these developments is, of course, overdetermined, but there can be no doubt that they are connected, perhaps profoundly, to the transition that is underway.

Certain other trends bear watching. One could argue, for instance, that the entire movement of postmodernism in the arts is a consequence of this same macroscopic shift. For what is postmodernism at root but an aesthetic that rebukes the idea of an historical time line, as well as previously uncontested assumptions of cultural hierarchy. The postmodern artifact manipulates its stylistic signatures like Lego blocks and makes free with combinations from the formerly sequestered spheres of high and popular art. Its combinatory momentum and relentless referencing of the surrounding culture mirror perfectly the associative dynamics of electronic media.

One might argue likewise, that the virulent debate within academia

123

over the canon and multiculturalism may not be a simple struggle between the entrenched ideologies of white male elites and the forces of
formerly disenfranchised gender, racial, and cultural groups. Many of
those who would revise the canon (or end it altogether) are trying to
outflank the assumption of historical tradition itself. The underlying
question, avoided by many, may be not only whether the tradition is
relevant, but whether it might not be too taxing a system for students to
comprehend. Both the traditionalists and the progressives have valid arguments, and we must certainly have sympathy for those who would try
to expose and eradicate the hidden assumptions of bias in the Western
tradition. But it also seems clear that this debate could only have taken
the form it has in a society that has begun to come loose from its textual
moorings. To challenge repression is salutary. To challenge history itself, proclaiming it to be simply an archive of repressions and justifica-
tions, is idiotic.*

Then there are the more specific sorts of developments. Consider
the multibillion-dollar initiative by Whittle Communications to bring
commercially sponsored education packages into the classroom. The
underlying premise is staggeringly simple: If electronic media are the
one thing that the young are at ease with, why not exploit the fact? Why
not stop bucking television and use it instead, with corporate America
picking up the tab in exchange for a few minutes of valuable airtime for
commercials? As the *Boston Globe* reports:

---

*The outcry against the modification of the canon can be seen as a plea for old reflexes
and routines. And the cry for multicultural representation may be a last-ditch bid for
connection to the fading legacy of print. The logic is simple. When a resource is threatened—made scarce—people fight over it. In this case the struggle is over textual power
in an increasingly nontextual age. The future of books and reading is what is at stake,
and a dim intuition of this drives the contending factions.

As Katha Pollitt argued so shrewdly in her much-cited article in *The Nation:* If we
were a nation of readers, there would be no issue. No one would be arguing about
whether to put Toni Morrison on the syllabus because her work would be a staple of
the reader's regular diet anyway. These lists are suddenly so important because they
represent, very often, the only serious works that the student is ever likely to be exposed to. Whoever controls the lists comes out ahead in the struggle for the hearts and
minds of the young.

Here's how it would work:

Participating schools would receive, free of charge, $50,000 worth of electronic paraphernalia, including a satellite dish and classroom video monitors. In return, the schools would agree to air the show.

The show would resemble a network news program, but with 18- to 24-year-old anchors.

A prototype includes a report on a United Nations Security Council meeting on terrorism, a space shuttle update, a U2 music video tribute to Martin Luther King, a feature on the environment, a "fast fact" ('Arachibutyrophobia is the fear of peanut butter sticking to the roof of your mouth') and two minutes of commercial advertising.

"You have to remember that the children of today have grown up with the visual media," said Robert Calabrese [Billerica School Superintendent]. "They know no other way and we're simply capitalizing on that to enhance learning."

Calabrese's observation on the preconditioning of a whole generation of students raises troubling questions: Should we suppose that American education will begin to tailor itself to the aptitudes of its students, presenting more and more of its materials in newly packaged forms? And what will happen when educators find that not very many of the old materials will "play"—that is, capture student enthusiasm? Is the *what* of learning to be determined by the *how?* And at what point do vicious cycles begin to reveal their viciousness?

A collective change of sensibility may already be upon us. We need to take seriously the possibility that the young truly "know no other way," that they are not made of the same stuff that their elders are. In her *Harper's* magazine debate with Neil Postman, Camille Paglia observed:

Some people have more developed sensoriums than others. I've found that most people born before World War II are turned off by the modern media. They can't understand how we who were born after the war can read and watch TV at the same time. But we *can.* When I wrote my book, I had earphones on, blasting rock music or Puccini and Brahms. The soap operas—with the sound turned down

—flickered on my TV. I'd be talking on the phone at the same time. Baby boomers have a multilayered, multitrack ability to deal with the world.

I don't know whether to be impressed or depressed by Paglia's ability to disperse her focus in so many directions. Nor can I say, not having read her book, in what ways her multitrack sensibility has informed her prose. But I'm baffled by what she means when she talks about an ability to "deal with the world." From the context, "dealing" sounds more like a matter of incessantly repositioning the self within a barrage of on-rushing stimuli.

Paglia's is hardly the only testimony in this matter. A *New York Times* article on the cult success of Mark Leyner (author of *I Smell Esther Williams* and *My Cousin, My Gastroenterologist*) reports suggestively:

> His fans say, variously, that his writing is like MTV, or rap music, or rock music, or simply like everything in the world put together: fast and furious and intense, full of illusion and allusion and fantasy and science and excrement.
>
> Larry McCaffery, a professor of literature at San Diego State University and co-editor of Fiction International, a literary journal, said his students get excited about Mr. Leyner's writing, which he considers important and unique: "It speaks to them, somehow, about this weird milieu they're swimming through. It's this dissolving, discontinuous world." While older people might find Mr. Leyner's world bizarre or unreal, Professor McCaffery said, it doesn't seem so to people who grew up with Walkmen and computers and VCR's, with so many choices, so much bombardment, that they have never experienced a sensation singly.

The article continues:

> There is no traditional narrative, although the book is called a novel. And there is much use of facts, though it is called fiction. Seldom does the end of a sentence have any obvious relation to the beginning. "You don't know where you're going, but you don't mind taking the leap," said R. J. Cutler, the producer of "Heat," who invited

Mr. Leyner to be on the show after he picked up the galleys of his book and found it mesmerizing. "He taps into a specific cultural perspective where thoughtful literary world view meets pop culture and the TV generation."

My final exhibit—I don't know if it qualifies as a morbid symptom as such—is drawn from a *Washington Post Magazine* essay on the future of the Library of Congress, our national shrine to the printed word. One of the individuals interviewed in the piece is Robert Zich, so-called "special projects czar" of the institution. Zich, too, has seen the future, and he is surprisingly candid with his interlocutor. Before long, Zich maintains, people will be able to get what information they want directly off their terminals. The function of the Library of Congress (and perhaps libraries in general) will change. He envisions his library becoming more like a museum: "Just as you go to the National Gallery to see its Leonardo or go to the Smithsonian to see the Spirit of St. Louis and so on, you will want to go to libraries to see the Gutenberg or the original printing of Shakespeare's plays or to see Lincoln's hand-written version of the Gettysburg Address."

Zich is outspoken, voicing what other administrators must be thinking privately. The big research libraries, he says, "and the great national libraries and their buildings will go the way of the railroad stations and the movie palaces of an earlier era which were really vital institutions in their time . . . Somehow folks moved away from that when the technology changed."

And books? Zich expresses excitement about Sony's hand-held electronic book, and a miniature encyclopedia coming from Franklin Electronic Publishers. "Slip it in your pocket," he says. "Little keyboard, punch in your words and it will do the full text searching and all the rest of it. Its limitation, of course, is that it's devoted just to that one book." Zich is likewise interested in the possibility of memory cards. What he likes about the Sony product is the portability: one machine, a screen that will display the contents of whatever electronic card you feed it.

I cite Zich's views at some length here because he is not some Silicon Valley research and development visionary, but a highly placed executive at what might be called, in a very literal sense, our most conservative public institution. When men like Zich embrace the electronic future, we can be sure it's well on its way.

Others might argue that the technologies cited by Zich merely represent a modification in the "form" of reading, and that reading itself will be unaffected, as there is little difference between following words on a pocket screen or a printed page. Here I have to hold my line. The context cannot but condition the process. Screen and book may exhibit the same string of words, but the assumptions that underlie their significance are entirely different depending on whether we are staring at a book or a circuit-generated text. As the nature of looking—at the natural world, at paintings—changed with the arrival of photography and mechanical reproduction, so will the collective relation to language alter as new modes of dissemination prevail.

Whether all of this sounds dire or merely "different" will depend upon the reader's own values and priorities. I find these portents of change depressing, but also exhilarating—at least to speculate about. On the one hand, I have a great feeling of loss and a fear about what habitations will exist for self and soul in the future. But there is also a quickening, a sense that important things are on the line. As Heraclitus once observed, "The mixture that is not shaken soon stagnates." Well, the mixture is being shaken, no doubt about it. And here are some of the kinds of developments we might watch for as our "proto-electronic" era yields to an all-electronic future:

1. *Language erosion.* There is no question but that the transition from the culture of the book to the culture of electronic communication will radically alter the ways in which we use language on every societal level. The complexity and distinctiveness of spoken and written expression, which are deeply bound to traditions of print literacy, will gradually be replaced by a more telegraphic sort of "plainspeak." Syntactic masonry is already a dying art. Neil Postman and others have already suggested what losses have been incurred by the advent of telegraphy and television—how the complex discourse patterns of the nineteenth century were flattened by the requirements of communication over distances. That tendency runs riot as the layers of mediation thicken. Simple linguistic prefab is now the norm, while ambiguity, paradox, irony, subtlety, and wit are fast disappearing. In their place, the simple "vision

thing" and myriad other "things." Verbal intelligence, which has long been viewed as suspect as the act of reading, will come to seem positively conspiratorial. The greater part of any articulate person's energy will be deployed in dumbing-down her discourse.

Language will grow increasingly impoverished through a series of vicious cycles. For, of course, the usages of literature and scholarship are connected in fundamental ways to the general speech of the tribe. We can expect that curricula will be further streamlined, and difficult texts in the humanities will be pruned and glossed. One need only compare a college textbook from twenty years ago to its contemporary version. A poem by Milton, a play by Shakespeare—one can hardly find the text among the explanatory notes nowadays. Fewer and fewer people will be able to contend with the so-called masterworks of literature or ideas. Joyce, Woolf, Soyinka, not to mention the masters who preceded them, will go unread, and the civilizing energies of their prose will circulate aimlessly between closed covers.

2. *Flattening of historical perspectives.* As the circuit supplants the printed page, and as more and more of our communications involve us in network processes—which of their nature plant us in a perpetual present—our perception of history will inevitably alter. Changes in information storage and access are bound to impinge on our historical memory. The depth of field that is our sense of the past is not only a linguistic construct, but is in some essential way represented by the book and the physical accumulation of books in library spaces. In the contemplation of the single volume, or mass of volumes, we form a picture of time past as a growing deposit of sediment; we capture a sense of its depth and dimensionality. Moreover, we meet the past as much in the presentation of words in books of specific vintage as we do in any isolated fact or statistic. The database, useful as it is, expunges this context, this sense of chronology, and admits us to a weightless order in which all information is equally accessible.

If we take the etymological tack, history (cognate with "story") is affiliated in complex ways with its texts. Once the materials of the past are unhoused from their pages, they will surely *mean* differently. The printed page is itself a link, at least along the imaginative continuum, and when that link is broken, the past can only start to recede. At the same time it will become a body of disjunct data available for retrieval and, in the hands of our canny dream merchants, a mythology. The more we grow rooted in the consciousness of the now, the more it will seem utterly extraordinary that things were ever any different. The idea of a farmer plowing a field—an historical constant for millennia—will be something for a theme park. For, naturally, the entertainment industry, which reads the collective unconscious unerringly, will seize the advantage. The past that has slipped away will be rendered ever more glorious, ever more a fantasy play with heroes, villains, and quaint settings and props. Small-town American life returns as "Andy of Mayberry"—at first enjoyed with recognition, later accepted as a faithful portrait of how things used to be.

3. *The waning of the private self.* We may even now be in the first stages of a process of social collectivization that will over time all but vanquish the ideal of the isolated individual. For some decades now we have been edging away from the perception of private life as something opaque, closed off to the world; we increasingly accept the transparency of a life lived within a set of systems, electronic or otherwise. Our technologies are not bound by season or light—it's always the same time in the circuit. And so long as time is money and money matters, those circuits will keep humming. The doors and walls of our habitations matter less and less—the world sweeps through the wires as it needs to, or as we need it to. The monitor light is always blinking; we are always potentially on-line.

I am not suggesting that we are all about to become mindless, soulless robots, or that personality will disappear altogether into an oceanic homogeneity. But certainly the idea of what it means to be a person living a life will be much changed. The figure-ground model, which has always featured a solitary self before a background that is the society of other selves, is romantic in the extreme. It is ever less tenable in the world as it is becoming. There are no more wildernesses, no more lonely homesteads, and, outside of cinema, no more emblems of the exalted individual.

The self must change as the nature of subjective space changes. And one of the many incremental transformations of our age has been the slow but steady destruction of subjective space. The physical and psychological distance between individuals has been shrinking for at least a century. In the process, the figure-ground image has begun to blur its boundary distinctions. One day we will conduct our public and private lives within networks so dense, among so many channels of instantaneous information, that it will make almost no sense to speak of the differentiations of subjective individualism.

We are already captive in our webs. Our slight solitudes are transected by codes, wires, and pulsations. We punch a number to check in with the answering machine, another to tape a show that we are too busy to watch. The strands of the web grow finer and finer—this is obvious. What is no less obvious is the fact that they will continue to proliferate, gaining in sophistication, merging functions so that one can bank by phone, shop via television, and so on. The natural tendency is toward streamlining: The smart dollar keeps finding ways to shorten the path, double-up the function. We might think in terms of a circuit-board model, picturing ourselves as the contact points. The expansion of electronic options is always at the cost of contractions in the private sphere. We will soon be navigating with ease among cataracts of organized pulsations, putting out and taking in signals. We will bring our terminals, our modems, and menus further and further into our former privacies; we will implicate ourselves by degrees in the unitary life, and there may come a day when we no longer remember that there was any other life.

While I was brewing these somewhat melancholy thoughts, I chanced to read in an old *New Republic* the text of Joseph Brodsky's 1987 Nobel Prize acceptance speech. I felt as though I had opened a door leading to the great vault of the nineteenth century. The poet's passionate plea on behalf of the book at once corroborated and countered everything I had been thinking. What he upheld in faith were the very ideals I was saying good-bye to. I greeted his words with an agitated skepticism, fashioning from them something more like a valediction. Here are four passages:

> If art teaches anything . . . it is the privateness of the human condition. Being the most ancient as well as the most literal form of private

enterprise, it fosters in a man, knowingly or unwittingly, a sense of his uniqueness, of individuality, of separateness—thus turning him from a social animal into an autonomous "I."

The great Baratynsky, speaking of his Muse, characterized her as possessing an "uncommon visage." It's in acquiring this "uncommon visage" that the meaning of human existence seems to lie, since for this uncommonness we are, as it were, prepared genetically.

Aesthetic choice is a highly individual matter, and aesthetic experience is always a private one. Every new aesthetic reality makes one's experience even more private; and this kind of privacy, assuming at times the guise of literary (or some other) taste, can in itself turn out to be, if not a guarantee, then a form of defense, against enslavement.

In the history of our species, in the history of Homo sapiens, the book is an anthropological development, similar essentially to the invention of the wheel. Having emerged in order to give us some idea not so much of our origins as of what that sapiens is capable of, a book constitutes a means of transportation through the space of experience, at the speed of a turning page. This movement, like every movement, becomes flight from the common denominator . . . This flight is the flight in the direction of "uncommon visage," in the direction of the numerator, in the direction of autonomy, in the direction of privacy.

Brodsky is addressing the relation between art and totalitarianism, and within that context his words make passionate sense. But I was reading from a different vantage. What I had in mind was not a vision of political totalitarianism, but rather of something that might be called "societal totalism"—that movement toward deindividuation, or electronic collectivization, that I discussed above. And from that perspective our era appears to be in a headlong flight *from* the "uncommon visage" named by the poet.

Trafficking with tendencies—extrapolating and projecting as I have been doing—must finally remain a kind of gambling. One bets high on the validity of a notion and low on the human capacity for resistance and for unpredictable initiatives. No one can really predict how we will adapt to the transformations taking place all around us. We may discover, too, that language is a hardier thing than I have allowed. It may flourish among the beep and the click and the monitor as readily as it ever did on the printed page. I hope so, for language is the soul's ozone layer and we thin it at our peril.

# 9

# Perseus Unbound

L IKE IT OR NOT, interactive video technologies have muscled their way into the formerly textbound precincts of education. The videodisc has mated with the microcomputer to produce a juggernaut: a flexible and encompassing teaching tool that threatens to overwhelm the linearity of print with an array of option-rich multimedia packages. And although we are only in the early stages of implementation—institutions are by nature conservative—an educational revolution seems inevitable.

Several years ago in *Harvard Magazine,* writer Craig Lambert sampled some of the innovative ways in which these technologies have already been applied at Harvard. Interactive video programs at the Law School allow students to view simulated police busts or actual courtroom procedures. With a tap of a digit they can freeze images, call up case citations, and quickly zero-in on the relevant fine points of precedent. Medical simulations, offering the immediacy of video images and instant access to the mountains of data necessary for diagnostic assessment, can have the student all but performing surgery. And language classes now allow the learner to make an end run around tedious drill repetitions and engage in protoconversations with video partners.

The hot news in the classics world, meanwhile, is Perseus 1.0, an interactive database developed and edited by Harvard associate professor Gregory Crane. Published on CD-ROM and videodisc, the program holds, according to its publicists, "the equivalent of 25 volumes of ancient Greek literature by ten authors (1 million Greek words), roughly 4,000 glosses in the on-line classical encyclopedia, and a 35,000-word on-line Greek lexicon." Also included are an enormous photographic database (six thousand images), a short video with narration, and "hundreds of descriptions and drawings of art and archeological objects." The package is affordable, too: Perseus software can be purchased for about $350. Plugged in, the student can call up a text, read it side by side with its translation, and analyze any word using the Liddell-Scott lexicon; he can read a thumbnail sketch on any mythic figure cited in the text, or call up images from an atlas, or zoom in on color Landsat photos; he can even study a particular vase through innumerable angles of vantage. The dusty library stacks have never looked dustier.

Although skepticism abounds, most of it is institutional, bound up with established procedures and the proprietorship of scholarly bailiwicks. But there are grounds for other, more philosophic sorts of debate, and we can expect to see flare-ups of controversy for some time to come. For more than any other development in recent memory, these interactive technologies throw into relief the fundamental questions about knowledge and learning. Not only what are its ends, but what are its means? And how might the means be changing the ends?

From the threshold, I think, we need to distinguish between kinds of knowledge and kinds of study. Pertinent here is German philosopher Wilhelm Dilthey's distinction between the natural sciences (*Naturwissenschaften*), which seek to explain physical events by subsuming them under causal laws, and the so-called sciences of culture (*Geisteswissenschaften*), which can only understand events in terms of the intentions and meanings that individuals attach to them.

To the former, it would seem, belong the areas of study more hospitable to the new video and computer procedures. Expanded databases and interactive programs can be viewed as tools, pure and simple. They give access to more information, foster cross-referentiality, and by reducing time and labor allow for greater focus on the essentials of a problem. Indeed, any discipline where knowledge is sought for its application rather than for itself could only profit from the implementation of these technologies. To the natural sciences one might add the fields of language study and law.

But there is a danger with these sexy new options—and the rapture with which believers speak warrants the adjective—that we will simply assume that their uses and potentials extend across the educational spectrum into realms where different kinds of knowledge, and hence learning, are at issue. The realms, that is, of *Geisteswissenschaften*, which have at their center the humanities.

In the humanities, knowledge is a means, yes, but it is a means less to instrumental application than to something more nebulous: understanding. We study history or literature or classics in order to compose and refine a narrative, or a set of narratives about what the human world used to be like, about how the world came to be as it is, and about what we have been—and are—like as psychological or spiritual creatures. The data—the facts, connections, the texts themselves—matter insofar as they help us to deepen and extend that narrative. In these disciplines the *process* of study may be as vital to the understanding as are the materials studied.

Given the great excitement generated by Perseus, it is easy to imagine that in the near future a whole range of innovative electronic-based learning packages will be available and, in many places, in use. These will surely include the manifold variations on the electronic book. Special new software texts are already being developed to bring us into the world of, say, Shakespeare, not only glossing the literature, but bathing the user in multimedia supplements. The would-be historian will step into an environment rich in choices, be they visual detailing, explanatory graphs, or suggested connections and sideroads. And so on. Moreover, once the price is right, who will be the curmudgeons who would deny their students access to the state-of-the-art?

Being a curmudgeon is a dirty job, but somebody has to do it. Someone has to hoist the warning flags and raise some issues that the fast-track proselytizers might overlook. Here are a few reservations worth pondering.

1. Knowledge, certainly in the humanities, is not a straightforward matter of access, of conquest via the ingestion of data. Part of any essential understanding of the world is that it is opaque, obdurate. To me, Wittgenstein's famous axiom, "The world is everything that is the case," translates into a recognition of otherness. The past is as much about the disappearance of things through time as it is about the recovery of traces and the reconstruction of vistas. Say what you will about books, they

not only mark the backward trail, but they also encode this sense of obstacle, of otherness. The look of the printed page changes as we regress in time; under the orthographic changes are the changes in the language itself. Old-style textual research may feel like an unnecessarily slow burrowing, but it is itself an instruction: It confirms that time is a force as implacable as gravity.

Yet the multimedia packages would master this gravity. For opacity they substitute transparency, promoting the illusion of access. All that has been said, known, and done will yield to the dance of the fingertips on the terminal keys. Space becomes hyperspace, and time, hypertime ("hyper-" being the fashionable new prefix that invokes the nonlinear and nonsequential "space" made possible by computer technologies). One gathers the data of otherness, but through a medium which seems to level the feel—the truth—of that otherness. The field of knowledge is rendered as a lateral and synchronic enterprise susceptible to collage, not as a depth phenomenon. And if our media restructure our perceptions, as McLuhan and others have argued, then we may start producing generations who know a great deal of "information" about the past but who have no purchase on pastness itself.

Described in this way, the effects of interactive programs on users sound a good deal like the symptoms of postmodernism. And indeed, this recent cultural aesthetic, distinguished by its flat, bright, and often affectless assemblages of materials may be a consequence of a larger transformation of sensibility by information-processing technologies. After all, our arts do tend to mirror who we are and anticipate what we might be becoming. Changes of this magnitude are of course systemic, and their direction is not easily dictated. Whether the postmodern "vision" can be endorsed as a pedagogic platform, however, is another question.

2. Humanistic knowledge, as I suggested earlier, differs from the more instrumental kinds of knowledge in that it ultimately seeks to fashion a comprehensible narrative. It is, in other words, about the creation and expansion of meaningful contexts. Interactive media technologies are, at least in one sense, anticontextual. They open the field to new widths, constantly expanding relevance and reference, and they equip their user with a powerful grazing tool. One moves at great rates

across subject terrains, crossing borders that were once closely guarded. The multimedia approach tends ineluctably to multidisciplinarianism. The positive effect, of course, is the creation of new levels of connection and integration; more and more variables are brought into the equation.

But the danger should be obvious: The horizon, the limit that gave definition to the parts of the narrative, will disappear. The equation itself will become nonsensical through the accumulation of variables. The context will widen until it becomes, in effect, everything. On the model of Chaos science, wherein the butterfly flapping its wings in China is seen to affect the weather system over Oklahoma, all data will impinge upon all other data. The technology may be able to handle it, but will the user? Will our narratives—historical, literary, classical—be able to withstand the data explosion? If they cannot, then what will be the new face of understanding? Or will the knowledge of the world become, perforce, a map as large and intricate as the world itself?

3. We might question, too, whether there is not in learning as in physical science a principle of energy conservation. Does a gain in one area depend upon a loss in another? My guess would be that every lateral attainment is purchased with a sacrifice of depth. The student may, through a program on Shakespeare, learn an immense amount about Elizabethan politics, the construction of the Globe theater, the origins of certain plays in the writings of Plutarch, the etymology of key terms, and so on, but will this dazzled student find the concentration, the will, to live with the often burred and prickly language of the plays themselves? The play's the thing—but will it be? Wouldn't the sustained exposure to a souped-up cognitive collage not begin to affect the attention span, the ability if not willingness to sit with one text for extended periods, butting up against its cruxes, trying to excavate meaning from the original rhythms and syntax? The gurus of interaction love to say that the student learns best by doing, but let's not forget that *reading* a work is also a kind of doing.

4. As a final reservation, what about the long-term cognitive effects of these new processes of data absorption? Isn't it possible that more may be less, and that the neural networks have one speed for taking in— a speed that can be increased—and quite another rate for retention?

Again, it may be that our technologies will exceed us. They will make it not only possible but irresistible to consume data at what must strike people of the book as very high rates. But what then? What will happen as our neural systems, evolved through millennia to certain capacities, modify themselves to hold ever-expanding loads? Will we simply become smarter, able to hold and process more? Or do we have to reckon with some other gain/loss formula? One possible cognitive response—call it the "S.A.T. cram-course model"—might be an expansion of the short-term memory banks and a correlative atrophying of long-term memory.

But here our technology may well assume a new role. Once it dawns on us, as it must, that our software will hold all the information we need at ready access, we may very well let it. That is, we may choose to become the technicians of our auxiliary brains, mastering not the information but the retrieval and referencing functions. At a certain point, then, we could become the evolutionary opposites of our forebears, who, lacking external technology, committed everything to memory. If this were to happen, what would be the status of knowing, of being educated? The leader of the electronic tribe would not be the person who knew most, but the one who could execute the broadest range of technical functions. What, I hesitate to ask, would become of the already antiquated notion of wisdom?

I recently watched a public television special on the history of the computer. One of the many experts and enthusiasts interviewed took up the knowledge question. He explained how the formerly two-dimensional process of book-based learning is rapidly becoming three-dimensional. The day will come, he opined, when interactive and virtual technologies will allow us to more or less dispense with our reliance on the sequence-based print paradigm. Whatever the object of our study, our equipment will be able to get us there directly: inside the volcano or the violin-maker's studio, right up on the stage. I was enthralled, but I shuddered, too, for it struck me that when our technologies are all in place—when all databases have been refined and integrated—that will be the day when we stop living in the old hard world and take up residence in some bright new hyperworld, a kind of Disneyland of informa-

139

tion. I have to wonder if this is what Perseus and its kindred programs might not be edging us toward. That program got its name, we learn from the brochure, from the Greek mythological hero Perseus, who was the explorer of the limits of the known world. I confess that I can't think of Perseus without also thinking of Icarus, heedless son of Daedalus, who allowed his wings to carry him over the invisible line that was inscribed across the skyway.

# 10

# Close Listening

In the beginning, before any words, a sudden splash. The sound of agitated water, rushing. Then, in quick segue, a woman's voice: "The rented Toyota, driven with such impatient exuberance by The Senator, was speeding along the unpaved unnamed road, taking the turns in giddy skidding slides, and then, with no warning, somehow the car had gone off the road and had overturned in black rushing water . . ." Amanda Plummer reads the opening passage of Joyce Carol Oates's *Black Water* at a headlong clip. Too quickly, perhaps. Certainly a beat or two ahead of what I can deal with just now, here. But I try to keep up. The narrative spins out in widening recursive loops. The Senator and his date, Kelly Kelleher—ha!—are racing to catch the July 4 ferry. I'm starting to shift my thoughts and local agitations to the *here* of Oates's story. The paradox is too rich: The Senator and Kelly going hell-for-leather in his Toyota while I sit wedged in traffic in my own, my windows up in the ninety-degree heat so that I can listen to them go plunging into the icy black stream. Hurtling I'm not; my car is a scale on a glittering snake that is winding its length along the whole Eastern seaboard. Indeed, it was this prospect that pushed me to inject the cassette into the player and the phantasmic life of Kelly Kelleher into my own.

This is the confession of a former audio book virgin. Sure, I had listened to the occasional tape of a famous poet reading famous poems, or tuned in to those radio mysteries that are impossible to avoid if you drive through the Midwest late at night. But I had never thought to listen to an actual book on cassette. Books, for me, have always been about covers and pages and grappling with the syntactical rigors of stationary prose. The passivity of listening seemed to me on a par with the passivity of television watching. How could it fail to reduce any work of merit to, at best, a companionable blur, a string of easy cadences in the ear?

Yet here I was, inching past the traffic rotary and heading toward the defunct train yard by Cambridge's Alewife Station. Outside the window, raw urban scurf—billboard signs for appliances and the glare of the liquor mart. Inside, in the corolla of my Corolla, the overheated drama of a young woman's destiny: "Am I going to die?—like this?" Kelly's story is punctuated every so often by the reverb-enhanced voicing of her thoughts. A tacky effect, I think; but this is the critic's detached judgment. The fact is that I am also being seduced, or maybe drugged. For the sharp, pleasurable, slightly disorienting experience has the effect of a designer pharmaceutical. Bumpers and horns, brake pedal and gas, but at the same time I am completely absorbed in the story. "Am I going to die?—like this?" I have to know. A long-dormant memory trace flares out. Is it the feeling of being read to as a child, or something deeper, more ancient? I don't get the time to plumb it. As the Senator and Kelly meet during a flashback and hit it off, I hit the gas. The light turns green and the traffic breaks. Amanda Plummer's voice fades as I jockey for position in the westbound chariot race.

Audio books—for me such an anomalous encounter—are a billion-dollar-a-year industry. According to the 1994 edition of *Words on Cassette,* more than 55,000 audio titles are available from roughly 1,400 publishers. We are in the first stages of a phenomenon that may prove as socially transformational as the paperback revolution of the 1960s. First there was the American love affair with the cassette, that painless, portable gizmo that allowed us to listen to things while we were otherwise occupied. Music broke in the habit, and now comes the spoken word. What makes it all possible, maybe even necessary, are the changes in the way we live. The microchip may have split time open like an atom, but nevertheless we seem to have less of the stuff—real time—than ever. Prophets and promoters have long promised that technology would set us free, creating vast quantities of leisure time; the fantasy has backfired. Instead we have swelling pockets of empty time; our lifestyles have us in harness, we are unable to move, spiritually gridlocked. So we look to technology to undo what it has wrought. Although the audio book was originally designed for the blind and infirm, it is now targeted to Americans who commute. And with the average commute now as long as forty-five minutes a day, publishers are tilling fertile ground.

My experience with Oates's novel unsettled me, but it also piqued my curiosity. So I listened and listened—listening takes time—and drove and drove. I quickly realized that listening while driving is infinitely preferable to listening while walking, sitting in a chair, or chopping vegetables. To be ambulatory, even with headphones on, is still to be in a live environment—too distracting. Sitting still is too much like being in a classroom: The pencil doodles, the mind drifts. But driving ... There is something about moving while in an enclosure, with scenery slipping past—the soul lays itself open for seduction by the word. And this, finally, was my question, the point of my search: Is *seduction* what this version of the literary encounter is about? Is listening to books an extension of reading, or is it a simplification, yet another ingenious way of turning everything into entertainment?

So I drove—past blighted roadsides, through open country, jerking behind rows of bumpers, and pelting along open highways—and as I drove I was lulled by the fluid ease of it all. But whenever I realized what I was doing, I grew appalled at my submissiveness. This was something new, possibly portentous—a McLuhanesque wrinkle in the collective sensibility. Change the medium and you change the message, right? Here we are, centuries removed from the ways of our progenitors, smugly evolved past the tribal storytelling of the oral tradition, partaking again of the pleasures of that ancient mode. Everything in creation has changed, but the triad endures: the voice, the story, the listener.

We should not, of course, push the similarities too far. Our driver has his windows up, his ventilation blasting; several thousand dollars' worth of machinery guide his progress past high-rises and service stations. The shepherd hunkers by the communal fire, giving ear to what the teller embroiders from the tribal archive. Listening to a cassette in your car is not the same as gathering with your mates on a charred log, or even cozying up around the Victorian tea table. It is more like stepping into a disembodied trance.

I have come to listening late, and I have come tentatively; my biases are those of a reader. It was my predilection for the printed page, as well as for the indrawn and somewhat secretive nature of the reading act, that led me to become a literary critic. I have more than a few times gone public with my grumpy notions that our growing immersion in various circuitries is cutting us off from the civilizing powers of the written word, that electronic books and interactive videos will leach away our capacities for reflection, and so on.

But those are still mainly scenarios projected on the future—the audio book is now. The range of audio titles roughly parallels that of printed books, with everything from *Beginning Passamaquoddy* to *How to Love Yourself: Cherishing the Incredible Miracle That You Are* to *The Brothers Karamazov* read by that husky-voiced diva Debra Winger. You can hear Deborah Tannen's *That's Not What I Meant,* complete with staged vignettes and piano-bar music tinkling in the background. And then there are the pairings of book and reader—Arlo Guthrie reading Woody's *Bound for Glory,* John Malkovich giving eerie intonation to Anne Tyler's *The Accidental Tourist,* or Lou Diamond Phillips narrating James Fenimore Cooper's *The Last of the Mohicans* (the choice of Daniel Day-Lewis for the film role confirms that you need three names before you can touch that property). Dudley Moore is a perfect choice for Oscar Wilde's *The Happy Prince,* but what about Hollywood firebrand Ed Asner as the reader of Curt Gentry's *J. Edgar Hoover: The Man and the Secrets?* I recently heard a tape of actor Tony Roberts doing Dashiell Hammett's *The Maltese Falcon.* Consider the loops here: Woody Allen's sidekick in *Play It Again, Sam* makes Spade sound like Bogart, and throws in convincing renditions of Lorre and Greenstreet too. The listener gets half-remembered images from the original film and then an overlay of the images that later spoofed those images. Underneath it all, somewhere, is Hammett's text.

Even given my Luddite disposition, I find that the medium has a number of attractions. Listening is, no matter the work, a partaking of the fruits of another's imagination. One listener might be caught in the web of the latest Elmore Leonard while another can plug into Seamus Heaney reciting verses in his buttery brogue. Either option is superior to the vacuous monitoring of your neighbor's exhaust pipe.

But once we grant the audio book its attractions, we are still confronted with the question of its *whatness*. This is no mere epiphenomenon; it is a full-fledged trend. As life gets more complex, people are likely to read less and listen more. The medium shapes the message and the message bears directly on who we are; it forms us. Listening is not reading, but what *is* it?

The origins of literature were, of course, oral. And although literature is grounded in the idea of speech (we can't read without hearing words in our auditory imagination), the fact is that the invention of the written sign kicked off a process of evolution. The storyteller was naturally constrained by the attention of his listeners; thus the tales were often formulaic, built around repetitions and mnemonic tags, and structured to maximize suspense. But the word on the page is implicitly a memory device, and it long ago liberated the writer to pursue nonformulaic incentives. Our more serious literature incorporates levels of difficulty—in narrative sequence, referentiality, syntax, and linguistic density—and presupposes a reader who is free to hover over a phrase, reach for a dictionary, and dart back. Indeed, modern literature can be plotted along a complexity curve, and past a certain point on that curve the prose is likely to elude even the most dedicated listener. Novels such as E. L. Doctorow's *Ragtime* and Terry McMillan's *Waiting to Exhale* can be ingested with relative ease, whereas writers like Virginia Woolf and Thomas Pynchon are likely to flummox their listeners. What all this means is that the limitations of the medium may substantially narrow the spectrum of the literary. Certain works will not circulate within the culture in spoken form.

The complexity curve is not, moreover, a static construct. Works of an earlier period, even works that may once have been staples of the family reading circle, slip from our audial grasp. We are no longer at ease with the extended sentence or with too many complex or compound constructions; syntax has been virtually streamlined out of existence.

There are also the more elusively subjective barriers. As I listened to Saul Bellow reading *Herzog,* I found I was up to pace in certain places, riveted by passages of description, dialogue, or animated narration. But as soon as he launched into one of his flights of philosophical or moral

conjecture—which are perhaps my main incentive for *reading* Bellow—
I became disgruntled, fidgety. Not because I couldn't apprehend the
words, but because these were the very places in my reading where I
would stop my finger at the margin and gaze out into the middle distance. We don't just speed a thought through our neural network—we
inhale it, hold it, wait for it to send ripples through the whole of our
being. Rewinding the tape is no solution.

Pace is a serious problem; since paid readers are under obligation to
get through the text expeditiously, they cannot linger. But this enforced
relentlessness underscores the degree to which reading is an ever-
modulating engagement. Until I listened to a book on tape, I didn't realize how much I depend on the freedom to slow down, speed up, or
stop altogether while reading. With certain writers, I might pause significantly a dozen times over the course of a few paragraphs: once for comprehension, several times more to savor a phrase, and one or more
times because something drives me off the page and out into my life—a
half-remembered face, the look of a spot by a certain lake, a whiff of
autumn in the summer air. For me this is the true life of reading—the
ulterior life, that slow, painful, delicious excavation of the self by way of
another's sentences. I can lift up and hover while listening, to be sure,
but always at the risk of losing my way. If I chase a memory, I miss
something; when I tune in again I am slightly wobbly from trying to
catch up. The only way to combat this distraction is to restrict the radius
of the private flights: buzz like a bee around the words, but don't dare go
winging out over the clover.

Reading, because we control it, is adaptable to our needs and
rhythms. We are free to indulge our subjective associative impulse; the
term I coin for this is *deep reading:* the slow and meditative possession
of a book. We don't just read the words, we dream our lives in their
vicinity. The printed page becomes a kind of wrought-iron fence we
crawl through, returning, once we have wandered, to the very place we
started. Deep listening to words is rarely an option. Our ear, and with it
our whole imaginative apparatus, marches in lockstep to the speaker's
baton.

When we read with our eyes, we hear the words in the theater of our
auditory inwardness. The voice we conjure up is our own—it is the

sound-print of the self. Bringing this voice to life via the book is one of the subtler aspects of the reading magic, but hearing a book in the voice of another amounts to a silencing of that self—it is an act of vocal tyranny. The listener is powerless against the taped voice, not at all in the position of my five-year-old daughter, who admonishes me continually, "Don't read it like *that*, Dad." With the audio book, everything— pace, timbre, inflection—is determined for the captive listener. The collaborative component is gone; one simply receives.

Both the reader's inner voice and the writer's literary or stylistic voice are, obviously, sexed. When I read a male writer, I simply adjust my vocalization to the tone of the text; when I read a woman, I don't attempt an impersonation, but I am aware that my voicing is a form of translation. But when I listened to a cassette of John Cheever's stories read by an expressive female voice, I just couldn't take it. Midway through "The Enormous Radio" I had to pop the tape from the machine to keep her from wreaking havoc on my sense of Cheever. Cheever's prose is as imprinted with his gender as Virginia Woolf's is with hers. Nor could I get past the bright vigor of the performing voice; I missed the dark notes, the sense of pooling shadows that has always accompanied my readings of the man.

Sometimes, to be sure, the fit is excellent—either because the reader achieves the right sort of neutrality, allowing the voice to become a clear medium for the text, or because the interpretation somehow accords with my own expectations. Then, too, I have had the pleasure of hearing an author rendering his or her own work. Indeed, listening to certain remastered recordings of the "greats," I have experienced the skin-prickling illusion of proximity (*I am actually listening to James Joyce* . . . ). The author can open up a work in ways that no other reader can. To hear the theatrically arch accents of Nabokov as he serves up *Pale Fire* is to discover new rifts of comedy in the novel. And when I heard John Updike's voice catch slightly at a climactic moment of his superb divorce story "Separating," I felt a momentary parting of that membrane that supposedly divides art from life. At moments like this I find myself wavering, questioning the fixity of my assumptions.

Most of my audio gripes have to do with the loss of the reader's perquisites, or better, his rights. But with the issue of abridgment we are also talking about the rights of the work itself. With some definite exceptions, books on cassette have been cut; in some cases gutted. The percentage of the loss varies. A short work like Oates's *Black Water*, on two cassettes, is designated "slightly abridged"; with longer novels we miss up to half the text. In these cases we are asked to commit a rhetorical fallacy: to take the part in place of the whole. What gets cut? The longueurs, certainly. The hard parts, often, but also those sometimes flat but nevertheless all-important scenes that help to prepare the climactic moments. We have to ask: What is the value of a symphony from which half of the second and all of the third movements have been cut? To what extent is the listener entitled to claim the experience of the work?

I was genuinely appalled when I one day slipped a cassette of Malcolm Lowry's *Under the Volcano* into my player. The tape was an abridgment, but what stopped me cold was the *nature* of the abridgment; it began with chapter two. Lowry's complex and retrospective opening had been scuttled without a trace. What was lost—certainly for the listener unfamiliar with the book—was all suggestion of the author's circular scheme. Lowry had meant his novel to turn like a wheel; everything in it is keyed to the concept of circularity, making chapter one absolutely indispensable. No amount of civilized gnashing by reader Christopher Cazanove could make up the deficit.

Everything about modern (or is it postmodern?) life carries us away from the state that is propitious for deep reading. The generations now coming up, reared on music and visual media, have reflexes and combinatory capacities that are something new in the world. They perform acts of multitrack cognitive juggling that leave their elders tied in knots. As Camille Paglia affirms, "Baby boomers have a multi-layered, multi-track ability to deal with the world." And what is this ability but a new evolutionary acquisition, a neural response to changed environmental conditions? In itself it is neither good nor bad. But we have to see that it does not bode well in the long run for certain kinds of concentrated or deep reading. Multitrack sensibilities will likely be less and less able to perform the single-track tasks demanded by the silent page; so it is not farfetched to suppose that a good part of the future of literature will be bound up with the audio process.

This prospect leaves me feeling strangely divided; as much as it pains my old bookish soul to say so, I find certain virtues in the listening experience. For one thing, some literary works *do* play very well in the audio format. Short stories, which tend to be more focused, often work beautifully. I have heard stories by Updike, Welty, and Carver—all artists highly attuned to word sounds and sentence rhythms—that achieve a delightful resonance. The prose of Garrison Keillor, for whom the printed page is less an avenue to his vision than a detour around it, is actually improved by spoken rendition.

Nor should we feel altogether hopeless about books that are perched higher on the complexity curve. Although it is true that a first hearing may not convey the full aesthetic experience of a given piece of writing, the audio medium makes it very easy, even tempting, to go back and listen again. I am far more likely to insert a cassette for a second hearing than I am to reread a novel from the top.

I find I have been listening to James Joyce's beautiful and densely woven story "The Dead" over and over, and listening to it in different ways—as a narrative, as a portrait of a place and time. I approach the story like a difficult piece of music, first acquainting myself with the structure and then listening further for the tonal, textural, and harmonic subtleties. And truly, with a writer like Joyce, language can make a kind of music, with vowels and consonants and rhythmic shifts piping an intricate accompaniment to the other senses.

Audio books remind us of the sound of literature. For unless we are pledged to reading a work with exceptional attentiveness, voicing it inwardly with care and monitoring its slightest inflections, we tend to gulp the words at something close to the speed of garble. Too often we read serious books at the same rate at which we read the morning paper, stripping the sentences for their sense and jamming phrases together like the pleats of a compressed accordion. It can be tonic in the extreme to hear well-written prose enunciated, fleshed-out to its intended proportions. An evocative reading can capture the shifting tension that exists between sound and sense; it can unearth the overlooked sentence rhythm and whet the blade of irony.

Reading is different from listening, yes, but in listening's limitations I have found unexpected pleasures. When you read, both eye and ear are engaged; when you listen, the eye is free. Slight though the freedom may seem, it can declare itself resoundingly. The listener can attain a peculiar exaltation—a vivid sense of doubleness, of standing poised on a wire between two different realities.

I felt that exaltation quite recently. I had been to Concord's Walden Pond for an afternoon swim and I was taking my usual back-country route home. I was wet-haired, relaxed from the water, and the speed limit signs were there to be ignored. In this mood, I put a cassette of Thoreau's *Walden* into the player. Said the master (in the voice of Michael O'Keefe):

> Every morning was a cheerful invitation to make my life of equal
> simplicity, and I may say innocence, with Nature herself. I have been
> as sincere a worshipper of Aurora as the Greeks. I got up early and
> bathed in the pond: that was a religious exercise, and one of the best
> things which I did. They say that characters were engraven on the
> bathing tub of King Tching-thang to this effect: "Renew thyself completely
> each day; do it again and again, and forever again."

It was high summer. The road was open and the countryside was in bloom. I sped through an arcade of trees as the voice went on to retail the terms of our daily enslavement. I felt myself soaring. The words streamed in unmediated, shot like some kind of whiskey into my soul. I had a parenthesis of open country, then came the sentence of the highway. But the state held long enough to allow a thought: In the beginning was the Word—not the written or printed or processed word, but the *spoken* word. And though it changes its aspect faster than any Proteus, hiding now in letter shapes and now in magnetic emulsion, it remains. It still has the power to lay us bare.

# 11

# Hypertext: Of Mouse and Man

I HAVE A FRIEND, R., who is not only an excellent short-story writer and philosopher of the art, but who is also a convert to the sorcery of the microchip. R. has had a nibbling interest in hypertext—for some the cutting edge in writing these days—and he had me over to his studio recently so that I could get a look at this latest revolutionary development. Our text was Stuart Moulthrop's *Victory Garden,* an interactive novel by a writer who has been called one of the leading theoreticians of the genre. R. sat me down in a chair in front of his terminal, booted up, and off we went.

Or did we? In fact it was not one of those off-you-go kinds of things at all. What we had in front of us was a spatialized table of contents in the form of a map of an elaborate garden. There were mazelike paths and benches and nooks, each representing some element, or strand, of the novel. This was the option board. The reader was invited to proceed by inclination, choosing a character, focusing on a relationship, engaging (or not) a relevant subplot, and deciding whether to snap backward or forward in time. A kind of paralysis crept over me. I was reminded of Julio Cortázar's *Hopscotch,* where the reader learns that he can follow the chapters in a number of different sequences. But this was stranger, denser. The extent of the text was concealed (and in that sense lifelike). It was also stylistically uninspired. I felt none of the tug I had felt with Cortázar's novel, none of the subtle suction exerted by masterly prose. Still, I did not give up. I tipped up and back in my chair, clicked and clicked again, waiting patiently for the empowering rush that ought to come when worlds open upon other worlds and old limits collapse.

It was hard, I confess, to square my experience with the hype surrounding hypertext and multimedia. Extremists—I meet more and more of them—argue that the printed page has been but a temporary habitation for the word. The book, they say, is no longer the axis of our intellectual culture. There is a kind of aggressiveness in their proselytizing. The stationary arrangement of language on a page is outmoded. The word, they say, has broken from that corral, is already galloping in its new element, jumping with the speed of electricity from screen to screen. Indeed, the revolution is taking place even as I type with the antediluvian typewriter onto the superseded sheet of paper. I am proof of the fact that many of us are still habit-bound, unable to grasp the scope of the transformation that is underway all around us. But rest assured, we will adjust to these changes, as we do to all others, by increments; we will continue to do so until everything about the way we do business is different. So they say. Those with a lesser stake in the printed word, for whom the technologies are exciting means to necessary ends—to speed and efficiency—will scarcely notice what they are leaving behind. But those of us who live by the word, who are still embedded in the ancient and formerly stable reader-writer relationship, will have to make our difficult peace.

In a widely-discussed essay in the *New York Times Book Review*—entitled, terrifyingly, "The End of Books" (June 21, 1992)—Robert Coover addressed the new situation. He began boldly:

> In the real world nowadays, that is to say, in the world of video transmissions, cellular phones, fax machines, computer networks, and in particular out in the humming digitalized precincts of avant-garde computer hackers, cyberpunks and hyperspace freaks, you will often hear it said that the print medium is a doomed and outdated technology, a mere curiosity of bygone days and destined soon to be consigned forever to those dusty unattended museums we now call libraries. Indeed, the very proliferation of books and other print-based media, so prevalent in this forest-harvesting, paper-wasting age, is held to be a sign of its feverish moribundity, the last futile gasp of a once-vital form before it finally passes away forever, dead as God.

His ground set out, Coover soon focuses his attention on hypertext, which is, in this newly enormous landscape, focus enough. Here is his description of the term:

> "Hypertext" is not a system but a generic term, coined a quarter of a century ago by a computer populist named Ted Nelson to describe the writing done in the nonlinear or nonsequential space made possible by the computer. Moreover, unlike print text, hypertext provides multiple paths between text segments, now often called "lexias" in a borrowing from the pre-hypertextual but prescient Roland Barthes. With its webs of linked lexias, its networks of alternate routes (as opposed to print's fixed unidirectional page-turning) hypertext presents a radically divergent technology, interactive and polyvocal, favoring a plurality of discourses over definitive utterance and freeing the reader from domination by the author. Hypertext reader and writer are said to become co-learners or co-writers, as it were, fellow travelers in the mapping and remapping of textual (and visual, kinetic, and aural) components, not all of which are provided by what used to be called the author.

This is the new picture, background and foreground, and we members of the literary community had better stop thinking of it as a science-fiction fantasy.

Ground zero: The transformation of the media of communication maps a larger transformation of consciousness—maps it, but also speeds it along; it changes the terms of our experience and our ways of offering response. Transmission determines reception determines reaction. Looking broadly at the way we live—on many simultaneous levels, under massive stimulus loads—it is clear that mechanical-linear technologies are insufficient. We require swift and obedient tools with vast capacities for moving messages through networks. As the tools proliferate, however, more and more of what we do involves network interaction. The processes that we created to serve our evolving needs have not only begun to redefine our experience, but they are fast becoming our new cognitive paradigm. It is ever more difficult for us to imagine how people ever got along before fax, e-mail, mobile phones, computer networks, etc.

What is the relevance of all this to reading and writing? This must now be established—from scratch.

Words read from a screen or written onto a screen—words which appear and disappear, even if they can be retrieved and fixed into place with a keystroke—have a different status and affect us differently from words held immobile on the accessible space of a page. Marshall McLuhan set out the principles decades ago, charting the major media shifts from orality to print and from print to electronic as cultural watersheds. The basic premise holds. But McLuhan's analysis of the print-to-electronics transformation centered upon television and the displacement of the printed word by transmissions of image and voice. But what about the difference between print on a page and print on a screen? Are we dealing with a change of degree, or a change of kind? It may be too early to tell. At present, while we are still poised with one foot in each realm, it would seem a difference of degree. But as electronic communications eventually supplant the mechanical, degree may attain critical mass and become kind. Or less than kind.

Reading over Coover's description of hypertext, we have to wonder: Are our myriad technological innovations to be seen as responses to collective needs and desires, or are they simply logical developments in the inexorable evolution of technology itself? Do the hypertext options arrive because we want out of the prison-house of tradition (linearity, univocality, stylistic individuality), or are they a by-product of breakthroughs in the field? Is hypertext a Hula-Hoop fad or the first surging of a wave that will swell until it sweeps away everything in its path? If it is indeed a need-driven development—a reflection of a will to break out of a long confinement, to redefine the terms and processes of expression—then we may be in for an epic battle that will transform everything about reading, writing, and publishing.

The subject comes up a great deal in conversation these days. Disputants, many of them writers, say to me, "Words are still words—on a page, on a screen—what's the difference?" There is much shrugging of the shoulders. But this will never do. The changes are profound and the differences are consequential. Nearly weightless though it is, the word printed on a page is a thing. The configuration of impulses on a screen is not—it is a manifestation, an indeterminate entity both particle and wave, an ectoplasmic arrival and departure. The former occupies a position in space—on a page, in a book—and is verifiably there. The latter, once dematerialized, digitalized back into storage, into memory, cannot be said to exist in quite the same way. It has potential, not actual, locus. (Purists would insist that the coded bit, too, exists and can be found, but its location is not evident to the unassisted and uninstructed senses.) And although one could argue that the word, the passage, is present in the software memory as surely as it sits on page x, the fact is that we register a profound difference. One is outside and visible, the other "inside" and invisible. A thing and, in a sense, the idea of a thing. The words on the page, however ethereal their designation, partake of matter. The words removed to storage, rendered invisible, seem to have reversed expressive direction and to have gone back into thought. Their entity dissolves into a kind of neural potentiality. This fact—or, rather, this perception on the part of the screen reader—cannot but affect the way the words are registered when present. They may not be less, but they are as different as the nearly identical pieces of paper currency, the one secured by bullion-holdings at Fort Knox, the other by the abstract guarantees of the Federal Reserve System.

The shape of a word—its physical look—is only its outer garb. The impulse, the pulse of its meaning, is the same whether that word is incised in marble, scratched into mud, inscribed onto papyrus, printed onto a page, or flickered forth on a screen. Or is it? Wouldn't we say that the word cannot really exist outside the perception and translation by its reader? If this is the case, then the mode of transmission cannot be disregarded. The word cut into stone carries the implicit weight of the carver's intention; it is decoded into sense under the aspect of its imperishability. It has weight, grandeur—it vies with time. The same word, when it appears on the screen, must be received with a sense of its weightlessness—the weightlessness of its presentation. The same sign, but not the same.

Seeing is believing—or so they say. In fact, the proposition is nonsensical. Seeing is knowing, whereas believing is trusting to the existence of something we cannot see. But belief can be stronger than knowing. When we trust to the unseen, we confer power. Dieties and subatomic particles and, more recently, the silicon pathways webbed into microchips—all of these we invest with a potency that we do not always grant to more objectively verifiable phenomena. Thus, the words on the page, though they issue from the invisible force field of another's mind, are insulated between covers, while the words on the screen seem to arrive from some collective elsewhere that seems more profound, deeper than a mere writer's subjectivity. But this does not necessarily invest the words themselves with a greater potency, for the unseen creative self of the writer is conflated with the unseen depth of the technology and, in the process, the writer's independent authority is subtly undermined. The site of veneration shifts; in the reader's subliminal perception some measure of the power belonging to the writer is handed over to the machine. The words on the screen, in other words, are felt to issue from a void deeper than language, and this, not the maker of the sentences, claims any remnant impulse to belief.

The page is flat, opaque. The screen is of indeterminate depth—the word floats on the surface like a leaf on a river. Phenomenologically, that word is less absolute. The leaf on the river is not the leaf plucked out and held in the hand. The words that appear and disappear on the screen are naturally perceived less as isolated counters and more as the constituent elements of some larger, more fluid process. This is not a matter of one being better or worse, but different.

There is a paradox lurking in this metamorphosis of the word. The earlier historical transition from orality to script—a transition greeted with considerable alarm by Socrates and his followers—changed the rules of intellectual procedure completely. Written texts could be transmitted, studied, and annotated; knowledge could rear itself upon a stable base. And the shift from script to mechanical type and the consequent spread of literacy among the laity is said by many to have made the Enlightenment possible. Yet now it is computers, in one sense the very apotheosis of applied rationality, that are destabilizing the authority of the printed word and returning us, although at a different part of the spiral, to the process orientation that characterized oral cultures.

Process. As a noun, "a series of actions, changes, or functions that bring about an end or result." As a verb, "to put through the steps of a prescribed procedure." Although the word is both noun and verb, in this context its verbal attributes are dominant. The difference between words on a page and words on a screen is the difference between product and process, noun and verb. The word processor is not, never mind what some writers say, "just a better typewriter." It is a modification of the relation between the writer and the language.

The dual function of print is the immobilization and preservation of language. To make a mark on a page is to gesture toward permanence; it is to make a choice from an array of expressive possibilities. In former days, the writer, en route to a product that could be edited, typeset, and more or less permanently imprinted on paper, wrestled incessantly with this primary attribute of the medium. If he wrote with pencil or pen, then he had to erase or scratch out his mistakes; if he typed, then he either had to retype or use some correcting tool. The path between impulse and inscription was made thornier by the knowledge that errors meant having to retrace steps and do more work. The writer was more likely to test the phrasing on the ear, to edit mentally before committing to the paper. The underlying momentum was toward the right, irrevocable expression.

This ever-present awareness of fixity, of indelibility, is no longer so pressing a part of the writer's daily struggle. That is, the writing technology no longer enforces it. Words now arrive onto the screen under the aspect of provisionality. They can be transferred with a stroke or deleted altogether. And when they are deleted it is as if they had never been. There is no physical reminder of the wrong turn, the failure. At a very fundamental and obvious level, the consequentiality of bringing forth language has been altered. Where the limitations of the medium once encouraged a very practical resistance to the spewing out of the unformulated expression, that responsibility has now passed to the writer.

To theorize along these lines is to court ridicule. Present the average reader with prose originally written onto the screen and prose typed onto the page, and he will wonder what is the difference. *The words are the same, of course. More or less.* Yet at some level, perhaps molecular, they are not the same. The difference? It must originate in the writer, more precisely in the writer in the act of composition. A change in procedure must be at least subtly reflected in the result. How could it not? More than a few writers have explained to me just how the fluidity and alterability made possible by the medium have freed them to write more, to venture their sentences with less inhibition. And the fact that one can readily move sentences, paragraphs, even whole sections, from one place to another has allowed them to conceive of their work—the process of it—in more spatial terms. These would seem to be gains; but gains, we know, always come with a price. Which in this case would be the removal of focus from the line and a sacrifice of some of the line-driven refinements of style. With a change in potential, an incorporation of a greater awareness of the whole, the tendency of stylistic attention to be local and detail-oriented decreases. I'm talking about abstract tendencies, not about the practice of individual writers. One can still be a consummate fabricator of phrases and sentences—but one must be willing to work against the grain of the technology.

Writing on the computer promotes process over product and favors the whole over the execution of the part. As the writer grows accustomed to moving words, sentences, and paragraphs around—to opening his lines to insertions—his sense of linkage and necessity is affected. Less thought may be given to the ideal of inevitable expression. The expectation is no longer that there should be a single best way to say something; the writer accepts variability and is more inclined to view the work as a version. The Flaubertian tyranny of *le mot juste* is eclipsed, and with it, gradually, the idea of the author as a sovereign maker.

Roland Barthes once wrote an influential essay entitled "The Death of the Author" (which chimes, I see, with Coover's "End of the Book") in which he argued, in essence, that the individual writer is not so much the creative originator as he is the site for certain proliferations of language; that the text, by the same token, is a variegated weaving of strands from prior texts and not a freestanding entity. Barthes's pitch was extreme, calculated to provoke, and he did not really have electronic communications in mind—but it is in part the arrival of the new technologies that has made his writings so prescient.

The changes brought about by the wholesale implementation of the word processor and, more radically, the various hypertext options, are really just part of a much larger set of societal circumstances, all of which are modifying the traditional roles of writer and reader. The decline of the prestige of authorship—something all writers feel and lament—has much to do with the climate of our current intellectual culture, a climate in which all manifestations of *author*-ity are seen as suspect. Deconstruction and multiculturalism advance arm in arm, the former bent upon undermining the ideological base upon which aesthetic and cultural hierarchies have been erected, the latter proposing a lateral and egalitarian renovation of the canon. Together they convincingly expose the "greatness" of authors and works as complex constructs, not so much unimpeachable artistic attainments as triumphs of one set of cultural forces over others.

The idea of individual authorship—that one person would create an original work and have historical title to it—did not really become entrenched in the public mind until print superseded orality as the basis of cultural communication (and maybe this "public mind" only came into being at this point). So long as there was a spoken economy, the process, the transmission, had precedence over the thing transmitted. The speaker passed along what had been gathered and distilled from other oral sources. As the print technology gained ground, however, all that changed. Fixity brought imprimatur. Verbal perfectability, style, and the idea of ownership followed. The words on the page, chiseled and refined by a single author, aspired to permanence. The more perfect, the more inevitable the expression seemed, the greater the claim that the author could lay upon posterity. Think of the bold boasting in Shakespeare's sonnets, born of the recognition that so long as words survived (were read) the subject and the poet would both enjoy a kind of afterlife. Everything hinged upon the artistic power of the work itself.

In literary legend, Gustave Flaubert is seen as the paradigmatic maker and his *Madame Bovary* as the ultimate made thing. His contortions on the way to writing the perfect book, a book meditated down to its least syllable, a book that would suffer from the slightest modification of word order or punctuation, are legendary. His belief in the adequacy of language to experience had to be absolute; without it he would have had to go mad from the contemplation of unrealized possibility. Style—word order, word sound, periodic rhythm, etc.—was arbitrariness surmounted. The printed page was an objective, immutable thing; the book was an artifact. With the divestment of the creator's authority and the attenuation of the stylistic ideal, the emphasis in writing has naturally moved from product to process. The work is not intended to be absolute, nor is it received as such. Writing tends to be seen not so much as an objective realization as an expressive instance. A version. Looking from the larger historical vantage, it almost appears as if we are returning to the verbal orientation that preceded the triumph of print.

The word processor can be seen as a kind of ice-breaker for that inchoate thing that is hypertext—which is, as Coover notes, a "generic" term for writing on a computer that avails itself of some of the capacities of that technology. Hypertext is more than just an end run around paper; it is a way of giving the screen, the computer software, and the modem a significant role in the writing process.

In some ways hypertext resembles the now-familiar word processor operation. Text does not visibly accumulate, but scrolls in from and back out to oblivion. Words do not lie fixed against the opaque page but float in the quasidimensional hyperspace. Not only can they be moved or altered at will, but any part of the text can theoretically mark the beginning of another narrative or expository path. The text can be programmed to accommodate branching departures or to incorporate visual elements and documents. The lone user can sculpt texts as she wishes, breaking up narratives, arranging lines in diverse patterns, or creating "windows" that allow readers to choose how much information or description they want. And on and on.

No less significantly, the hypertext writer need not work alone. The technology affords the option of interactive or collaborative writing. And this, even more than the fluidity or the candy-store array of choices offered by the medium, promises to change our ideas about reading and writing enormously in the years to come. Already users can create texts in all manner of collaborative ways—trading lines, writing parallel texts that merge, moving independently created sets of characters in and out of communal fictional space. Coover described in his essay how he and his students established a "hypertext hotel," a place where the writers were free to "check in, to open new rooms, new corridors, new intrigues, to unlink texts or create new links, to intrude upon or subvert the texts of others, to alter plot trajectories, manipulate time and space, to engage in dialogue through invented characters, then kill off one another's characters or even sabotage the hotel's plumbing."

But while Coover sustains an attitude of exploratory optimism throughout, he does concede that he is himself enough a creature of the book to feel a certain skepticism about this brave new world. He notes what he sees as certain obvious problems:

> Navigational procedures: how do you move around in infinity without getting lost? The structuring of the space can be so compelling and confusing as to utterly absorb the narrator and to exhaust the reader. And there is the related problem of filtering. With an unstable text that can be intruded upon by other author-readers, how do you, caught in the maze, avoid the trivial? How do you duck the garbage? Venerable novelistic values like unity, integrity, coherence, vision, voice, seem to be in danger. Eloquence is being redefined. "Text" has lost its canonical certainty. How does one judge, analyze, write about a work that never reads the same way twice?

Worthy, commonsensical questions. The problem is similar to that uncovered by Nietzsche: How do we ascertain or uphold values if God is dead and everything is permitted? In the case of hypertext it is not God who is gone, but the author, the traditional originator of structure and engineer of meanings. The creator who derived his essential prestige from the power of fiat: Let there be no world but this. If the game is wide open, if everything is possible between reader and writer, then how do we begin to define that game? Or do we define it at all? Does the idea of literature vanish altogether in the new gratification system of exchanged and shared impulses?

I sat in R.'s studio and did my dutiful best to get in past the wall of my resistance to hypertext. But I was still stymied. The battery of directions and option signals all but short-circuited any capacity I may have had to enter the life of the words on the screen. I was made so fidgety by the knowledge that I was positioned in a designed environment, with the freedom to rocket from one place to another with a keystroke, that I could scarcely hold still long enough to read what was there in front of me. Granted, what prose I did browse was not of a quality to compel entry by itself—it needed the enticement of its "hyper" element—but I realized that it would be the same if Pynchon or Gass had written the sentences. For the effect of the hypertext environment, the ever-present awareness of possibility and the need to either make or refuse choice, was to preempt my creating any meditative space for myself. When I read I do not just obediently move the eyes back and forth, ingesting verbal signals, I also sink myself into a receptivity. But sitting at my friend's terminal I experienced constant interruption—the reading surface was fractured, rendered collagelike by the appearance of starred keywords and suddenly materialized menu boxes. I did not feel the exhilarating freedom I had hoped to feel. I felt, rather, an assault upon what I had unreflectingly assumed to be my reader's prerogatives.

This is a matter that has not been sufficiently addressed—the *ungainliness* of the interaction. Not only is the user affronted aesthetically at every moment by ugly type fonts and crude display options, but he has to wheel and click the cumbersome mouse to keep the interaction going. This user, at least, has not been able to get past the feeling of being infantilized. No matter how serious the transaction taking place, I feel as though my reflexes are being tested in a video arcade. I have been assured that this will pass, but it hasn't yet. I still register viscerally the differential between the silken flow of information within the circuits and the fumbles and fidgets required to keep it from damming up. The interactive text, I suppose, cannot be any better than its reader's capabilities allow it to be.

Granted, the technology is still in its infancy. Many of the irritants will in time be refined away, and skilled writers will generate works of great cunning and suggestiveness. And readers will eventually acclimate themselves to texts encoded with signals. But even then, when trained reader encounters skilled writer, will that reader ever achieve that meditative immersion that is, for me, one of the main incentives for reading?

My guess is that the "revolution" scenarios, staple features of the New-Age "hacker" magazines, are premature and do not take into account the conservative retraction of the elastic. Innumerable possibilities will be tested—vast interactive collaborations, video inserts, much entrepreneurial fizz—but most of them will blow away like smoke in the wind. Remaining behind will be the incentives that really work—the brilliant, ingenious, artistic productions that are not merely technical *tours de force* but which have something to communicate, which reach the interactive reader in something more than just a cerebral way. As with all systemic processes, a natural ecology will assert itself, preserving what is useful and eliminating what is not.

Still, if the shift from typewriter to word processor altered the writer's sense of stylistic imperative, then hypertext can be seen as delivering a mighty blow to the long-static writer-reader relationship. It changes the entire system of power upon which the literary experience has been predicated; it rewrites the contract from start to finish. Coover states that hypertext "presents a radically divergent technology, interactive and polyvocal, favoring a plurality of discourses over definitive utterance and freeing the reader from domination by the author," but his tonal matter-of-factness belies the monumentality of the assertion. This "domination by the author" has been, at least until now, the *point* of writing and reading. The author masters the resources of language to create a vision that will engage and in some way overpower the reader; the reader goes to the work to be subjected to the creative will of another. The premise behind the textual interchange is that the author possesses wisdom, an insight, a way of looking at experience, that the reader wants.

A change in this relation is therefore not superficial. Once a reader is enabled to collaborate, participate, or in any way engage the text as an empowered player who has some say in the outcome of the game, the core assumptions of reading are called into question. The imagination is liberated from the constraint of being guided at every step by the author. Necessity is dethroned and arbitrariness is installed in its place.

Consider the difference. Text A, old-style, composed by a single author on a typewriter, edited, typeset, published, distributed through bookstores, where it is purchased by the reader, who ingests it the old way, turning pages, front to back, assembling a structure of sense deemed to be the necessary structure because from among the myriad existing possibilities the author selected it. Now look at Text B, the hypertext product composed by one writer, or several, on a computer, using a software program that facilitates options. The work can be read in linear fashion (the missionary position of reading), but it is also open. That is, the reader can choose to follow any number of subnarrative paths, can call up photographic supplements to certain key descriptions, can select from among a number of different kinds of possible endings. What is it that we do with B? Do we still call it reading? Or would we do better to coin a new term, something like "texting" or "word-piloting"?

We do not know yet whether hypertext will ever be accepted by a mass readership as something more than a sophisticated Nintendo game played with language. It could be that, faced with the choice between univocal and polyvocal, linear and "open," readers will opt for the more traditional package; that the reading act will remain rooted in the original giver-receiver premise because this offers readers something they want: a chance to subject the anarchic subjectivity to another's disciplined imagination, a chance to be taken in unsuspected directions under the guidance of some singular sensibility.

I stare at the textual field on my friend's screen and I am unpersuaded. Indeed, this glimpse of the future—if it is the future—has me clinging all the more tightly to my books, the very idea of them. If I ever took them for granted, I do no longer. I now see each one as a portable enclosure, a place I can repair to to release the private, unsocialized, dreaming self. A book is solitude, privacy; it is a way of holding the self apart from the crush of the outer world. Hypertext—at least the spirit of hypertext, which I see as the spirit of the times—promises to deliver me from this, to free me from the "liberating domination" of the author. It promises to spring me from the univocal linearity which is precisely the constraint that fills me with a sense of possibility as I read my way across fixed acres of print.

# PART III

# Critical Mass:
# Three Meditations

# 12

# The Western Gulf

W E CHOOSE THE THINGS we write about for various reasons
—some because they irritate us into thought, others because
they confirm us in what we have been thinking already. Some subjects
are close to us and we want to underscore that proximity; others are distant and we wish to draw them in closer, or else to study the terms of
their distance.

I decided to write about Lionel Trilling's *The Liberal Imagination*
for several of these reasons. On the one hand, its underlying inquiry
into the conditions of American literary and intellectual culture put it
very near to my own recent preoccupations. On the other hand, its assumptions and overall mode of address suggest to me how much has
changed since Trilling's day. (*The Liberal Imagination* was published in
1950.) The changes, enormous and culturally all-encompassing, have
made that text compellingly remote to me. Its tone, its implicit terms,
its particular references all harken back to a world "before." Before
what? Part of the point of these meditations will be just this: to locate
the transformations that allow us to speak in terms of a before and after.
In any case, the remoteness of Trilling's book is not, for me, the remoteness of the unknown, but rather of something once familiar that has receded nearly out of reach. I want to catch its meanings—some—before
they are entirely gone, to try to search out what has happened in our
culture, particularly our literary culture, and to guess at what may yet be
in store.

My anchor point to the present, encountered serendipitously while
I was writing notes on Trilling, is a remark by novelist Don DeLillo, who

in a recent *Paris Review* interview was asked about the fate of the novel. Said DeLillo, "We're all one beat away from becoming elevator music." Not a sanguine assessment, but it's one that in my less optimistic moods I share. We will need to reckon with it.

Most of the sixteen essays in *The Liberal Imagination* were originally written piecemeal for journals or as lectures. Yet when they are read through from start to finish and allowed to mix in the mind, they not only disclose a thematic unity, but they seem to ramify, one perspective deepening another, an aside here fleshing out an observation made there. This may help to explain how a book cobbled together out of diverse pieces for specific occasions came to have the impact it did. It is a testimony to the fundamentally organic coherence of Trilling's sensibility, and reveals that whatever else he was thinking upon he was also urgently occupied with the problem of humanism and its ongoing viability. *The Liberal Imagination* at once reflects and criticizes a literary and intellectual culture that had reached its apogee. We see this in retrospect. The years that followed the book's publication, while each bright with its own stars and excitements, nevertheless appear to be dropping like terraces, one below the next. There have been greater works, and fiercer intellects, but there has been ever less of a coherent and receptive social environment in which they could have any kind of impact.

We now stand many terrace steps down and after us it will be worse—the idea of the literary intellectual threatens to become altogether implausible. What has happened? Although answering may not have been his immediate project, Trilling had enough critical acumen, and was sensitive enough to the pulsations that run through the culture to inscribe a great many useful observations in his essays. And as we draw away from the book and its times, certain elements lose their urgency—the Freudian, for example—while those more relevant to our plight seem to stand out in greater relief. They mark a trail of their own and ultimately face us forward to our present.

Let me begin where Trilling does, with the preface, a short piece of reflective prose which was, we can be sure, written last. Written, that is, once Trilling had assessed the contents of his collection and was ready to plant the suggestions of how it might be read and to emphasize the terms of its mattering.

The most striking thing in these pages is Trilling's calm, utterly confident assertion of certain connections. The tone is deceptive, for later in the book Trilling is clearly arguing the case—his articles of faith are not foregone conclusions. And indeed to us, four decades later, they are unthinkable:

> Goethe says somewhere that there is no such thing as a liberal idea, that there are only liberal sentiments. This is true. Yet it is also true that certain sentiments consort only with certain ideas and not with others. What is more, sentiments become ideas by a natural and imperceptible process. "Our continued influxes of feeling," said Wordsworth, "are modified and directed by our thoughts, which are indeed the representatives of all our past feelings."

He adds:

> If this is so, if between sentiments and ideas there is a natural connection so close as to amount to a kind of identity, then the connection between literature and politics will be seen as a very immediate one. And this will seem especially true if we do not intend the narrow but the wide sense of the word politics . . . as the politics of culture, the organization of human life toward some end or other, toward the modification of sentiments, which is to say the quality of human life.

For dyed-in-the-wool humanists—even for inveterate readers of belles-lettres, that now nearly extinct genre once represented by writers like Edmund Wilson, Irving Howe, and Mary McCarthy—there is nothing new or startling here. The eye glides easily over these assertions of faith, the more so as they are couched in a supple and confident prose. But a moment's sustained attention must bring us up short. For the late-modern reader, the citizen of our mad pre-millennium, the truth is otherwise. The gyre has widened enough to carry the falcon away; the ideas seem fantastical. There is now very little connection between our literature and our politics, even if we construe "politics" in the most general way. Indeed, we may not even *have* sentiments of the sort invoked by Trilling. The hallmark of our postmodern culture is a shrugging sense of anarchy, of elements slipping into and out of combination for no clear reason. That a writer's expression, a literature, should bear importantly on what the author calls "the quality of human life" is unthinkable—it is a subject for mockery. Our collective faith in literature, that joining place of sentiments and ideas, has dissolved. And we read as if on papyrus the grand closing sentence of the preface:

> To the carrying out of the job of criticizing the liberal imagination, literature has a unique relevance, not merely because so much of modern literature has explicitly directed itself upon politics, but more importantly because literature is the human activity that takes the fullest and most precise account of variousness, possibility, complexity, and difficulty.

But in fact, Trilling in his preface is being either sly or disingenuous. For if these opening declarations trumpet what sounds like a faith, the essays that follow show the critic to be a good deal more worried and embattled. The vision of the preface turns out to be just that, a vision—or else an effort by Trilling to harry himself back into a hopefulness he feels he might be losing. Again and again in his various reflections we catch the note of apprehension, the argumentative insistence that belies the pose of Olympian serenity. The book is, in the last analysis, quite anxious about the fate of literature, and by extension—if the continuities pledged to in the preface are assumed—about the larger cultural and societal enterprise. *The Liberal Imagination* is a brave but dark book, a venturesome bid to salvage what is almost lost. If anything connects it to our time it is the ill-concealed valedictory note. We now live in the culture that Trilling went in dread of.

Trilling's short essay, "The Function of the Little Magazine," while hardly the most searching or speculative of the lot, does set out the contours of his concern most concisely. Written as an introduction to *The Partisan Reader* (1946), the piece sketches out the state of things literary in the years directly following World War II. He writes, "Here is an epitome of our cultural situation. Briefly put, it is that there exists a great gulf between our educated class and the best of our literature."

This gulf, he asserts, "did not open suddenly." He then harks back, somewhat nostalgically, to an earlier era. His characterization, because it will have some use as a point of reference, deserves to be cited at some length. Taking his cue from some personal reflections left by William Dean Howells, Trilling writes:

> The Ohio of Howells' boyhood had only recently emerged from its frontier phase and in its manner of life it was still what we call primitive. Yet in this Ohio, while still a boy, Howells had devoted himself to the literary life. He was unusual but he was not unique or lonely . . . Literature had its large accepted place in this culture. The respectable lawyers of the locality subscribed to the great British quarterlies. The printing office of Howells' father was the resort of the village wits, who, as the son tells us "dropped in, and liked to stand with their backs to the stove and challenge opinion concerning Holmes and Poe, Irving and Macaulay, Pope and Byron, Dickens and Shakespeare." Problems of morality and religious faith were freely and boldly discussed. There was no intellectual isolationism, and the village felt, at least eventually, the reverberations of the European movement of mind.

I have found that whenever I suggest, either in conversation or in some more public forum, that there has been a decline in the quality of our literary or intellectual life, I am immediately, and sometimes angrily, countered by someone who demands to know when things have ever been better. If I answer, as I often do, that an epoch like the one described here may have had more to offer, at least in certain essential ways, I hear that we have never been so rich in bounty as we are now; that more books are printed, sold, and circulated at present than ever before in the history of the world. This I don't dispute, but I still side with Trilling. We need to calculate on the basis of something other than the numerical availability of printed works. I fall back on what is finally an unverifiable impression—that for all of our supposed riches, our culture *feels* impoverished; it lacks the kinds of animation that regular exposure to ideas and works of imagination supplies; and it is without an affirmative circulation of mental and spiritual energies. I say this and I am told, again, that it has never been this way, that I have created my own chimera of the past.

Trilling insists in his essay, "In the nineteenth century, in this country as in Europe, literature underlay every activity of mind." And soon after, he makes what seems to me a most suggestive point:

> Of two utterances of equal quality, one of the nineteenth and one of the twentieth century, we can say that the one of the nineteenth century had the greater *power*. If the mechanical means of communication were then less efficient than now, the intellectual means were far more efficient. There may even be a significant ratio between the two.

That last sentence is important enough to warrant repeating: "There may even be a significant ratio between the two." Isn't this the crux of it all? That the whole question of intellectual and artistic mattering has far less to do with the quantitative availability of ideas and expressions, and much more with their impact upon the individual and, through him, the society? That what matters is not the sound but the resonance of the sound? (It frustrates me deeply that Trilling should have ventured such a telling insight but not gone on to explore it.)

Trilling did not devote much attention to this power equation in any of his writings, not so far as I have read. Doubtless in the late forties and early fifties there was little evidence of the kinds of transformations that would overwhelm us in more recent decades. Even his word, "mechanical" has now an antique ring to it. We recall that there was a time when the world clattered forward on engines and meshing gears. What palpability, what logic-driven noise! Now the world slips around us fluently, scarcely clinging, melding archives of information with the instantaneousness of electricity flaming through a circuit. And that inverse ratio is greater than ever. Never so much utterance, so much flow, and never before so little sense of connection or mattering. The gulf that Howells saw opening up in his later years between literary culture and the rest of society is so vast that one no longer thinks of it as a gulf.

When Trilling wrote his essay on the little magazine, he still professed a slight degree of hope. The falling off in energy of literary movements, a function of the declining power of the word, was not yet deemed permanent. But it could well turn out that way. "There are circumstances that suggest it might become so. After all, the emotional space of the human mind is large but not infinite, and perhaps it will be pre-empted by the substitutes for literature—the radio, the movies, and certain magazines—which are antagonistic to literature not merely because they are compelling genres but also because of the political and cultural assumptions that control them." Again, we are put in mind of horse and buggy days. *Radio? Movies? Magazines?* What would the temperate sage of Columbia conclude if he were alive today, free to surf the churning electronic swells, ride the brilliant image cataracts, or study the retinal flickers in the eyes of a whole generation interacting with the fantasia of the latest from Sega or Nintendo?

Trilling says many more cogent and relevant things in this essay, then swerves around to make his central point about the absolute necessity in such an age of a journal like *Partisan Review*. Its aim—and now Trilling echoes his preface—is to "organize a new union between our political ideas and our imagination." Implicit is his belief in a continuum between the affective and intellectual parts of our being. The place where the gulf can be bridged, the rift healed, is the printed page; the medium of restoration, language. A small-circulation journal like *Partisan Review* shows that in principle the synthesis can be effected; it holds out the possibility for the rest of the culture.

The *Partisan Review* of that era was more than just an influential journal. To its readers and writers it was a lofty enterprise, a Weimar asserting itself against the mounting forces of mass culture. In these golden days, the memoirists tell us, writers were still esteemed, ideas were important enough to be contested tooth and nail, and the project of forging an enlightened culture was not altogether unthinkable. No more. The faith that mobilized our last true band of freelance intellectuals has dissolved. The writers and thinkers themselves have either gotten old or have died and, as Russell Jacoby laments in his study, *The Last Intellectuals*, no group even remotely comparable has emerged to fill the vacuum. Trilling, Wilson, Rahv, McCarthy, Lowell, MacDonald, Dupee, Kazin, Howe, Hardwick, Jarrell, Schwartz, Bellow—they were the last of their kind. The new intellectual, notes Jacoby, is an altogether different creature: an academic, a tenured specialist who writes not for the educated lay public but for other specialists. The reasons for the disappearance of the freelance intellectual are many—everything from rising urban rents to shrinking publication possibilities—but the main factor has been the unprecedented expansion of colleges and universities in the postwar period. The urban *luftmensch* (literally "the man who lives on air") has become the briefcase-toting scholar on his or her way to deliver a paper at a conference. The consequence is that we have lost the last link that could connect the thinking person and the culture at large.

Trilling doubtless had a suitably complex explanation for the gulf that had opened up between the forces of sensibility and intellect (the so-called "liberal imagination") and the vast *other* that constitutes our society, but in this book he ventures no explicit analysis. He does, however, greet the reader with one very fundamental suggestion, one that we meet up with in various guises in the essays. This is, quite simply, Trilling's estimate of the essential American character. As often happens, he appears to be discussing a crucial literary distinction and discloses only gradually that he has something far more encompassing in mind.

The first essay in the book, "Reality in America," makes a point that subsequent essays will augment and elaborate. Trilling begins with a carefully staged discussion of Vernon Parrington, using the senior critic as an emblem of what he will argue is not only a disfiguring bias in American thought, but in the society itself. Parrington, he writes, "still stands at the center of American thought about American culture because . . . he expresses the chronic American belief that there exists an opposition between reality and mind and that one must enlist oneself in the party of reality." Trilling's insistent repetition of the word "American" signals that he does not regard this as a universal characteristic.

In the second section of "Reality in America," Trilling zeroes in and gives point to his assertion. He sets up Theodore Dreiser and Henry James as representatives of the two extremes and then looks at how each has been received by the critical establishment:

> To James no quarter is given by American criticism in its political
> and liberal aspect. But in the same degree that liberal criticism is
> moved by political considerations to treat James with severity, it
> treats Dreiser with the most sympathetic indulgence. Dreiser's liter-

ary faults, it gives us to understand, are essentially social and political virtues. It was Parrington who established the formula for the liberal criticism of Dreiser by calling him a "peasant": when Dreiser thinks stupidly, it is because he has the slow stubbornness of a peasant; when he writes badly, it is because he is impatient of the sterile literary gentility of the bourgeoisie. It is as if wit, and flexibility of mind, and perception, and knowledge were to be equated with aristocracy and political reaction, while dullness and stupidity most naturally suggest a virtuous democracy, as in the old plays.

Trilling's whole agenda can be discerned here: his liberal's thrust against what he sees as the core weakness of liberalism—its fear of appearing elitist; the hint of an alliance with a European Enlightenment sensibility where philosophical and aesthetic issues are concerned; and, though we cannot know it fully yet, his rallying behind the banner of Henry James, an American who fled to Europe for the nutrients his native land could not give him. We might also note the echo between the so-called "reactionary" qualities Trilling lists—"wit, and flexibility of mind, and perception, and knowledge"—and the attributes he confers upon literature in his preface, where he calls it "the human activity that takes the fullest and most precise account of variousness, possibility, complexity, and difficulty." No question about it, Trilling's literary ideal is, in the Parrington scheme of things, aristocratic.

The tensions inherent in Trilling's aristocratic liberalism lend interest to the often laborious argumentation of his essay "The Princess Casamassima," on Henry James's novel of the same name. Here we see Trilling making his most ingenious gambit on behalf of mind and sensibility; he shows us what can be done with the deft jujitsu moves of paradox. As he does so often, the critic turns an occasion of particular focus into a platform for expressing a more generally applicable position.

Trilling makes his case with great care—indeed, it is a *tour de force* reading of James's novel. Basically, Trilling takes up where he left off in "Reality in America." His tactic is to read James in defiance of the conventional conceptions about him and to show that the reality sense of the "virtuous democracy" is severely limited.

Well into the essay, Trilling asserts "A writer has said of *The Princess*

*Casamassima* that it is 'a capital example of James's impotence in matters sociological.' The very opposite is so. Quite apart from its moral and aesthetic authority, *The Princess Casamassima* is a brilliantly precise representation of social actuality." What James has achieved, writes Trilling, is the creation of a protagonist, Hyacinth, who appears to be utterly disconnected from the vital dramas of political life, and then to devise for him "a situation in which he must choose between political action and the fruits of the creative spirit of Europe." He chooses the latter, as one would expect, but then James moves to vex his critics. He allows Hyacinth a sacrificial and heroic death that shows him bound to, not divorced from, the world around him. As Trilling puts it, "James even goes so far as to imply that the man of art may be closer to the secret center of things when the man of action is quite apart from it." Bulky Dreiser and practical Parrington are pushed aside; James, the paraphrastic dandy, is given the mantle.

James's novel is obviously a parable of sorts for Trilling, a ratifying of his hope for himself. So long as he can argue that there is a continuum between intellect and sensibility and the rougher business of the world, he can insist on the power and relevance of the artist. That fundamental continuity must be affirmed and reaffirmed, for without it the artist is doomed to irrelevance and the critic to sterility.

As we read through the whole of *The Liberal Imagination* we begin to grasp the iconic centrality of Henry James in Trilling's scheme of things. It is James we are to summon up when the critic enumerates the failings of Sherwood Anderson; James's refined subtlety is there to hold against the fervid simplifications of Kipling. And it is James who is, ultimately, the American gateway to the intelligence of the European novel—a gateway the modern novelist must pass through if he hopes to stall the decline of the whole compromised genre.

In the essay "Manners, Morals, and the Novel," Trilling gives a memorable formulation of his idea of the novel's dependence on the tensions arising from the stratification of class. That idea has little currency these days, although it was revitalized briefly in altered form in Tom Wolfe's controversial polemic, "Stalking the Billion-Footed Beast," in which he proposed to novelists that they return to the social chronicling practiced by the great nineteenth-century writers, only using status rather than class as their basis. When Trilling looks at social class as a foundation for the novel, he looks through a philosophical lens. Via class we approach most directly the novel's reason for being— the moral interrogation of the real versus the illusory. We need the backdrop of social stratification so that we may witness the interplay of manners. "The great novelists knew that manners indicate the largest intentions of men's souls as well as the smallest and they are perpetually concerned to catch the meaning of every dim implicit hint. . . . The novel, then, is a perpetual quest for reality, the field of its research being always the social world, the material of its analysis being always manners as the indication of the direction of man's soul."

How strange all this sounds! And what a turn the novel has taken since Trilling set down these lofty injunctions. Nothing in his analysis even suggests the possibilities of minimalism, metafiction, or the various other incarnations assumed by the postmodern novel. This is not because Trilling was not perceptive as a reader of societal or aesthetic trends. It has more to do with his, and everyone else's, inability to grasp the monumental transformation that was just getting underway and that would, in a few short decades, entirely rewrite the terms under which reality was apprehended by both artist and ordinary citizen. He could not have known how soon that tangible and dimensional order, the *real,* the stage set since the dawn of time for all of our human dramas, would be subjected to vast forces of mediation. Trilling, writing in 1947, could be excused for not seeing what another writer (just then doing work in English literature) would in 1964 announce:

> Today, after more than a century of electronic technology, we have extended our central nervous system itself in a global embrace, abolishing both space and time as far as our planet is concerned. Rapidly, we approach the final phase of the extensions of man—the technological simulation of consciousness, when the creative process of knowing will be collectively and corporately extended to the whole of human society, much as we have already extended our senses and our nerves by the various media.

The writer is Marshall McLuhan, and his book, published thirty years ago, is *Understanding Media*. And if I began this reflection by placing Trilling and his liberal humanism nearly out of reach of the contemporary sensibility, it is largely because the changes prophesied by McLuhan have mostly come to pass; they have so changed our understanding of reality that these broodings about class and manners seem themselves part of some long-forgotten novel.

But this is a topic for a subsequent meditation. My intent here is to try to recreate how things concrete and abstract seemed to people before the onset of the electronic deluge. And for this purpose Trilling is an excellent guide. For he not only held to the faith in societal connectedness and in the capacity of the arts to play a worthy humanizing role, but he was also attuned enough to what Auden called "the age of anxiety" to know that all bedrock certainties were subject to tremor and that an aesthetically and socially barbarous future was a distinct possibility.

Trilling's essay "Art and Fortune" sounds just this unsettled note. He begins, "It is impossible to talk about the novel nowadays without having in our minds the question of whether or not the novel is still a living form." The critic tells us in the next paragraph that *he* does not believe that the novel is dead, but there is a distinct cautiousness in his tone. He does not want the reader to suppose that he is about to swoop down to save the form from its eulogists. Trilling then offers what he sees as the three current explanations advanced by those who believe the novel to have expired.

> The first is simply that the genre has been exhausted, worked out in the way that a lode of ore is worked out—it can no longer yield a valuable supply of its natural matter. The second explanation is that the novel was developed in response to certain cultural circumstances which now no longer exist but have given way to other circumstances which must be met by other forms of the imagination. The third explanation is that the circumstances to which the novel was a response still do exist but we either lack the power to use the form, or no longer find value in the answers that the novel provides, because the continuing circumstances have entered a phase of increased intensity.

What is interesting is that forty-five years have passed since Trilling first delivered "Art and Fortune" as a talk. In that half century, the novel, while maybe not in the healthiest condition ever, still soldiers on. It is criticism, precisely of the Trilling sort—belletristic, pitched to the intelligent reader—that has gone into eclipse. The great critics have mostly died; the former venues have either shrunk, disappeared, or become commercial. In the cultural spot where Trilling and others stood and jousted, there is a great and distressing silence. The fathers and mothers are no longer there to tell us what to think. Listening to the pundits on TV or reading them in the editorial pages is not the same. Whether criticism died of one of the novel's terminal illnesses is uncertain. Was the genre finally exhausted? I would not think it could be until interest in literature and ideas was spent, but maybe that has been the case. Did criticism arise in response to circumstances that no longer obtain? Yes, if those circumstances are seen to have been conducive to a postwar hunger for serious culture. But whatever collective appetite was once there is there no longer. Finally, do we no longer find value in the answers that criticism provides? It saddens me to nod, but this is obviously what has happened. The answers hold no value because the questions have changed. The answers did not take into account a transformed societal situation; they spoke to assumptions of genteel literacy that had no bearing on a circuit-driven mass culture. Criticism refused to address the crisis of reading—the overthrow of the authority of the book and writer—and it died of irrelevance.

And Trilling's views on the survival of the novel? As so often, his argument is obscure, Jamesian in its indirectness. And indeed, James figures prominently. Trilling finally ends up appealing to the Master's own distinction between the terms "reality" and "romance." James defined reality as "the things we cannot possibly not know" and then tells us that the romantic "stands for the things that, with all the facilities in the world, all the wealth and all the courage and all the wit and all the adventure, we never *can* directly know; the things that can reach us only through the beautiful circuit of thought and desire."

Look closely: We are back to the Dreiser/James standoff, with Trilling seeking out the future of the novel in a commitment to the Jamesian ideal, which, oddly, will be reflected in (a) a return to story-

179

telling; (b) implementation of a naturalistic prose that rejects the poetic experimentation of someone like Djuna Barnes; (c) an avoidance of experimental wrestling with form; and (d) an explicit way of dealing with ideas. Ideas, for Trilling, as for James, need not be "pallid and abstract and intellectual." Rather, they represent a kind of psychological complication arising from character and situation.

This insistence on the place of ideas in the novel is really the only thing that distinguishes Trilling's view of the novel from, say, Dreiser's. His criteria are otherwise quite conservative and appear to be in opposition to the central impulses of modernism, which had everything to do with formal and linguistic experimentation.

The appeal to sensibility, to "the beautiful circuit of thought and desire," feels very dated now, the more so as the novel could be said, with few exceptions, to have gone the Dreiserian path. But this does not mean, invoking competitive terms, that the party representing the tangibles has won out over the party of the intangibles. It sooner means that, given the transformations that have been wreaked upon society by electronic media, among other things, the novelist has found it all but impossible to render inwardness coherently. We are fractured and fragmented, dissolved and distracted. The term "sensibility," standing for a coherent inwardness, has slipped from usage; I flinch at its archaism whenever I use it. Everything in contemporary society discourages interiority. More and more of our exchanges take place via circuits, and in their very nature those interactions are such as to keep us hovering in the virtual now, a place away from ourselves.

Trilling could not have foreseen any of this, not at the time he was writing. Television had just broken out of the laboratories; it was seen as a quaint extension of radio. Trilling still thought the old way, framing issues in terms of ideologies, trusting that one could work through to conclusions along paths carved out by reason. He, like everyone of his time, could not imagine that thought could be affected by something other than thought, that the whole human matrix might one day be changed.

Measuring our distance from Trilling, we also measure our distance from humanism, that once-grand growth that had its roots in the Renaissance, that took man as the measure of all things, and that looked forward to the marriage of reason and spirit. Humanism survived so long as there was a clear organic link between the individual and his society. Its great crisis, which some, like critic George Steiner, argue that it did not survive, came with the Nazi holocaust and the mass exterminations ordered by Stalin. The problem was not that humanism could not admit the idea of evil, but that it had no purchase on atrocities that were carried out in assembly-line fashion, by bureaucrats, against every norm of human accountability hitherto known.

That problem, the destruction of the natural balance between the individual and his society, a balance that morally presupposes account-ability, has worsened dramatically. Every technological development now wrenches us further out of scale, mocks further the Renaissance ideal that influenced us for so long. In Trilling's essays, in his final lame but beautiful insistence on an art pledged to the circuit of "thought and desire," we see the final foundering of that faith. The critic would assert a continuum between sentiments and ideas and between ideas and the vast turning gears of society. We cannot even imagine the possibility. He believed in the civilizing power of a liberal education, in an immer-sion in the best that has been thought and written. We are no longer so sure. Not only has the prestige of reading diminished radically in the past few decades, but the idea that there are certifiably "great" works is under siege. "All is changed," as Yeats wrote in quite a different context, "changed utterly."

Reading *The Liberal Imagination,* if we are lucky enough to have turned up a copy (the work has slipped out of print), we are most struck by Trilling's stance—his tone, his references, the assumptions he makes about his audience. We may be surprised by the realization that he is writing not for his fellow academic but for the intelligent layman; that there was once a small but active and influential population of such readers, enough for publishers to count on, enough to support a literary culture outside the university radius. These readers were assumed to have a broad general acquaintance with literary classics—James, Austen, Dickens, Flaubert—as well as modern works by writers like Hemingway, Forster, Mann, and Sartre. They would have the rudi-ments of Freudian psychology, Marxist science, philosophy (certainly a smattering of Descartes, Kant, Bergson, and Nietzsche), classical history

(Tacitus, Polybius, Thucydides), and so on. Not a great deal to ask, but how many readers like that are out there now? Some, of course. But do we ever think of them as forming a constituency, as representing a cultural power, as representing anything besides a quirky exception to the norm?

The isolated reader may remain, but the audience is gone and is not likely to reappear. And this loss impinges heavily, very heavily, on the quality of our cultural life. It assures that there will be a sharp split between extremes—between an academic elite and a mass population—with no mediating center. I do not believe that the overtaking of print by electronic communications, the development that has helped to sink the humanistic culture Trilling espoused, will bridge the rift. If anything, it will lead to further scattering, greater ruptures, a growing sense of cultural displacement.

I chose Trilling as my subject because to me he represents our culture at a moment of anxious wakefulness—and at a critical turning point. To move from Tilling to the present, as we are about to do, is to plot a downward curve. Alvin Kernan's title, *The Death of Literature,* suggests where the nadir lies. We need to study it, to exact a look at the worst, before we can search out the terms and conditions under which some cultural vitality may yet survive.

# 13

# The Death of Literature

I F LIONEL TRILLING'S *Liberal Imagination* shows us the last flaring of a humanist's faith in the power and prestige of the literary enterprise, Alvin Kernan's *Death of Literature* (1990) gives us the certificate of expiration of that faith. Reading Kernan directly after Trilling, we may feel as though we have hurried through some revolving door of decades, and indeed we have—nearly fifty years have passed, carrying at least a normal century's worth of changes in their wake. The juxtaposition of texts is startling, though not as startling as it might have been had Trilling himself not been so wary about the survival of the practices and values he cherished.

*The Death of Literature* does not advance any polemical purpose, not even in the sly manner of Trilling; it does not pit one set of assumptions against another, and does not try to win anything except the reader's assent. Kernan is the defeated humanist, gracious in defeat, telling us what happened. "Literature," he lets us know straight off, "has in the past thirty years or so passed through a time of radical disturbances that turned the institution and its primary values topsy-turvy." A forthright assertion, but also somewhat misleading. For if the diagnosis that follows is to be taken seriously, then literature has not "passed through" anything—it has, like Nietzsche's God, been finished off. Hence the square solemnity of the title, and hence the marshaling of perspectives that lead one to concur and to close the book with the feeling that a new dark age may be upon us.

Just what has happened since Trilling's less-than-rousing profession of hope for literature's future? Kernan begins with a high-altitude survey. The traditional romantic and modernist literary values, he ventures, have been completely reversed. He means, among other things, that the author, once the fount of imagination, the stable center of operations, has been demoted, divested of *authority*; that the historical tradition, represented by the canon, is being disintegrated, and literary history is criticized for being a "diachronic illusion"; that the structure and language of the literary work are undergoing deconstruction; that criticism, formerly subservient to the arts of the imagination, has declared independence and now arrogates to itself equal status; that television and the electronic entertainment culture have encroached upon the preserves of the literary, steadily pushing works of language to the margins . . . And on and on. One does not have to listen hard to hear echoes of the familiar conservative rant, echoes that grow amplified later when Kernan points to the infiltration of academe by various leftist ideologies. But to call something "conservative" is not always to call it untrue. Not only are many of Kernan's assertions on the mark, but so, to a significant degree, is the overall assessment. Literature and the humane values we associate with it have been depreciated, reincarnated in debased form. They have not been extinguished, for our culture will always need to pay lip service to them, but they have been rendered safely, nostalgically, irrelevant.

Think about it. Where in our society do we get so much as an inkling that writers matter? Or their books? A writer needs to have a three-million-dollar bounty on his head before he makes it into the news. And who really heeds those depictions, those more serious renderings of reality, that sit spine-out on the upper shelves of bookstores? The challenging writer is archaic—she goes begging for a publisher, and when she finds one she goes begging for attention. Difficult books have always depended on loyal coteries, but as these have dwindled we find publishers less and less willing to take a chance. Our culture is ruled by the pocketbook, by the psychology of the bottom line. The result is that our arts increasingly cater to the lowest common denominator; they express recognitions that are likely to appeal to a more general audience. And this is how cultural values are shaped and promulgated. Does it matter to be smart or cultivated, or to think about things subtly and at depth? Where do we find any confirmation that artistic refinement or discrimination are desirable—for social purposes or just for themselves? We don't find it anywhere. Certainly not outside whatever small circle of the like-minded we have been able to draw around ourselves. Is literature dead? From the large-scale societal perspective, yes. It is no longer a source of energies or a place of shared recognitions. If literature survives at all, it is as retreat for those who refuse to assimilate to American mass culture.

But, says the cynic—as if this constituted a worthy counterargument—hasn't literature always been dead? I don't think so. It was not dead in William Dean Howells's Ohio as Trilling evoked it. There may have been fewer books and fewer schools, but the public faith in ideas and authors—in the power resident in thoughtful expression—was exponentially greater. And even in Trilling's diminished 1950s one could, if inclined, find circuits quick with literary and intellectual activity. More important, these circuits still mattered. Serious writers were read and honored—at least lip service was paid to them. Thinkers were tapped for their insights by the administrative sector. One could think and write with a sense of mission, not a fear of irrelevance.

What happened? Kernan begins with a grand overview: "The death of literature looks like the twilight of the gods to conservatives or the fall of the Bastille of high culture to radicals, but my argument is, to put it simply, that we are watching the complex transformations of a social institution in a time of radical political, technological, and social change." He then takes up, from a historical vantage, some of the developments that have brought us to our present circumstance.

Kernan wisely begins by reflecting upon the historical evolution of the idea of "literature." I say "wisely" because this tactic persuades us that he will be speaking not with rue about some vanished Eden, but rather with a pragmatist's understanding that literature is a variable construct, a socially determined entity, and not a given.

According to Kernan, and others before him, what we think of as literature really originated in the eighteenth century, prompted in large part by the expansion of mechanized printing and the rise of general literacy. He then discusses the process whereby the verbal arts take on a romantic prestige, rising like cream over the milk of the printed word. In the nineteenth and early twentieth centuries, literature attains the status of art. Moreover, it becomes more powerful and more real as it becomes a social institution, an academic discipline complete with a legitimating history. And although scientific rationalism is increasingly accepted as the official mode of knowledge in modern society, the artist long retains his romantic prestige. He is the keeper of an intuitive power that counters society's shift toward increasing mechanization. But then gradually this begins to change.

In recent decades, Kernan finds, romantic ideas and ideals have lost their vigor; they have been overwhelmed by the utilitarianism they once successfully resisted. The spread of leftist, i.e., Marxist modes of analysis has, in his view, brought about a change in our understanding. We no longer see literature as independent of the capitalist state; it is in cahoots, and works to perpetuate its ideologies. Hence the powerful reaction by academic deconstructionists, feminists, multiculturalists, etc. This will not be the last time that Kernan lays part of the blame at the feet of the sixties' social radicalism.

In his chapter "*Lady Chatterley* and 'Mere Chatter about Shelley': The University Asked to Define Literature," Kernan looks more closely at the academicization of literature, taking up its early struggles for validation: how in England it long suffered as a subdiscipline of the more acceptably rigorous field of philology; how there and in America it suffered because it could not demonstrate its *wissenschaft*, the principles that would legitimate it for scholarly study. Against this background, Kernan establishes—as have Terry Eagleton and others—how the academic pursuit of literature became pledged to formalism. By adopting strict and teachable modes of close reading, the professoriat was able to sell its discipline as one subject to sound methodological procedures. But, as Kernan writes, "Formalism has now passed in turn, and at the moment, the most energetic types of academic literary activity—feminist, deconstructive, new-historicist, Marxist, and psychoanalytic—share a social conception of literature described succinctly by Terry Eagleton as 'modes of feeling, valuing, perceiving and believing which have some kind of relation to the maintenance and reproduction of social power.'"

This, as may be imagined, has led to a sense of destabilization, with so many competing isms that there exists no definitional core to the study of literature. The problem, according to Kernan, besets the discipline at every turn. As a case in point, the obscenity trial in England of *Lady Chatterley's Lover,* which called upon the leading writers and scholars to give some comprehensible definition of literature, yielded an embarrassing array of divergent responses. The upshot was that even those who practice and preach the stuff cannot agree on what it is. But while this would seem to prove that literature is a soft subject, a cognitive blur, I would only point out that a term's indefinability is not always an indicator of its lack of importance. That panel of "experts" would have had an equally hard time settling on a meaning for "love" or "God"—yet surely these terms are not without their existential potency. But Kernan's point is more about academic defensibility, and the consensus seems to be that literary pedagogy cannot stand toe-to-toe with the hard sciences.

The chapter "Authors as Rentiers" takes a different tack. Here Kernan is interested in exploring the professionalization of criticism. He is struck in particular by the treason of the critics: When literature found itself under assault, these individuals, who all along had seen their task as one of legitimation, rose up. They turned, declaring the host body to be in an infernal alliance with capitalist ideology, the patriarchy, and so on.

> The Bastilles of the old literature, the reality of "literature," the creativity of the author, the superiority of authors and literary works to critics and readers, and the integrity of the literary art work, have now all been stormed. The attackers carried many banners, but all were associated with the political radicalism of recent decades, and all drew their authority in varying ways and degrees from two closely connected skepticisms, structuralism and post-structuralism or deconstruction, which were the enabling philosophies of the new left.

I am hard put to disagree with Kernan's first sentence; from the academic perspective, all that he claims has happened has. But I cannot follow him in blaming the leftists, who, or so it seems to me, have as much invested in myths of coherence (the Marxist, the Freudian) as anyone else. I would argue that both structuralism and deconstruction are to be grasped as the inevitable intellectual accompaniment to the fragmenta-

tion and collapse of formerly coherent systems in the face of the communications revolution. Deconstruction is a far better analogue for the
replacement of mechanized systems by circuitries than it is for the assault upon capitalist ideology by leftist radicals. The linguistic indeter-
minacy at the heart of the philosophy allows it to mirror developments
in the culture at large—a culture in which image and presentation have
assumed a substantiality formerly unthinkable.

Kernan does eventually address himself to some of these issues. In
"Technology and Literature: Book Culture and Television Culture," he
outlines some salient features of this massive process of transformation.
Assenting to the basic model proposed decades ago by Marshall
McLuhan, Kernan finds that we are presently changing over from a
print society to an electronic society, a process which, if it has not yet
eliminated the book, is rapidly relegating it to a minor role in the cultural marketplace. He quotes James Kaplan: "The very concept of the
book as an object to be lingered over and palpated, something that seeps
into the soul, has changed. The printed, bound book now represents
one stage in a process which turns out that most unliterary of all quantities: product."

With this diminution of role comes a major sacrifice of authority.
Kernan reports that his students now believe that the computer screen
holds more in the way of truth than does the printed page. That is, they
trust it more. What does he mean? What difference can there be between signs on a screen and signs on a page? Anyone who asks this seriously has yet to grasp the nature of the revolution taking place around
us. Because of the triumph of the screen and the digital program, the
printed page is now a diminished thing. We see it as opaque, finite, not
connected to what we postulate to be the near-transcendental totality of
the data bank. The book dead-ends us in ourselves, whereas the screen
is a sluice into the collective stratum, the place where all facts are known
and all lore is encoded. Kernan makes a similar point, but he mistakenly
invokes television. Television is but one tributary stream in what is now
the bogglingly vast flow of electronic data. If we substitute for TV the
larger term "electronic interaction," Kernan's following observation
makes more sense: "At the deepest level the worldview of television is
fundamentally at odds with the worldview of a literature based on the

printed book. As television watching increases therefore, and more and more people derive, quite unconsciously, their sense of reality and their existential situation in it from television, the assumptions about the world that have been identified with literature will become less and less plausible, and in time will become downright incredible."

This is perhaps the most devastating formulation of the causes of literature's demise. Beside it the rise of deconstruction and other assaulting isms are as nothing. For, in a different climate, literature could well defend itself on its implicit merits. But where the underpinnings have been knocked away, where the rules of the game have been rewritten from top to bottom, there would not seem to be much of a basis from which literature can mount a self-defense. The field no longer belongs to the printed word. And as literature is, in some sense, the apotheosis of the printed word, it is hardly surprising that it should be losing its place in the "knowledge tree."

The knowledge tree, as Kernan explains, is a conception deriving from the Enlightenment era, when the various branches of learning were divided up and assigned their respective places on a schematic branch-bearing tree. This apportionment of place and influence can be seen to underlie both the classification systems of libraries and "the academic structure of major universities as recorded in the catalog with its listing of divisions, departments, and curricula." Kernan continues, "The university not only in general objectifies human intelligence—a matter that always needs reinforcement—but, in the divisions and departments of study, certifies certain modes of knowledge as genuine—astronomy, not astrology—and orders them in relation to one another." And, given the ways in which societal changes have impinged on academic culture, "It remains to be seen whether literature can maintain its place in society's knowledge tree."

This is more or less where Kernan leaves us—holding the end of the question mark like the handle of an umbrella, convinced that the old securities of art will fail us as soon as the weather turns bad. Not a cheerful place to land. But as individuals with an investment in the survival of literary values, we cannot afford to shrug off Kernan's pessimism. We need to explore the terms of the worst-case scenario and see where it leaves us.

This might be the place for a good news/bad news sound bite. The good news is that Kernan's dark assessment focuses mainly on the declining place of literature in the sphere of academe; he does not really extend his analysis into the general culture. The bad news is that, alas, things are not that much better outside the ivied walls. Indeed, what makes Kernan's conclusion so devastating is that the university was long perceived as the last stronghold of serious literature, and yet its overall societal role has been eroding for decades. Let me put it another way. If serious literature were alive and well in the culture (written, published, circulated, read, and discussed), then there would be less reason to fret about the state of things in our institutions of higher learning. But in truth, the voltage is low. Although there are occasional encouraging surges, spurts of interest in novels by African-American women or in worthy works given sudden profile by films (I think of Ishiguro's *Remains of the Day* and Wharton's *Age of Innocence*), these are less a testimony to a keen literary appetite and more the happy consequence of extraliterary events. This is not to depreciate those reading experiences or to wish them away, only to suggest that they do not mark any societal rededication to the word.

The overall situation is bleak and getting bleaker. Talk to anyone engaged in editing, publishing, or teaching the written word. Although significant works still get written, it is harder than ever for them to get published; or, once published, distributed; or once distributed, sold; or once sold, read. The mega-mergers in the communications industry have turned the infamous "bottom line" into a bullwhip that gets cracked over the heads of acquisitions editors. And while serious readers still exist and demonstrate laudable independence—they alone keep literature alive—they also constitute an older section of the population. Book buying and reading have fallen off radically among the under-thirty crowd. And who can guess what the numbers will look like as new generations come of age? These will be the kids born into a preexisting electronic environment, who have soaked in the ambient media options with mother's milk and who have been conditioned to see the book as just one resource among many. It makes perfect sense that trade publishers who once dealt exclusively with printed matter are now diversifying as fast as they can into audio books, CD-ROM, and anything else that will hedge the losses incurred by their paper "product."

There are, then, two ways of looking at the declining prestige of literary culture. One is on the basis of content. The works themselves—the worlds they encode and present—are felt by many to lack relevance. Readers are leaving the book as churchgoers have been leaving the church—because they no longer feel the need of what is to be gotten there. Is literature offering us less, or is it that what is offered is no longer deemed as vital to our well-being?

The other perspective would be that literature has suffered no decline—it is as fit and relevant as ever—but the climate of late modernity, the press of new concerns, has rendered us less able to engage that relevance. Our lives are busy, distracted, multitracked, stressed. We may have altered our cognitive apparatus—speeding up, learning to deal with complex assaults of stimuli—in such a way that we can no longer take in the word as it is meant to be taken in. The price of retooling for the electronic millennium is a sacrifice of the incompatible aptitudes required for reading and meditative introspection. Who among us can generate regularly the stillness and concentration and will to read Henry James, or Joseph Conrad, or James Joyce, or Virginia Woolf as they were meant to be read? And which one of us, when able to do so, does not feel immured in a privacy that has nothing to do with the real business of the world?

The value of literature survives, as W. H. Auden said of poetry, "In the valley of its saying where executives / Would never want to tamper"—but it is a value that fewer and fewer people feel they cannot live without. If, by contrast, more people felt the need, they would buy and read, and if they did so, if they bought in droves, then publishers would not feel the lash of the bottom line. And all things would be well, or better. But alas, it is not so. Literature—serious fiction and poetry and the discourse that has always accompanied them and helped make them a way of talking about important and difficult aspects of our universal experience—all of literature now occupies the place marked out by Auden as the estate of poetry. Which is to say: It is not extinct, it has its partisans, it makes its small noise, but does so as the big parade of the rest of the world goes clattering by.

And here again we are back to Trilling's observation in "Reality in America" about the "chronic American belief that there exists an opposition between reality and mind and that one must enlist oneself in the party of reality." In that essay Trilling used "reality" to refer to the material, the palpably manifest, that which Dreiser lumberingly got his hands around. Things are somewhat different now. The dominant reality that we all live in the midst of, and in terms of, is not so much the reality of smokestacks and bricks, of hard durable goods—it is the reality of impulses and mediated information. Reality comes in over the screen, the phone line, the fax, the radio. But for all the difference this makes, we are collectively no more hospitable to the mind than before. Don't forget: When Trilling speaks of mind he does not mean the exercise of capacity for abstract intellection. He really means inwardness, sensibility, the incessant making of discriminations regarding human character, values, affections, and so forth. The Dreiserian citizen is alive and well. Astonishingly, we are able to carry on the business of living without too much distracting fuss about meaning or purpose. If we can't, if the automatic pilot falters and we are overwhelmed by doubts or incapacities, we take the self in for repairs—to a therapist or a doctor who can prescribe the right pharmaceuticals. But this meltdown, this excessive preoccupation with intangibles, is felt by the majority to indicate an imbalance, a lack of fitness. That we live all day among buttons and signals instead of tools and materials has not brought us appreciably closer to the interior. It has, if anything, made us less available to the kinds of self-inspection that enlightened living would demand.

I grant that I am looking at the dark side. But this does not mean that I have adopted Kernan's title, "death of literature," as my own mantra. Although I pull naturally toward the graver side of the spectrum, I am not entirely without hope. I will explain my reasons shortly.

First, however, I need to recapitulate and underline my two principal assumptions. One, I believe that, as Marshall McLuhan originally theorized (and as Kernan has reaffirmed), we are in the midst of an epoch-making transition; that the societal shift from print-based to electronic communications is as consequential for culture as was the shift instigated by Gutenberg's invention of movable type. If this fact has not yet struck home, if everyone is not yet agog over it, it is in part because the news of the change is still being delivered slowly, piecemeal, by way of the entrenched agencies of print. This circuit-driven renovation is happening in every sector, on every level, and the momentum will not slacken until the electronic web has woven itself into every potentially profitable crevice. Ten, fifteen years from now the world will be nothing like what we remember, nothing much like what we experience now. We will still wear clothes and live in dwellings, but our relation to the space-time axis will be very different from what we have lived with for millennia. We will be swimming in impulses and data—the microchip will make us offers that will be very hard to refuse. And the old, solid, dense, obstacle-ridden world that we know from historical legend (or, if we are old enough, from our youth) will recede into memory.

My second assumption, which pertains to literature, is that while circuit and screen are ideal conduits for certain kinds of data—figures, images, cross-referenced information of all sorts—they are entirely inhospitable to the more subjective materials that have always been the stuff of art. That is to say, they are antithetical to inwardness. There are a number of reasons for this, but the main one has to do with time. Quite simply, inward experience, including all aesthetic experience, unfolds in one kind of time; electronic communications, of their very nature, depend upon—indeed *create*—another. The time of the self is deep time, duration time, time that is essentially characterized by our obliviousness to it. To the degree that we immerse ourselves in a book, listen to music, sink into the visual realm of a painting—to that degree we surrender our awareness of the present as a coordinate on a grid. We relinquish the governing construct of the now, exchanging it for content, feeling, and absorption. All circuit-driven communications, by contrast, are predicated upon instantaneousness. To use them, to interact with them, requires that we enter a kind of virtual *now*—the perpetual present tense of the impulse, of the beep, the flickering cursor. We often hear people speak of cyberspace, a term for that peculiar no-place wherein data are held and through which they pass, the place we inhabit when we are on-line. I propose that we coin the companion term "cybertime" so that we can designate the limbo we suspend ourselves in as we perform these operations.

If our world is being refashioned from top to bottom by circuit-driven technologies, if our activities will be ever more completely governed by these same technologies, and if their fundamental nature is opposed to the inward orientation of all true art, then we are in great danger of collectively sacrificing a very precious, indeed a defining part of our experience. The philosopher Martin Heidegger, who was deeply interested in the problem of technology, called it the "forgetting of being" and saw it as the malaise of our age. What I undertook to discuss as the "death of literature" is finally so much more than that. The phrase can be considered as a shorthand tag for the progressive atrophy of all that defines us as creatures of spirit.

This is as far as I want to go in the direction of darkness. While I think about these matters often, I do not in my heart of hearts embrace their necessity. As I suggested earlier, I am not altogether without hope. Let me explain why.

To speak seriously and with a genuine sense of finality about the death of literature is to speak of the eclipse of a whole set of cultural impulses. I do not anticipate a future utterly without books, or bereft of all discourse about ideas, or entirely given over to utilitarian pursuits. No, what I fear is a continued withering-away of influence, a diminution of the literary which brings about a flattened new world in which only a small coterie traffics in the matters that used to be deemed culturally central. My nightmare scenario is not one of neotroglodytes grunting and wielding clubs, but of efficient and prosperous information managers living in the shallows of what it means to be human and not knowing the difference. I fear a world become sanitized and superficial, in which people have forgotten the primal terms of existence—the terrors and agons—and in which the existential unknown is banished outside the pulsing circulation system of data. A world so immersed in the lateral present that the depths and the difficulties of history have become a chimera, a media resource. A world in which history is Spielberg's *Schindler's List* and Schindler himself has been swallowed up by the attractive screen presence of Liam Neeson.

The truth is that I am divided in myself. What I express here is only my fever dream of the future, not my whole imagining. I set it down to purge myself, and to serve as a warning. I can also imagine some less-dire scenarios that depend upon a more generous estimate of human nature.

I do believe, like any good Freudian, that there is an economy of the psyche, that our attributes and impulses are not undivided, but have their counterparts and opposites. We are, in other words, host to a full array of drives, and these rise and fall as they carry on their long-term battles for ascendancy. I also believe (although some of my observations may appear to belie this) that we are, as a species, wired for meaning. Avoid self-inquiry as we may, there remains a powerful part of the psyche that needs, indeed, creates meaning. We all share a dread and fascination with the unknown; we are haunted by time and memory; we are shot through with spiritual impulses. The Dreiserian sense of reality as tangible may be dominant, and we may disparage the Jamesian preoccupation with ideas and stirrings of sensibility, but they live in us nonetheless. And the more we tamp them down, ignore them, the greater the repression charge they accumulate. Right now it is the Dreiserian side of our nature that our electronic technologies are serving. The data that flow through the circuits, abstract as they may be, are data about that reality, as are the images that wash across our high-resolution screens. The circuit does not serve the ghost of Henry James very well. But that ghost is not about to go away—and in this I place whatever small faith I have in the future of literature.

If we are wired for meaning, and if psyche is a closed system—two big ifs—then it follows, as Freud would agree, that repressed elements return. They rebound, burst forth, erupt, very possibly in unexpected ways. Our relentless focus on external matters, our near-exclusive preoccupation with vaulting the techno-hurdles—which are necessary, of course, to bring about any substantial societal transformation—may be creating what firefighters call a "backdraft": a depletion so severe that it can result in a sudden explosion. We witnessed one such blast in the 1960s in the emergence, seemingly overnight, of a counterculture. Journalists and pop historians have, I think, routinely misunderstood what happened then. The sixties were only incidentally about drugs or sexual experimentation or rock and roll—these were epiphenomena. They were about protest, yes, in part against our government's intervention in Southeast Asia, but no less against the social structures that stood in the way of the pursuit of meaning. The counterculture represented a kind of American Revolution against the tyranny of tired elders—a revolution on behalf of emotional expression, spirituality, modes of exchange and cooperation not based on capital. The sixties were about turning away from kinds of industry and commerce that had crippled the natural human reflexes; they were thus about communal living, rural enterprise, and migration. The period was excessive, often lending itself to caricature—face paint and beads and peace signs and LSD tripsters—and they have not worn well in the historical chronicle. But their excessive, deformed character was largely a result of the force of the blast, of the backdraft. The impulses, blown out so suddenly, took on shapes that were occasionally grotesque. Had they emerged more gradually, or had they not been so repressed in the first place . . . But then, things can always be imagined differently.

I linger on this period because it is relevant to our situation. These are different times, and there are different forces at work, but we are again in a period of extreme imbalance. Our societal and cultural energies are being disproportionately exerted on behalf of outward things. We embrace the computer revolution, the information highway, with the zeal of children presented with a new toy. We are, I believe, in typical American fashion, approaching another crisis. A crisis of meaning. Not this year or next year. It will take some time for the strands of the fiber to be stretched, and for the fizz of new headline developments to build—all the new linkages, mergers, innovations; all the forecasts about the arrival of the electronic millennium. But slowly, steadily, we may see the pressure build, and with it the awareness in individuals of a vacancy at the subjective core, a gnawing sense of need. Certain suppressed fears will grow until they reach the awareness threshold—mainly the fear that this much-touted capability is lacking something essential, that all the tapping of keys and monitoring of monitors cannot slake some irrational deeper wanting. And when the crisis does come, no chip or screen will have a solution for it. It will flash forth as an insistent need, a soul craving, and nothing binary will suffice.

I predict three possible outcomes, or collective reactions to this crisis. One, a return to religion—to churches, temples, ashrams—to all the places that have traditionally served as repositories of the sacred. Whatever else they may be, our religions are grand stories that make a place for us. Two, I would expect to see a rush to therapy, the resort of choice for those who are experiencing a sense of emergency in secular terms. People will pay and pay to counter the distracted drift of the perpetual present with some explanatory narrative that has a purchase on time, on history. The fragmented self will be brought to trained professionals for reconstitution.

And three, I see the possibility of a genuine resurgence of the arts, of literature in particular. This may be wishful thinking—our electronic conditioning may leave us unfit for the rigors of stationary words on a page—but grant me the wish. For literature remains the unexcelled means of interior exploration and connection-making. The whole art— fiction, poetry, and drama—is fundamentally pledged to coherence, not just in terms of contents, but in forms as well. The structures of language represent a doorway back into duration. This is what makes reading so very difficult in the cultural present: We cannot easily get off the rails of one kind of time to reexperience another. But perhaps when the need is strong enough we will seek out the word on the page, and the work that puts us back into the force field of deep time. The book—and my optimism, you may sense, is not unwavering—will be seen as a haven, as a way of going off-line and into a space sanctified by subjectivity. So long as there is a natural inclination toward independent selfhood, so long will literature be able to prove the reports of its death exaggerated.

# 14

# The Narrowing Ledge

BACK IN THE ROMANTIC DAYS of Hollywood hype, there was a film—no, a *movie*—called *Youngblood Hawke.* It was based on a novel of that name by Herman Wouk, which was in turn loosely based on the story of Thomas Wolfe, that prolific colossus of prewar American fiction. James Franciscus played the eponymous Hawke with the kind of tight intensity that was then—this was in 1964—in vogue. I remember in particular some early sequences. Hawke, a young man living in rural isolation, is in the grip of inspiration. Through the long night he sits at his desk working on his novel. Typing, maybe even writing longhand. He is in a fever; he must get his vision onto the page. When he finishes the book, he wraps it in brown paper and posts it to a New York publisher. Time passes. Then one day he opens the mailbox and finds the letter we all dream about. His novel has been accepted—he must come to New York right away! The rest of the story, as I recall, obeys the conventions. The novel is published, wins great acclaim, and the humble small-town boy becomes the talk of the town, prey to venal dealmakers and hard, sophisticated women.

But I'm not interested here in the fine points of the plot or the morality of the tale it unfolds. I am far more intrigued by how thoroughly all of the terms of the premise have changed. Granted, *Youngblood Hawke* is a Hollywood fantasy, but if you factor out the romanticism you still get an image of the writer's idealized status in the culture of the time. The fact that Franciscus is playing a heroic lead speaks volumes. And indeed, there was a time when writers worked in isolation and spoke in terms of realizing their visions on the page; when

editors at publishing houses actively sought and worked to refine literature of quality; when that literature could land in the marketplace and
perhaps make a splash, elevating the author to a certain cultural star-
dom. There was a time (1961) when publisher Alfred A. Knopf himself
could print on the front dust jacket of a massive two-volume novel
called *The Demons* the following:

> One evening in September 1957, looking over the TLS and running
> my eye down a four-column article called "The Austrian Scene," I
> was arrested by the following: "To talk of demons is to think of
> Heimito von Doderer's *Dämonen,* a book which seals his reputation
> as the most formidable German-speaking novelist now living."
> Strong words these, and they sent me hot-footedly after the Doderer
> novel. It turned out to be a volume of 1,348 pages, offering the most
> formidable problems to a translator, and the certainty of a huge
> printing, paper, and binding bill to the publisher who would attempt
> to bring it out in English. Nevertheless, I couldn't deny that I would
> feel very sad indeed if it were to appear on any other list than ours.

When people argue, as they do often these days, about whether
writing and publishing and reading have really changed—the optimists
accusing the pessimists of false nostalgia—they would do well to read
Mr. Knopf's statement closely and to think hard about what it suggests
about shifts in our literary culture. This culture has mutated, by degrees,
of course, so as to be almost unrecognizable from the days when the independent house of Knopf ruled the roost. And yet people tell me all the
time that there's no real problem—more books are published and sold
than ever in the past, that work of quality has the same chance it ever
did, and so forth.

They are wrong. Everything has changed in the past quarter century, with the changes hitting their real momentum in the past decade
or so. Today's Youngblood Hawke is not banging keys at a rude table,
but most likely sits ensconced before his terminal, processing. When he
finishes his masterwork, he does not get out the brown paper and
string—he sends the book (or maybe just the disk) to his agent. Fed Ex,
of course. And if that agent can land the book, there are negotiations;
agent and publisher tussle over ad budgets, film and electronic rights,

and promo tours. The editor will seldom, as Thomas Wolfe's legendary Maxwell Perkins did, work with the manuscript to bring it to final artistic completion; the editor's main function these days is acquisition. And when publication time comes, the odds of today's young writer taking New York by storm are slim, to say the least. His book has a two-month window, and unless the reviews are prodigal with praise, unless there is a carefully choreographed twelve-city reading tour with TV and radio talk-show spots, the book will probably disappear—it will get shipped back to the publisher and await its afterlife as a remainder.

But even these shifts, significant as they are, are as nothing to the real transformation, which is that of the cultural context. There is no denying that a terrible prestige-drop has afflicted books themselves. They have moved from center to margin; the terms of their mattering are nothing like they used to be. You do not have to be a writer, a publisher, or a critic to see this. Anyone who pays attention knows that writing and reading are not what it's about these days. It is almost impossible to imagine a major trade publisher thinking as Knopf did, saying of a difficult and important work, "I couldn't deny that I would feel very sad indeed if it were to appear on any other list than ours."

What has happened? The explanation must be many-stranded, for what we have are many forces in complex interrelation. On the publishing front, with the rash of corporate takeovers of formerly independent companies, economics have almost entirely displaced any notion of cultural service. What gets printed and how is in the last analysis determined by the stockholder; the quarterly profit/loss statement cares not whether it is James Joyce or Joyce Elbert there on the page—just so the figures are good.

We can also blame the massive inroads made by the electronic media culture. The technologies of entertainment—MTV, video games, expanded channel options, and VCRs—have arrived with great fanfare, diminishing audiences for the book, allowing watching and playing to supplant reading as a dominant home activity. The gathered concentration of the act is no longer our central cultural paradigm. Moreover, these technologies have begun to exert a conditioning impact upon their users. They not only take up time that might have once belonged to the book, but they make it harder, once we do turn from the screen, to engage the single-focus requirement of reading. Reading is taught, of course, and books are assigned in school, but any teacher you ask will tell you that it is getting harder and harder to sell the solitary one-on-one to students. The practice itself is changing. Already it is clear that the new reading will be technology-enhanced. CD-ROM packages are on the way—some are already out—to gloss and illustrate, but also to break the perceived tedium of concentration by offering interactivity options and the seductions of collage-creation. Don't just crack your brain on *Hamlet,* but pull up pictures of famous actors and directors and read some sidebar interviews, even view clips of scenes in performance. After interactivity has made its first full inroad there will be no going back.

And so we ride the transformation. At the university level, where cultural attitudes are shaped and disseminated, we find that the premises that used to underwrite literature and buttress its prestige—premises about the centrality of author and text—are under attack. The legacy of the 1980s was a demolition of textual sovereignty and an assault on the very idea of authorship (a generation of literature majors cut its teeth on Roland Barthes's essay "The Death of the Author"). And, of course, the canon itself, that collection of so-called "great" works legitimized by rank upon rank of white male gatekeepers, is coming unraveled even as I write.

These are just the headline developments, but taken together they explain a good deal about why Youngblood Hawke isn't feeling so well these days.

But to go further, I would suggest that Youngblood Hawke is no longer viable as fantasy not just because of changes in publishing and the arrival of diverse electronic playthings, but also because he has begun to lose his emblematic attractiveness. Mr. Hawke was, in the literary sphere, the apotheosis of subjective individualism. He was of the era of Ayn Rand's Howard Roark and Saul Bellow's Augie March. Hawke was projected as an independent man with a vision, who through determination and ability conquered all obstacles and scaled the heights. He represented, in other words, the American pioneer ideal—the frontiersman, the homesteader, the gunfighter, the industrialist. His day has passed because his particular virtues, his strength and dogged independence, have themselves become outmoded.

Again, the forces making the change are extremely complex. But the overall tendency can be identified. As our culture is rapidly becoming electronic, we are less and less what we were, a society of isolated individuals. We are hurrying to get on-line, and the natural corollary to this is that the idea of individuality must come under siege. If you take all of our technological innovations of the past two decades—certainly those in the fields of computing and communications—you cannot fail to see that their collective tendency is to breach the wall of isolated selfhood and to swamp us in an element of connectedness. This connectedness can be either potential or actual—for whether we use our technologies (e-mail, beepers, computer networks) or not, our implicit social status is altered. And the momentum toward ever-greater interconnectedness is growing rapidly. In time we will all live, at least partially, inside a kind of network consciousness, subject at every level to mediation. How will we know this has happened? We will know by our sense of distance from the natural world, and by our loss of the experience of deep time. Our spells of unbroken subjective immersion will become rarer and rarer, and may even vanish altogether.

Although the attainment of network consciousness will mean many things, both good and bad, it will certainly spell the further decline of the kind of inwardness needed for serious reading. And this can only be bad news for the writing culture, at least as we understand it now.

We are evolving—at least, we are changing. The whole notion of inwardness, represented by the image of the serious artist, the rebel-explorer, is undergoing transformation. As technology gets more sophisticated, as it proliferates, and as population centers continue to grow, we will inevitably become more hive-like about our human engagements. Our collective ideals will change, as they have already this past quarter century. The old celebration of subjective individualism, romanticized in film and fiction, gratified certain societal needs. It was, in a sense, an evolutionary necessity: There were frontiers that needed conquering. Now we have other ideals to celebrate, ones that mirror our new situation. We no longer prize the loner, the dreamer, the disaffected protester, or the tormented misfit. These are now emblems of dysfunctionality. Our ads and speeches and TV specials are starting to promote speed, control, expertise, teamwork, and the ability to manage and direct vast quantities of information. Bill Clinton and Al Gore are the heroes of the new dispensation.

Of course, we see traces of the opposite as well. The transition to the on-line society, happening on so many levels at once, will not be effected without bumps or the provocation of certain contrary forces. Human nature does, it's true, bend toward ease; we do fall in with the pattern of progress, especially here in America. But there are also strongly conservative elements in our makeup. We invested a great deal in our ideals of individuality; they got us where we are and are part of our mythos. So we can expect that even as we slip into the web of neural linkages, we will also find ourselves susceptible to fantasies of the prior state. There is a law of compensation that is as absolute as anything described in physics. Our fantasies, banished from our own fidgety instrument-driven lives, will be, as they are already, the basis of our entertainment culture. As we get more boxed in, less physical in our engagements, the screen will douse us with more and more gunfire and spurting blood. The same person who passes his day moving information from place to place via codes punched into the terminal comes home to watch Schwarzenegger going hand-to-hand with spectacular evil. There is no contradiction. The discharge of the fantasy is what allows for such smooth bureaucratic functioning in the light of day.

Not everything, to be sure, gets enacted on the flat screen. Millions of readers still turn the pages of books, though not many of those books necessarily qualify as literature. More than a few people have asked me in the past year how I explain the enormous popular success of Robert James Waller's Madison County books. Although I haven't read either *The Bridges of Madison County* or *Slow Waltz in Cedar Bend,* I answer with full confidence: They are selling the reader a fantasy of individuality and freewheeling independence at a moment when we are all unconsciously trying to come to terms with the loss of those ideals in our lives. The books are not harbingers of anything; they are well-timed glances into the rearview mirror. The desire for self-assured subjective independence is bound to flare up in the eleventh hour, just when the societal space for it has all but disappeared.

But, to turn the focus back to the outlook for serious fiction, where do we stand? I have already suggested that things do not bode well for the enterprise just now. Not only for the reasons I suggested—economics, technology, and changing social ideals—but also for reasons pertaining more directly to writing itself. The writer, of fiction in particular, is now forced to face the crisis of subject matter. Serious literary works have always derived their artistic value, their importance, from the fact that they comprehended the changing terms of our world and gave us narratives that could help us understand the forces impinging on our lives. This core premise has been shaken, and a quick look at the history of the genre will make it clear why.

Once fiction emerged from its childhood and puberty in the oral storytelling tradition, it pledged itself to representation, to realism. Stendhal defined the novelist as a man carrying a mirror along a muddy road. In its glory days in the nineteenth century, the novel served mainly as a lens upon the intricate social choreography of a stratified society (see Eliot, Austen, Balzac, Tolstoy, Thackeray, et al.). In our century, as the stratified landmass tilted and buckled, the social compass constricted and the novel shifted its concern to the individual; it became the medium par excellence of psychological investigation (as in Woolf, Joyce, Conrad, Lawrence, Ford, Forster . . . ). And here the novel essentially remains: outwardly realistic in its depictions of milieu—of family as well as larger social networks—and psychological in its presentations of character.

Alas, this is no longer enough—and has not been for some time. For one thing, the novel (with a few important exceptions) has not been able to keep up with societal mutation. Some decades ago it lost its grip on the dominant features of contemporaneity and it has not been able to assess the impact of these features on the lives of individuals. For another thing, the law of diminishing returns has been operative, insuring that the old standby programs of fiction are less and less able to gratify readers. The result is a grand fatigue, a pervasive sense of genre depletion. The prestige of the art sinks yearly. Sad, but true: Fiction only retains its cultural vitality so long as it can bring readers meaningful news about what it means to live in the world of the present. Its other functions—escapism, reassurance, entertainment—are ultimately trivial.

This is not to say, of course, that the classics are useless, or that their readings of human character do not continue to bear upon the present. It *is* to say that the vitality of fiction—of literature—must be measured on the pulses in the here and now: How does the living writer serve the living reader? All the rest is scholarship.

The problem is one of representation, or representability. What no one seems to be acknowledging, what is at the root of the crisis of the art, is the fact that the nature of reality, of the average person's *experience* of reality, has changed, changed utterly. At some point in the last decades a condition of critical mass was attained. Incremental changes on many fronts combined with an alchemical subtlety and altered the whole feel of things. It was not just television or the moon-landing or the microchip—it was all these things, and a thousand others, exerting force on each other. The transformation? Fifty years ago the human environment was still more or less the natural environment. We had central heating and labor-saving devices and high-speed travel, but these were still only partial modifications of the natural given. It is the natural given that is now gone. Now, for better or for worse, we move almost entirely within a regulated and mediated environment. Our primary relation to the world has been altered.

Consider this fantasia of the average day of the average American businessman. He wakens to the sound of the clock radio, pads to the bathroom where he shaves his bristles to the background noise of a television news program, which tells him every minute what time it is and updates him almost as often on the weather. He finishes his coffee while he ties his tie, blasts a croissant in the microwave and carries it along to the car to enjoy on his way to work. The electric garage door lifts, the machine eases forth. Through tinted window glass he notes the look of the sky. The radio has more talk of the weather, some chatter about last night's ball game. He thinks about his office day as he hurtles along the expressway, zeroes in on priorities as he guides the car down the ramp into the office garage. An elevator then carries him into the building, and the business day begins. Check e-mail, listen to stored messages. Hours pass as he swivels in front of his computer. The long day unfolds in carpeted and climate-controlled rooms, under the crackle of fluorescents. If he has the energy, he takes an hour for racquetball. A yogurt and a roll. More calls, more moving of data. And as the sun sets over the glass towers of his metropolis, he hurries home to dinner, some Nintendo with the kids, and a few cold ones in front of "NYPD Blue." There are days, quite a few in fact, when our man does not set foot in what used to be known as the outdoors.

This *is* a bit overdone, granted, but there is truth in it, too. It is not my intention to pass judgment on this life—not here, anyway—but I will ask the obvious question. If you are a writer committed to the project of writing about your times, how do you write this life, this experience, into your fiction? How do you give Mr. Case's life a meaningful, never mind dramatic, contour? Well, you say, I would not choose to write about Mr. Case. And I agree, he's not optimum fiction fodder. But suppose that more and more people lived lives like this. And suppose this mode became the dominant reality of the times. What do you do then, as a writer pledged to exploring the present? Do you look for language that would accurately depict the monochrome nature of that experience? Or do you do something else—mock, ironize, wreak imaginative havoc?

Well, this is the problem facing the fiction writer in our time. Not only must he figure out what to do about the flatness of quotidian experience, but he must also deal with the fact that the greater part of human activities—which once may have stood out in relief—now take place on many tracks at once, with the individual in a state of distracted absorption. When we face our neighbor across the garden hedge we are more or less present to the exchange—gesturing, processing gestures, listening, offering our views—we are more or less *there*. The same two people talking on the phone are engaged in something altogether different. One is making faces at his daughter and stirring a pot on the stove; the other is adding up the charges from last month's phone bill. If you are a writer of fiction, unless the ironies of distraction *are* your point, you eschew describing the telephone conversation. And the hours that the protagonist spends noodling about in hyperspace, and the vacuousness of the afternoon commute, and . . . What *do* you write about? How do you tell the story of a man or woman living in the here and now, and tell it compellingly?

If you are Robert Stone, you remove your character from his electronic womb and set him afloat on the high seas so that he may find out what is really there, whether he has a heart, a soul. If you are Nicholson Baker, writing *The Mezzanine,* you take the banal features of the individual's life and you subject them to such a degree of aesthetic focus that they become intriguing. You modify scale, describe at length the plastic contours of the coffee cup, the topology of its die-stamped sipping lid. But if you are most other writers, you change the subject. You move into the past, into the 1950s or 1960s, say; or you betake yourself to some more rural place where the mediation is not yet so total; or you import some crime, some colorful street life. Any number of things. All of which amount to an implicit indictment of contemporaneity. For the daily life of the average American has become Teflon for the novelist.

You have a better chance of connecting with the present if you abjure realism and follow the path taken by writers like Don DeLillo, Thomas Pynchon, Paul Auster, William Gaddis, and a few others. Which is to say: make the irreality of the present part of the subject itself; irradiate situations with black humor and surrealistic touches.

All of these writers are writing as they do, I suspect, because they understand that the deeper truth of things can no longer be expressed in sequential realistic narrative. But these writers, with the possible exception of DeLillo and Auster, are little read. Their essentially dark outlook, and their recourse to elliptical stylistic techniques to register that outlook, makes their work daunting to readers raised on conventional fiction. Which is more than just a shame. It also reveals the central paradox facing the writer who would still try to address the present-day world in significant terms. Simply put, the more faithful you are to your truth, the more deeply you see into the dynamics of what is taking place on all sides, the less of a chance there is that your version of things will get published, or, if published, bought and read.

Youngblood Hawke is gone, along with the heroic posturings of Hemingway and Steinbeck. When Mailer tries on the act it looks quite silly. No one thinks any longer about writing the Great American Novel. To see what has become of Hawke, as of the early 1990s, we need only read Don LeLillo's *Mao II.* There we meet Bill Gray, writer as underground man. Gray is a brooding recluse, an old-school aspirant who is savvy enough to see how things stand with the art. Although he continues to write, to exercise his private compulsion, he does not publish. He makes searching and dispirited observations:

> The novel used to feed our search for meaning. . . . It was the great secular transcendence. The Latin mass of language, character, occasional new truth. But our desperation has led us toward something larger and darker. So we turn to the news, which provides an unremitting mood of catastrophe. This is where we find emotional experience not available elsewhere. We don't need the novel.

Bill Gray, the last novelist to still work on a typewriter.

The writer's social and cultural status is as low as it has been for centuries. If there is anything consoling to be said, it is that the *need* for the writer is right now probably as great as ever. As electronic communications continue to gain ascendence, as the logic of systems overwhelms independent initiative, as it must, then we will very likely enter upon a crisis of meaning such as has not been seen since the postwar period in Europe. The primary questions will again be asked with urgency, for insofar as we secure a sense of identity through what we do in the world, to that degree we will have to admit that we have lost existential purchase. The efficiency of the great circuits—which we will soon enough all be hooked into and serving—is a direct function of their abstractness. We may, it's true, evolve to accommodate their functioning, but the millennia of isolated selfhood, spooled in the genes, will not just vanish. Adaptation will not come without some storms of cognitive dissent.

Into the place of confusion comes, or should come, the writer. His art has the singular advantage that it can simulate inward process and explore states of consciousness in ways not available to film, music, or other expressive arts. The writer ought to be able, with some ingenuity, to find ways to dramatize—and maybe protest—this unprecedented collective occurrence. Here is the subject of subjects: the human individual facing the prospect of the erasure of independent selfhood. If the writer has ever needed a task fitted to his lofty aspirations, this is it: exploring the place of the renegade self in a world become inhospitable to the very idea of selves. As DeLillo puts it so tersely in *Mao II*, "The future belongs to crowds." Bill Gray, his protagonist, observes:

> There's a curious knot that binds novelists and terrorists. In the West
> we become famous effigies as our books lose the power to shape and
> influence. . . . Years ago I used to think it was possible for a novelist
> to alter the inner life of the culture. Now bomb-makers and gunmen
> have taken that territory. They make raids on human consciousness.
> What writers used to do before we were all incorporated.

The novelist worried about what tack to take in the future might find a
clue, a purpose, here. If literature is to survive, to gain back some of the
power it has ceded to terrorists and newsmakers of all descriptions, it
must become dangerous. That is, it must throw up a serious challenge
to the emergent status quo; it must shake and provoke people even as it
leads them back toward a reconnaissance of selfhood. The novel will not
endure because it can entertain (although certainly it can), but because
it offers an essential experience available nowhere else. Through language, which makes of the page a place of focus and immersion, the
writer gives the reader the deeper picture of things, the picture he might
assemble for himself if only he had the time, the concentration, and the
imaginative penetration.

This is a bet on long odds. It assumes that the writer will, for survival's sake, find new, perhaps nonrealist ways to capture the urgency of
changing circumstances. It assumes, too, that people will, out of a vestigial craving for meaning, or out of a sinking dread at what their lives
have become, turn again to writers for the news they need. If nothing
like this happens, then the writer will take a place beside the scrimshaw
artist in the museum of hallowed but ultimately useless crafts.

# Coda:

## *The Faustian Pact*

I'VE BEEN TO THE CROSSROADS and I've seen the devil there. Or is that putting it too dramatically? What I'm really saying is that I've been to the newsstand, again, to plunk down my money for *Wired*. You must have seen it—that big, squarish, beautifully produced item, that travel guide to the digital future. To read the magazine and to look at it (one does spend a great deal of time *looking* at *Wired*, checking out the ads, turning it this way and that to follow the little typographic trails) is almost to be persuaded that the future is here and that it can work. That ingenuity, design intelligence, and the capabilities of the microchip will soon liberate the world entirely from its sooty industrial roots. *Wired* gives us our old planet repackaged as a weightless environment, more dream than matter—information moving through cyberspace at the speed of thought (*intelligent* thought), with interactive resources putting people in control, allowing them to tailor the "fit" of their experience; digitally programmed words and visuals and sounds coalescing in ever-fresh multimedia combinations; pools of the like-minded gathering into networks, establishing grassroots power bases via Internet; virtual reality opening up realms of sensation, dazzling retreats just adjacent to our own ever more depleted world . . . and so on.

The ads and the graphics are finally more seductive than the excitable proselytizing of the writers. We are taken most by the *look* of it all—the compact, crisp, high-resolution design that inspires confidence, that allows us to revere the near-mystical power of the concealed microprocessors. Bold colors, sans serif type fonts, unexpected layouts. Everything orchestrated to say: *That was then, this is now.* Alongside

*Wired,* dominantly print-driven vehicles like *The New Yorker* or even *The Paris Review* look dowdy, Victorian. Unbroken columns of print suddenly seem like visual molasses.

Yes, I've been to the crossroads and I've met the devil, and he's sleek and confident, ever so much more "with it" than the nearest archangel. He is casual and irreverent, wears jeans and running shoes and maybe even an earring, and the pointed prong of his tail is artfully concealed. Slippery fellow. He is the sorcerer of the binary order, jacking in and out of terminals, booting up, flaming, commanding vast systems and networks with an ease that steals my breath away. I don't hate him—I admire and fear him, and I wonder, as I did in high school when confronted with the smooth and athletic ones, the team captains and class presidents, whether I would not, deep down, trade in all this doubting and wondering and just be him.

I have heard pornographic books and magazines referred to as "masturbation aids." *Wired* is, for me, of that ilk—except that it does not get me thinking dirty thoughts, it just gets me thinking. But I use it as one might use something from the aforementioned category: to put me on a very specific mind-track. I buy the magazine and read it and study it in order to engage myself in what I think of as the argument of our time—the argument between technology and soul. Every time I open the covers and find myself slipping into that most beguiling reverie of the near future, I have to ask: Is this what we want? Do we know what we're doing? Do people understand that there might be consequences, possibly dire, to our embrace of these technologies, and that the myth of the Faustian bargain has not become irrelevant just because we studied it in school?

To me it is very clear that the process is well underway and that it is not likely to stop. From our president on down people are smitten, more than they have been with anything in a very long time. I can't open a newspaper without reading another story about Internet or the information highway. The dollar, not the poet, is the antenna of the race, and right now the dollar is all about mergers and acquisitions, as seen in the bidding war for Paramount, the fierce battles being waged for control of the system that will wire us each to each and will allow us, soon enough, to cohabit in the all-but-infinite information space. If we are separate on earth because of geography and physics (two bodies cannot inhabit the same space), we will be piled together like transparent wafers in cyberspace. The dollar is smart. It is betting that the trend will be a juggernaut, unstoppable; that we are collectively ready to round the corner into a new age. The dollar is betting, as it always does, against the soul.

*Soul*—a vast, elusive word, and I need to be careful not to use it indiscriminately. What do I mean by it? Although I don't want to rule out its religious sense, I am not using it, as believers have for centuries, to designate the part of ourselves that is held to be immortal. My use of soul is secular. I mean it to stand for inwardness, for that awareness we carry of ourselves as mysterious creatures at large in the universe. The soul is that part of us that smelts meaning and tries to derive a sense of purpose from experience. It is the *I* that speaks when we say, "I've always believed . . ." as opposed to the *I* we refer to when we say "I went to get the car fixed this morning." I don't know that I can get more precise about it—I don't know that precision is called for. Soul is our inwardness, our self-reflectiveness, our orientation to the unknown. Soul waxes in private, wanes in public. We feel it, or feel through it, when we are in sacral spaces, when we love, when we respond to natural or artistic beauty. Soul may be elicited in many ways. We comprehend it unthinkingly—we either know it as a resonance, a presence, or we deduce it, negatively, from a feeling of absence. When we cannot get clear, cannot feel the importance of something we know to be important; when we harken to images that take us from the present that we feel trapped in: images of childhood, of isolated retreat in nature. Except in situations we deem communal, where we have communion with other souls, soul is private. Solitary. Said Emily Dickinson, "The soul selects its own society." And as I write this I think that, yes, there is something Dickinsonian, something tremulous and antiquated about it all. I hear ticking clocks and footsteps in empty houses. The inward self collects around a center, defines itself in its separation from others. What an odd notion. I see Old Nick winking and I find myself wondering if we might not indeed be ready to push onto something new, to put behind us once and for all this melancholy business of isolated selves trudging through a vale of tears.

This is where I often end up when I start thinking about these things—I feel as though a train has gone racing by, leaving me on the platform watching the swirl of candy wrappers. Yet, were the train to stop for me, I would not get on. Something holds me back, a fear not unlike what I've known on the brink of certain relationships. Then I held back because I sensed that to plunge would be to change myself as a person. Not a bad thing necessarily, but just not what I wanted then. The disinclination I feel about the digital future is stronger, more certain, but the fear grows from the same root. I see the situation in Faustian terms, as an either/or. To embrace the microchip and all its magic would be to close myself off from a great many habits and attitudes, ones that define me to myself; I would have to reposition myself on the space-time axis. I would have to say good-bye to a certain way of looking at the world because that way is bound up with a set of assumptions about history and distance, and difficulty and solitude and the slow work of self-making—all of which go against the premises of instantaneousness, interactivity, sensory stimulation and ease that make the world of *Wired* attractive to so many.

I think, then, in terms of a face-off, a struggle, a war. But it is to a large degree a war inside myself. In the larger societal sphere there is no great contest. We already know that technological ingenuity will set the agenda and that Americans, never that deeply entrenched in tradition, will follow. We are accustomed to taking up interesting offers. And the nature of the whole electronic system is such that recalcitrance is discouraged. Think of the incursion of the tele-technologies—phone and TV—and, more recently, of the telephone answering machine. Our society exerts pressures that make it very hard not to play the game. The game underway now is the game called "on-line" and, bitter it is to say it, I am still on the platform watching the dance of the candy wrappers.

I know which way the future is going, but I cannot find it in myself to get in step. At times I take this situation, this refusal, very seriously— I think of it as a crisis at the very core of my life. At other times, though, it seems comic. I see myself as one of the histrionically gesturing actors in the movie *Singin' in the Rain*—a man from the era of silent films who cannot believe that the newfangled talkies are really going to carry the day. But with this difference: That in my heart I know that the change is already taking place. The question I face is not, as some would have it, whether I should get myself a computer, find myself a network, do whatever one does to be in step. To me it is more a question of how I want to position myself as history makes a swerve, not only ushering in new circumstances and alignments, but changing its own deeper nature as well. For once the world goes fully on-line, there will be no more history of the old kind. History as we all studied it in school depended not just on the idea of chronological sequence, but also on fixed coordinates of space and time. X did such and such a thing here at such and such a time. No more. Most events of significance—most displays of force— will take place off the space-time axis. In cyberspace, among numbers. Binary codes don't live in time in the same way that people do, yet it will be their movement and interaction that will determine movements in the outer scape. The slow conventions of narrative will be overwhelmed by simultaneity. The time line, that organizing fiction that served us for so long, will go the way of Ptolemaic reckoning; we will have it only as a vestige.

Dire prognostications. What is it that I envision? Not a revolution —this is not a revolutionary scenario. I see instead a steady displacement of old by new, a generational pressure that escalates, its momentum gathering as the members of the old dispensation age and die off. Gone are those crusty individualists, those Jason Robards figures who still tickle us in movies; disappearing are the ideals they once espoused. As they move off the stage, they are not being replaced by chosen successors, but by people who have come up shaped by radically different stimuli. Not that generations haven't since time immemorial shouldered their predecessors aside. But this time there is a difference. The rate of change, social and technological, has surpassed exponentially the gradually escalating rates of previous periods. There is a ledge, a threshold, a point after which everything is different. I would draw the line, imprecisely, somewhere in the 1950s. That was when television worked its way into the fabric of American life, when we grew accustomed to the idea of parallel realities—one that we lived in, the other that we stepped into whenever we wanted a break from our living. People born after the mid-1950s are the carriers of the new; they make up the force that will push us out of our already-fading rural/small-town/urban understanding of social organization. The momentum of change has already made those designations all but meaningless. And many think it is a good thing.

I see the wholesale wiring of America. I see ever more complex and efficient technological systems being interposed between the individual and the harsh constraints of nature. This electronic mesh is already changing absolutely the way we deal with information. In fact, it is changing our whole idea of what information is. Former scales and hierarchies are being renovated. The medium shapes the message. If it can't be rendered digitally, it can't be much good. Software codes are a sorting hopper; they determine what flies through the circuits and what doesn't. We will see how the movement and control, the shaping of data will become a more central occupation. We will all (except the poor and the refuseniks) spend more and more of our time in the cybersphere producing, sending, receiving, and responding, and necessarily less time interacting in a "hands-on" way with the old material order. Similarly, we will establish a wide lateral interaction, dealing via screen with more and more people at the same time that our sustained face-to-face encounters diminish. It will be harder and harder—we know this already—to step free of our mediating devices. There will be people who will never in their lives have the experience that was, until our time, the norm—who will never stand in isolated silence among trees and stones, out of shouting distance of any other person, with no communication implement, forced to confront the slow, grainy momentum of time passing. The ways of being that ruled individuals since individuals first evolved are suddenly, with a finger-snap, largely irrelevant. This is more astonishing than we generally admit. Where do those reflexes go, those codes inscribed in the chips of our cells, spooled and spun in our DNA? What happens to all of the genetic information we outgrow?

But back to Wired and its can-do boosterism, its fervid embrace of the future, its covert assumption of the inevitability of complete social transformation. The remarkable thing about Wired is that it presents a fully self-contained order, a closed circuit. Nowhere in its pages do we find any trace of the murky and not-so-streamlined world that we can still see outside our windows. No ice on the mittens, no fumbling for quarters while the bus (late) toils toward us through morning traffic. Everything is clean as a California research park. No sense of getting from here to there.

And what is wrong with this picture? What, apart from the obvious fact that the world has so many steps to take before it becomes the high-resolution place willed by the editors of the magazine? I am most struck by the assumption on the part of all concerned of a continuum and the lack of what might be called existential questioning. There is what feels like a collective trust that we will all slide along smoothly from A, the present, to B, the future, without having to understand the world anew. But of course we will. For the change from A to B is not, as many historical changes have been, one of degree. Here is a change of kind, a paradigm shift, a plummet down the rabbit hole.

The editors of *Wired* like to tap innovative and unorthodox minds, whether for more off-the-wall explorations (William Gibson, Douglas Coupland) or more practically-oriented discussions, like Mitchell Kapor's "Democracy and the New Information Highway," in which the guru thoughtfully and pragmatically addresses the vital issues of access and control. I would like to make a few observations about Kapor's article, not because he makes any points that I disagree with, but because I see operative in his presentation certain assumptions that I would never dream of making, but which underscore my point, that so many of the believers think that we are moving along a simple continuum, that we are merely replacing some tired old tools with some sensationally effective ones.

Kapor's teasing first paragraph (I am quoting from an adapted version of his piece that appeared in the *Boston Review*) is worth giving in full because it summarizes the fantasy, the vision that inspires the hundreds of thousands of workers in the high-tech vineyards and which percolates throughout the pages of a journal like *Wired*. It is, let me emphasize, a rhetorical ploy, a scenario Kapor blocks out so that he can get to his real opening point, which is that the struggle for the control of the system that will deliver this nirvana to us has created massive gridlock. Writes Kapor:

The visionaries sketched it out, the computer literati caught onto it, and now it's all over the mainstream media: a high-speed, fiber optic, "new information highway" carrying an expanding universe of information and entertainment into the home and the workplace. Thousands of movies, mail-order catalogues, newspapers and magazines, educational courses, airline schedules, and other information databases will be available with a few clicks of a remote control. Two-way video conferencing will revolutionize business meetings, visits to the doctor, and heart-to-heart talks.

A nice touch, that last phrase—but never mind. After showing us the bureaucratic and political impediments that have arisen to stall the realization of this best of all possible worlds, Kapor makes an interesting move. He sets up as his goal in matters electronic, "a decentralized democracy, founded on the primacy of individual liberty and committed to pluralism, equality, and community." He then identifies his ideal as Jeffersonian, and lets the identification stand without any deeper inquiry into the implications of such an identification.

I read Kapor's article with some interest, and I found that so long as my reaction stayed within the general thought-circuit of the piece, I was nodding in agreement. But I was also aware of a gradually mounting sense of disquiet, the source of which, I realized (and this is often true with the essays I read in *Wired*) was not to be found in what the work itself said, but outside, in the realm where assumptions and unstated issues reside.

First, I was troubled—obliquely, then more overtly—by Kapor's ready conflation of terms, those pertaining to the new information highway and those invoking the Jeffersonian vision of a participatory democracy. It is not that the discourses cannot be connected, but I understood Kapor as suggesting that the information highway can actually serve and enhance a Jeffersonian egalitarianism. And with that we part company. As I see it, the techno-web and the democratic ideal are in opposition. Our whole economic and technological obsession with getting on-line is leading us away—not from democracy necessarily, but from the premise that individualism and circuited interconnection are, at a primary level, inimical notions. Warring terms. Let me make what looks like a digression before returning to this idea.

In the later chapters of his intellectual autobiography, *The Educa-tion of Henry Adams*, Adams reports on the revelation he experienced at the Great Exposition of 1900. In the chapter entitled "The Dynamo and the Virgin," he adduces the two great forces that, in a manner of speak-ing, divide the world between them. One is the dynamo, the apotheosis of applied mechanics, of which he writes:

> The planet itself seemed less impressive, in its old-fashioned, deliber-ate, annual or daily revolution, than this huge wheel, revolving within arm's-length at some vertiginous speed, and barely murmur-ing—scarcely humming an audible warning to stand a hair's-breadth further for respect of power—while it would not wake the baby lying close against its frame.

The other force, the Virgin, the force of faith and inwardness, "was still felt at Lourdes, and seemed to be as potent as x-rays," but in rude America her influence was almost negligible. Still, it would be between dynamo and Virgin, those representative centers of opposing force, that our personal and societal fortunes would be sorted out.

Adams's formulation, construed metaphorically (maybe more metaphorically than he intended) has been in my thoughts often, first as an explanatory trope for our present-day situation, later as the template for a new trope, one more suited to our transformed culture. These days I don't think in terms of dynamo and Virgin, I think of circuit and ther-apist. The terms are less grand than Adams's, but they lend themselves better to the facts of our case. As the dynamo brought industrialism to its zenith in the middle of our century, so now has the microscopic mazework of the silicon chip extended the promise of a computerized future. And where the Virgin was once the locus of spirit and care, the protectress of the interior life, the new site of power, now secular, is the office of the trained therapeutic specialist.

Like Adams's two forces, mine are symbolic orders in opposition. But unlike his, mine connect; they are not mutually exclusive. Where the circuit makes possible, maybe inevitable, a life lived significantly through mediated interactions (e-mail, ATM banking, home shop-ping), often leading to an obscure sense of subjective dissolution, of unreality (once called "anomie"), the therapist is the agent of repair and reconstitution. The electronic involvement leaches out traditional meaning and a sense of self by shattering the basic space-time coordinates we have always oriented ourselves by; the therapeutic involvement looks to develop narratives that, if they cannot restore wholeness, can at least offer some compensation for its loss.

To put it yet another way, being on-line and having the subjective experience of depth, of existential coherence, are mutually exclusive situations, thus creating a link between circuit and therapist. Electricity and inwardness are fundamentally discordant. Electricity—and the whole circulatory network predicated upon it—is about immediacy; it is in the nature of the current to surmount impedances. Electricity is, implicitly, of the moment—*now*. Depth, meaning, and the narrative structurings of subjectivity—these are *not* now; they flourish only in that order of time Henri Bergson called "duration." Duration is deep time, time experienced without the awareness of time passing. Until quite recently, people on the planet lived mainly in terms of duration time. Time not artificially broken, but shaped around natural rhythmic cycles; time bound to the integrated functioning of the senses, the perceptions.

We have destroyed that duration. We have created invisible elsewheres that are as immediate as our actual surroundings. We have fractured the flow of time, layered it into competing simultaneities. We learn to do five things at once or pay the price. We have plunged ourselves into an environment of invisible signals and operations; we live in a world where it is as unthinkable to walk five miles to visit a friend as it was once unthinkable to speak across that distance through a wire.

The hardwiring of the nation is well underway. The infrastructure is being set into place; the control battles are now joined. The face-off between Viacom and QVC over the purchase of Paramount is only the most eye-catching instance of what is going on at all levels of the communications industry. We are not about to turn from the millennial remaking of the world—indeed, we are all excited to see just how much power and ingenuity we command. By degrees—it is happening year by year, appliance by appliance—we are wiring ourselves into a gigantic hive. Life in the near future will take place among an exciting and maddening and deeply distracting hum of signals. When everyone is on-line, when the circuits are crackling, the impulses speeding every which way like thoughts in a fevered brain, we will have to rethink our defini-tions of individuality and our time-honored ideals of subjective individ-ualism. And of the privacy that has always pertained thereto. It may already be time. But to undertake such a reconsideration of ourselves—our private and collective selves—we will have to dispense with certain illusions. One of the deepest and most fiercely held may be that pro-posed by the Jeffersonian paradigm.

I have no trouble, then, with anything *in* Mitchell Kapor's presenta-tion. But what alarms me, not just about his essay but in general, is that the terms of this most massive change are bandied about and accepted with no debate. No one is stepping forth to suggest that there might be something at stake, that the headlong race to wire ourselves might, in accordance with the gain-loss formulae that apply in every sphere of human endeavor like the laws of physics, threaten or diminish us in some way. To me the wager is intuitively clear: we gain access and effi-ciency at the expense of subjective self-awareness. I am not ready to trade, and I wonder how the man from Monticello would vote if we could get him back for a moment from the informationless realm of the dead.

My assessment is not optimistic. The devil may himself be at the crossroads, but we have already picked our direction and started toward it. There was not, however, a moment of choosing; no pact was signed with the blood of a virgin. We have—subtly, at times all but impercepti-bly—been conditioned; our preliminary technologies had us moving down that road before anyone even knew where it might lead. The elec-tronic future was not there in an envelope that we could either open or ignore; we have made it inevitable through countless acts of acquies-cence.

When we look at the large-scale shift, looking as if at a motion study, we can see not only how our situation has come about, but also how it is in our nature that it should have. At every step—this is clear—we trade for ease. And ease is what quickly swallows up the initial strangeness of a new medium or tool. Moreover, each accommodation paves the way for the next. The telegraph must have seemed to its first users a surpassingly strange device, but its newfangledness was overridden by its usefulness. Once we had accepted mechanical transmission over distances, the path was clear for the telephone. Again, a monumental transformation: turn select digits on a dial and hear the voice of another human being. And on it goes, the original inventions coming gradually, one by one, allowing the society to adapt. We mastered the telephone, the television with its few networks running black and white programs. And while no law required citizens to own or use either, they did in a remarkably short time achieve near-total saturation.

We are, then, accustomed to the trade; we take the step that will enlarge our reach, simplify our communication, and abbreviate our physical involvement in some task or chore. We do not as readily streamline our pleasures. Indeed, it is in the name of pleasure that we accept so many of these changes—we want more time for the pursuit of what we most enjoy.

The difference between the epoch of early modernity and the present is, to simplify drastically, that formerly the body had time to accept the graft, the new organ, whereas now we are hurtling forward willy-nilly, assuming that if a technology is connected with communications or information processing it must be good, we must need it—and that we had better get it lest we find ourselves stranded by the wayside, on some windy platform watching the express rattle by. I never cease to be astonished at the contemplation of what a mere two decades has brought us. Consider the evidence. Since the early 1970s we have seen the arrival—we have accepted, deemed all but indispensible—of personal computers, laptop computers, phone answering machines, calling cards, fax, cellular phones, VCRs, modems, Nintendo games, e-mail, voice mail, camcorders, CD players, smart environments, virtual reality technologies . . . Very quickly, with almost no pause between increments, these circuit-driven tools and entertainments have moved into our lives, and with minimum ruffling of the waters, really—which of course makes them seem natural, even inevitable. Marshall McLuhan called improvements of this sort "extensions of man," and this is their secret. We embrace them because they seem a part of us, an enhancement. They don't seem to challenge our power so much as add to it.

I am startled, though, by how little we are debating the deeper philosophical ramifications. We talk up a storm when it comes to policy issues (who should have jurisdiction, etc.), and there is great fascination in some quarters with the practical minutiae of functioning, compatibility, and so on. But why do we hear so few people asking whether we might not ourselves be changing and whether the changes are necessarily for the good? Maybe because our overall American bewitchment with technology is based on the assumption that improvements in the material sphere are intrinsically good. If this is so, it reveals that there is for us a fatal split, a great divide, between the so-called objective world and the private, subjective, existential realm. If we did not have this split we could not refrain from asking at every turn whether our outer decisions and deeds did not have significant inner consequences. We don't ask—at least not often, and not in any public way that I am aware of. But of course the connection is there. Of course the inner and outer are on a continuum; events in one sphere necessarily impinge on the other.

My explanation for this blithe indifference to inward consequences is simple. I believe that we are—biologically, neuropsychologically— creatures of extraordinary adaptability. We greet change and disturbance by reorganizing the internal economy; we assess the odds and play what our calculations tell us will be the winning hand. We fit ourselves to situations, whether of privation or beneficent surplus. And in many respects this is to the good. The species is fit because it knows *how* to fit.

But there are drawbacks as well. The late Walker Percy, whose prescience, concern, and humor I admire tremendously, made it his work to explore the terms of the great trade off. Over and over, in his fiction as well as his speculative essays, he asks the same basic questions. As he writes in the opening of his essay "The Delta Factor," "Why does man feel so sad in the twentieth century? Why does man feel so bad in the very age when, more than in any other age, he has succeeded in satisfying his needs and making over the world for his own use?" Why are we "lost in the cosmos?" Why do we feel so deeply, if unconsciously, disconnected? One of his answers is that the price of adaptation is habit, and that habit—of perception as well as behavior—distances the self from the primary things that give meaning and purpose to life. We are cut off from beauty, from love, from true passion, and from the spiritual.

In "The Loss of the Creature," Percy explored this paradox with great resourcefulness and nudged his reader with illuminating anecdotes:

> A man in Boston decides to spend his vacation at the Grand Canyon. He visits his travel bureau, looks at the folder, signs up for a two-week tour. He and his family see the tour, see the Grand Canyon, and return to Boston. May we say that this man has seen the Grand Canyon? Possibly he has. But it is more likely that what he has done is the one sure way not to see the canyon.

Percy's point here is that under these circumstances, true seeing is most unlikely, "because the Grand Canyon, the thing as it is, has been appropriated by the symbolic complex which has already been formed in the sightseer's mind." By habit. And it is just possible that this person at some level feels a lack, a sense of distance from authentic experience. Percy then asks how his sightseer might recover the experience that habits of thought and perception have denied him. "The tourist leaves the tour, camps in the back country. He arises before dawn and approaches the South Rim through a wild terrain where there are no trails and no railed-in lookout points. In other words, he sees the canyon by avoiding all the facilities for seeing the canyon."

The tourist—the contemporary individual—lives his life in the circuit of habit, and so long as he remains within that circuit he is unconscious of anything outside. He is unaware, to paraphrase Percy's beloved Kierkegaard, that he is in despair, cut off from the sources of authentic selfhood. For it is the nature of adaptation to keep us sane and functional through the exclusion of the whole class of deeper questions and doubts about meaning, permitting them, at most, a subthreshold presence which manifests itself as an occasional wistfulness, sadness, homesickness. But when that same person faces something as magnificent and challenging as the Grand Canyon, the tension is exacerbated. He feels his lack as an inchoate sort of failure.

All of which is to say that we accept these gifts of technology, these labor-saving devices, these extensions of the senses, by adapting and adapting again. Each improvement is, at bottom, an order of abstraction that we accommodate ourselves to. Abstraction is, however, a movement away from the natural given—a step away from our fundamental selves, selves rooted for millennia in an awe before the unknown, a fear and trembling in the face of the outer dark. We widen the gulf, and if at some level we fear the widening, we respond by investing more of our faith in these systems we have wrought.

We sacrifice the potential life of the solitary self by enlisting ourselves in the collective. For this, even more than the saving of labor, is finally what these systems are all about. They are not only extensions of the senses, they are extensions of the senses that put us in touch with the extended senses of others. The ultimate point of the ever-expanding electronic web is to bridge once and for all the individual solitude that has heretofore always set the terms of existence. Each appliance is a strand, another addition to the virtual place wherein we will all find ourselves together. Telephone, fax, computer-screen networks, e-mail, interactive television—these are the components out of which the hive is being built. The end of it all, the *telos,* is a kind of amniotic environment of impulses, a condition of connectedness. And in time—I don't know how long it will take—it will feel as strange (and exhilarating) for a person to stand momentarily free of it as it feels now for a city dweller to look up at night and see a sky full of stars.

Whether this sounds dire or not depends upon your assumptions about the human—assumptions, that is, in the largest sense. For those who ask, with Gauguin, "Who are we? Why are we here? Where are we going?"—and who feel that the answering of those questions is the grand mission of the species—the prospect of a collective life in an electronic hive is bound to seem terrifying. But there are others, maybe even a majority, who have never except fleetingly posed those same questions, who have repressed them so that they might "get on," and who gravitate toward that life because they see it as a way of vanquishing once and for all the anxious gnawings they feel whenever any intimations of depth sneak through the inner barriers.

In his justly celebrated essay, "The Work of Art in an Age of Mechanical Reproduction," Walter Benjamin sets forth the idea, now almost commonplace, that the copying and disseminating of, say, a painting robs it of its aura. "Even the most perfect reproduction of a work of art is lacking in one element: its presence in time and space, its unique existence at the place where it happens to be." This is common sense, and the viewer of the reproduction at some level accepts it as part of the bargain. A few paragraphs on, however, Benjamin introduces a more devastating formulation: "The situations into which the product of mechanical reproduction can be brought may not touch the actual work of art, *yet the quality of its presence is always depreciated*" (emphasis mine). This he explains by arguing that the reproduction compromises the "historical testimony" of the work—its material witness to time—a compromise that saps its authority.

Benjamin's full argument would require patient elaboration. I only wish to borrow its ruling assumption—that technological abstraction changes the status of the thing abstracted—and his key notion of "aura." Aura, like soul, is one of those terms that are easy to intuitively catch the sense of, but very hard to define satisfactorily. The aura is the uniqueness, the presence, the natural emanation of a thing—its spirit. The aura is there when we stand in front of the original of a painting, and is absent when we are before the copy—even if the copy is so faithful as to be nearly identical. The copy is not the actual record of the brush and paint, does not hold as a part of its history the artist's actual physical engagement with materials. Many will shrug and say, "So what? I enjoy the beauty and can supply the rest in my imagination." And they are not wrong, but their response does not obviate the distinction between the thing and its surrogate. That distinction, elusive though it may be, is what underwrites our value systems, aesthetic and otherwise. Moreover, it is a distinction that will soon enough become a live issue (it is already in the philosophy of Jean Baudrillard and others) as the relative value of "real" and "virtual" experiences is contested.

Benjamin writes lyrically but also with a certain slipperiness about aura. He attempts to distinguish between aura as it applies to historical objects (works of art) and the aura that belongs to natural objects. "We define the aura of the latter as the unique phenomenon of a distance, however close it may be. If, while resting on a summer afternoon, you follow with your eyes a mountain range on the horizon or a branch which casts its shadow over you, you experience the aura of those mountains, of that branch." The uniqueness, or presence, then, is understood as a separateness, a resistance—the quality of being-in-itself, the "otherness" that all things manifest.

But now Benjamin speaks of "the desire of contemporary masses to bring things 'closer' spatially and humanly, which is just as ardent as their bent toward overcoming the uniqueness of every reality by accepting its reproduction. Every day the urge grows stronger to get a hold of an object at very close range by way of its likeness, its reproduction."

Benjamin, in his analysis, concentrates on objects of human perception—man-made objects as well as natural ones. He does not direct much focus upon the subjects, the perceivers themselves. That is, he acknowledges how changed aesthetic engagement—made possible by film, for instance—alters the ways in which we see and understand reality. But he does not take the next big step and examine the aura—the uniqueness—of the individual himself; he does not ask how that aura may be affected by the individual's engagement with various technologies. This is a whole other subject, one that may not have been as pressing for Benjamin as it is for us, because in his time the forces of mediation—the technologies abstracting and deflecting natural human interactions—had not yet attained critical mass.

But the time has come and it may be worthwhile to apply some of Benjamin's terms to our own situation. To put it in simple terms: Do we each, as individuals, have an aura, a unique presence that is only manifest on site, in our immediate space-time location? And if we do, how is this aura affected by our myriad communications media, all of which play havoc with our space-time orientation?

These are uncomfortably loose and difficult questions. Although we all know what it is to feel the human presence of another person, who is going to argue for presence as an essential attribute? There is no verifying, quantifying, or analyzing it. How then would we begin to theorize about the change or depletion of presence, of aura? Only in the most bumbling fashion, I'd say.

I am taking it as a given that every person is blessed with aura, that he or she gives off the immediate emanation, or "vibes," of living. At any and every moment, our actions, our emotional disposition, our thoughts, our will all combine into what another person might experience as our presence. At earlier stages of history, before the advent of the sense-extending technologies, human interactions were necessarily carried out face to face, presence to presence. Before the telephone and the megaphone, the farthest a voice could carry was the distance of a shout. We could say, then, that all human communication is founded in presence. There was originally no severance between the person and the communication.

The telephone obviously altered that. It eliminated the need for a spatial proximity while keeping the time link intact. "It's raining here," says one person; the other, bemused by the miracle of distance surmounted, allows that the sun is shining where he sits. Bring in the answering machine, the voice mail, and the time link is cut. "This is Bill. It's about three o'clock and I wanted to ask you . . . " Add to this the possibility that Bill's friend is not even picking up the message at his home, but has punched in digits from the office, maybe even from the car phone, and you begin to see what a dispersal of presence contemporary communication involves.

But the telephone and answering machine are only a small part of the picture. A comparable set of transformations has taken place on every front. Hand-written letters gave way to typed letters, which became word-processed letters, a great many of them structured in advance by the software. And now e-mail chatter is making rapid inroads on the tradition of paper, envelope, and stamp. Photographs, home movies, camcorder records of the stages on life's way. Every set of technological advances, every extension of the senses, involves some distortion of the time-space axis—the here and now—that used to be the given.

And who can say what the effect of all these changes and enhancements will be? Where is there a platform, an unaffected point of vantage, from which one can make a disinterested assessment? The only procedure I can think of is the comparative one: to look at the state of things in the present and then draw comparison with what we know about various periods in the past. Which can be done readily enough. But if one then wishes to make value judgments, to calculate gain/loss formulas, all sorts of problems arise. Who is to say that any historical period is better than any other? Communications cannot be compared in isolation from everything else. And to argue for the nineteenth century, or the seventeenth, is preposterous. Sure, village life had its benefits—certain kinds of intimacy and cohesion—but village life also knew brutality, idiocy, and the horrors of disease. And so on.

Still, one has to hazard something about the times and their tendencies. Taking my cue from Benjamin, I would say that the net effect of all of our mediations of the real—of our abstracting and fragmenting of a formerly more direct engagement with the world—can be compared to that wreaked upon the original work of art by reproduction. That is, our various improvements not only mark a diminution of the function improved upon (as the telephone leached the power and immediacy from all human dialogue), but they also work to dissolve some of the fundamental authority of the *human* itself. We are experiencing the gradual but steady erosion of human presence, both of the authority of the individual and, in ways impossible to prove, of the species itself. The same processes that are bringing this depletion about are also making inevitable a most peculiar compensation: It is getting easier and easier to accept the idea of electronic tribalism—hive life. Subjective individualism is now not the goal but the impedance factor, but as that gets leveled, the movement of the impulse through the circuit gains force. Subjective individualism, what remains of it, is like aura—we now must think of it in terms of resistance, or, to cite Benjamin, "the unique phenomenon of a distance."

My core fear is that we are, as a culture, as a species, becoming shallower; that we have turned from depth—from the Judeo-Christian premise of unfathomable mystery—and are adapting ourselves to the ersatz security of a vast lateral connectedness. That we are giving up on wisdom, the struggle for which has for millennia been central to the very idea of culture, and that we are pledging instead to a faith in the web. What *is* our idea, our ideal, of wisdom these days? Who represents it? Who even invokes it? Our postmodern culture is a vast fabric of competing isms; we are leaderless and subject to the terrors, masked as the freedoms, of an absolute relativism. It would be wrong to lay all the blame at the feet of technology, but more wrong to ignore the great transformative impact of new technological systems—to act as if it's all just business as usual.

There is, finally, a tremendous difference between communication in the instrumental sense and communion in the affective, the soul-oriented, sense. Somewhere we have gotten hold of the idea that the more all-embracing we can make our communications networks, the closer we will be to that partaking that we long for deep down. For change us as they will, our technologies have not yet eradicated that flame of a desire not merely to be in touch, but to be, at least figuratively, embraced, known and valued not abstractly but in presence. We seem to believe that our instruments can get us there, but they can't. Their great power is all in the service of division and acceleration. They work in—and create—an unreal time that has nothing to do with the deep time we thrive in: the time of history, tradition, ritual, art, and true communion.

The devil no longer moves about on cloven hooves, reeking of brimstone. He is an affable, efficient fellow. He claims to want to help us all along to a brighter, easier future, and his sales pitch is very smooth. I was, as the old song goes, almost persuaded. I saw what it could be like, our toil and misery replaced by a vivid, pleasant dream. Fingers tap keys, oceans of fact and sensation get downloaded, are dissolved through the nervous system. Bottomless wells of data are accessed and manipulated, everything flowing at circuit speed. Gone the rock in the field, the broken hoe, the grueling distances. "History," said Stephen Dedalus, "is a nightmare from which I am trying to awaken." This may be the awakening, but it feels curiously like the fantasies that circulate through our sleep. From deep in the heart I hear the voice that says, "Refuse it."